P9-CQS-686

Learning
the
Word

A
made easy
handbook
on Studying the Bible

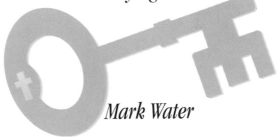

Mark Water

HENDRICKSON
PUBLISHERS

Learning the Word
Hendrickson Publishers, Inc.
P.O. Box 3473
Peabody, Massachusetts 01961-3473

A compilation of five
titles in the Made Easy
range:
*The Books of the Bible
made easy*
  – first printing 2001
Bible Study made easy
  – first printing 1999
*Key Bible Words made
easy*
  – first printing 2003
*Key Bible People made
easy*
  – first printing 2003
Bible Research made easy
  – first printing 1999

Designed and produced
by Tony Cantale
Graphics

First printing —
September 2004

Manufactured in
Hong Kong/China

**Acknowledgments:
Bible Research
made easy**
pp. 12-13 Extract taken
from *The NIV Study
Bible*, Hodder &
Stoughton, 1987. The
NIV Concordance,
copyright © 1982, 1984,
by The Zondervan
Corporation.

pp. 14-15 Extract taken
from *The NIV Study
Bible*, Hodder &
Stoughton, 1987. Color
Time Lines, copyright
© 1985, by The
Zondervan Corporation.

pp. 16-17 Extract taken
from *The NIV Study
Bible*, Hodder &
Stoughton, 1987.
Notes, copyright ©
1985, by The
Zondervan Corporation.

pp. 18-19 Extract taken
from *The NIV Study
Bible*, Hodder &
Stoughton, 1987. The
Center-Column Cross
Reference System,
copyright © 1984, by
The Zondervan
Corporation.

pp. 20-21 Extract taken
from *The Thompson
Chain - Reference Study
Bible NIV*, .B. Kirkbride
Bible Co., Inc. 1990.

pp. 24-27 Extracts
taken from *The New
Strong's Exhaustive
Concordance of the Bible*,
Thomas Nelson
Publishers, 1984

pp. 34-35 Extract taken
from *Vine's Complete
Expository Dictionary of
Old and New Testament
Words*, W.E. Vine,
William White Jr.,
Merrill F. Unger, ANG
Pub. 1990.

pp. 36-37 Extract taken
from *Easton's Bible
Dictionary*, M.G.
Easton, Nelson, 1991

pp 38-39 Extract taken
from *Nave's Topical
Bible*, Orville J. Nave,
Nelson, 1997

pp. 40-41 Extract taken
from *The International
Bible Commentary*,
(General Editor, F.F.
Bruce), Zondervan,
1986

pp. 42-43 Extract taken
from *The Message of
Acts*, John Stott, IVP,
1990

pp. 44-45 Extract taken
from *The New Unger's
Bible Handbook*, Revised
by Gary N. Larson,
Moody Press, 1984

pp. 46-47 Extract taken
from *The New Dictionary
of Theology* (edited by
S.B. Ferguson and D.F.
Wright), IVP, 1988

Photography supplied
by Artville, Todd Bolen,
Digital Stock, Foxx
Photos, Goodshoot,
Digital Vision,
C Moore, Photo Alto,
Photodisc and Tony
Cantale

Illustrations by
Tony Cantale Graphics

Introduction

The growing number of titles in the Made Easy series have sold nearly two million copies since their launch in 1998. Many readers have found them an ideal starting point in their reading and studying of the Bible.

In this second Made Easy handbook five titles about the Bible are now bound together in one volume:

- *The Books of the Bible made easy*
- *Bible Study made easy*
- *Key Bible Words made easy*
- *Key Bible People made easy*
- *Bible Research made easy*

As you use this handbook to increase your understanding of the Bible you will doubtless find yourself agreeing with the great 19th-century Baptist preacher's assessment of the Bible:

"Nobody ever outgrows Scripture;
the book widens and deepens with our years."

C.H. Spurgeon

The Books of the Bible made easy make it possible for you to have a bird's eye view of all sixty-six books of the Bible. Many books of the Bible are left unread. Just where is one supposed to start with 2 Chronicles, or Nahum the prophet, or John's second and third letters?

Here is a simple guide to lead you through each Old Testament and each New Testament book. No Bible book need remain a no-go area. Any parts of the Bible that were once uncharted waters for you can now be entered into with confidence and the certain knowledge that you will benefit from your reading.

The Books of the Bible made easy gives you:

• An instant overview of each Bible book
• A key verse for each book
• Information about how each book fits into the whole Bible
• Facts about when and why each book was written

Contents

Genesis
The book of beginnings

"In the beginning God created the heavens and the earth."
Genesis 1:1

Major theme
Beginnings of creation, Satan, sin, nations, peoples and God's plan to reclaim all of humanity.

Background and purpose
Genesis is the history of origins, including the creation of the world, the entrance of sin and death, and the rise of nations. It records the fall of human beings and the first prophecy of Christ's defeat of Satan and the reclaiming of humanity *(3:15)*.

Author
The book's author is not named, however, both Jews and Christians have attributed the first five books of the Bible to Moses.

Date
The exact date of writing is not known. Possibly Moses wrote it while in the wilderness, during the 40-year period in which God's children wandered aimlessly in the desert, when God met with Moses on Mount Sinai. The best guess is approximately 1400 BC.

4

Brief outline

1. Creation and the fall *1:1–5:32*

2. Noah and his descendants *6:1–11:26*

3. Abram (Abraham and his descendants) *11:27–25:18*

4. Issac *25:19–26:43*

5. Jacob and Esau *27:1–36:43*

6. The story of Joseph *37:1–50:26*

Important events
- **Creation** God is the Creator
- **Fall** Adam sins against God
- **Flood** God's judgment
- **Nations** After the building of the Tower of Babel God scatters people over the face of the earth.
- **Israel** The foundation of God's chosen people.

Christ in Genesis
- **Christ** is seen as a "type" in Genesis. He is depicted in various events and people.
- A "type" is an historical fact which illustrates a spiritual truth. For example: Adam is the head of the human race. Christ is the Head of the new creation.

Exodus
The book of departure

"Therefore, say to the Israelites: 'I am the Lord, and I will bring you out from under the yoke of the Egyptians. I will free you from being slaves to them, and I will redeem you with an outstretched arm and with mighty acts of judgment.'" *Exodus 6:6*

Major theme
Exodus records the slavery, deliverance and beginnings of the people of Israel on their journey to Canaan.

Background and purpose
Exodus describes God's actions as he liberated his enslaved people and molded them into a nation. Moses is the central figure. God chose him to miraculously lead the people of Israel out of Egypt, triumphing through the Red Sea into Sinai. God gives Moses the ten commandments on Mount Sinai. He directs the Israelites to make a chest, the ark of testimony (ark of the covenant), which is to be housed in the tabernacle.

Author
The book's author is not named, however, both Jews and Christians have attributed the first five books of the Bible to Moses.

Date
Approximately 1400 BC. The exact date of writing is not known. Possibly Moses kept an account of God's work which he then wrote out in the plains of Moab before he died.

Brief outline

1. The Israelites delivered from Egypt *1:1–15:21*

2. Traveling from the Red Sea to Mount Sinai *15:22–18:27*

3. Giving the Law and the covenant *19:1–24:18*

4. The tabernacle and instructions for worship *25:1–40:38*

5

Important events
- The Israelites are made slaves
- The ten plagues
- The Passover
- The escape from Egypt
- The giving of the ten commandments

Christ in Exodus
- The Passover lamb (*12:3*), is a type of Christ, who is the Lamb of God
- Manna (*16:4*), is a type of Christ.

Leviticus
The book of atonement

"'I am the Lord your God; consecrate yourselves and be holy, because I am holy.'"
Leviticus 11:44

Major theme
Leviticus carries on from the end of Exodus without a break, describing the God-given sacrificial rituals and practices for worship. Holiness and the perfection of God is portrayed throughout the book.

Background and purpose
The book answers the question: How can sinful humans approach a holy God? The words "holy" and "holiness" occur over 150 times. Leviticus is filled with laws defining the ways in which God's people are to worship. The people are instructed to keep their relationship with God alive, and to live holy lives.

Author
The author is not named. Throughout the book is the continuing statement, "The Lord spoke to Moses."

Date
Approximately 1400 BC. Much of the material recorded was given to Moses by God at Mount Sinai.

Brief outline

1. Regulations for sacrifices and offerings *1:1–7:38*

2. The priesthood and the tabernacle *8:1–10:20*

3. Cleanness and uncleanness *11:1–15:33*

4. The day of atonement *16:1–34*

5. Regulations about living *17:1–22:33*

6. Instructions for national life *23:1–27:34*

Important events

Regulations about sacrifices

The five annual feasts

1. The Feast of the Passover

2. The Feast of Pentecost

3. The Feast of Trumpets

4. The Day of Atonement

5. The Feast of Tabernacles

Christ in Leviticus
- Jesus is our great high priest.
- The scapegoat *(16:20-22)*, bore the sins of Israel, as Jesus bears our sins.

Numbers
Wandering in the desert

"'... not one of the men who saw my glory and the miraculous signs I performed in Egypt and in the desert but who disobeyed me and tested me ten times–not one of them will ever see the land I promised on oath to their forefathers.'" *Numbers 14:22-23*

Major theme
Two themes are apparent: God is faithful to his people, but disobedience is always punished.

Background and purpose
While Leviticus covers only a short period of time, Numbers covers nearly 39 years. It records Israel's movements from the last days at Mount Sinai, the wanderings around Kadesh-barnea, to the arrival in the plains of Moab in the fortieth year. This resulted from Israel's disbelief and disobedience to God. For Israel, what could have been an eleven-day journey became forty years of wandering in the desert.

This book is given the name "Numbers" in the *Septuagint*, the pre-Christian Greek translation of the Old Testament. This name is derived from the two occasions on which the Israelites were numbered, *chapters 1 and 39*.

Author
The book's author is not named. Traditionally, both Jews and Christians have attributed the first five books of the Bible to Moses.

Date
Approximately 1400 BC.

Brief outline

1. Israelites prepare to leave Mount Sinai *11–4:49*

2. More laws of God for the people *5:1–10:10*

3. Wandering in the wilderness, from Mount Sinai to Moab *10:11–21:35*

4. Events in Moab and summary of the journey from Egypt to Moab *22:1–33:49*

5. Instructions before crossing the Jordan *33:50–36:13*

Christ in Numbers
- The offering of the red heifer *(chapter 19)*, symbolizes salvation through Jesus' offering of himself.
- Jesus himself pointed to the bronze serpent *(21:1-9)*, and said, "So the Son of Man must be lifted up" *(John 3:14)*.

Deuteronomy
God's laws

"Love the Lord your God with all your heart and with all your soul and with all your strength."
Deuteronomy 6:5

Major theme
God renews his covenant with Israel on the plains of Moab just before they enter the Promised Land.

Background and purpose
The term deuteronomy signifies the "Second law." The original teaching of Moses (from God) is repeated, commented upon, explained and enlarged because those who first heard the teachings were now dead, except for Moses, Joshua, and Caleb. This book records three of Moses' speeches and his last words. Through this teaching Moses confirms Israel as God's people before handing over his leadership of them to Joshua. He tells them to remember God when they prosper and that they will be disciplined if they disobey God.

Author
The book's author is not named. However, both Jews and Christians have attributed the first five books of the Bible to Moses. It has been pointed out that Moses could hardly be the author of a book which records his own last words. But Moses could still be the author of everything except the introduction *(1:1-5)*, and the report of his death *(34)*. Jesus spoke about Moses being the author of this book *(Matthew 19:7-8; Mark 10:3-5; John 5:46-47)*.

Date
Approximately 1400 BC.

Brief outline

1. Review of the Israelites journey from Eygpt *1:1–4:43*

2. The ten commandments and loving God *4:44–6:25*

3. Moses' teachings from God reviewed *7:1–26:19*

4. Moses reviews Israel's pledged relationship with God *27:1–30:20*

5. Moses and his final days *31:1–34:12*

Christ in Deuteronomy
- Moses, probably more than any other Old Testament person, is a "type" of Jesus.
- Jesus quoted Scripture more often from the book of Deuteronomy than from any other Old Testament book.

8

Joshua
Conquering the Promised Land

"'Have I not commanded you? Be strong and courageous. Do not be terrified; do not be discouraged, for the Lord your God will be with you wherever you go.'" *Joshua 1:9*

Major theme
The account of how God kept his promise to bring his people into the Promised Land. The book's theme is "... take possession of the land the Lord your God is giving you for your own" *(1:11)*.

Background and purpose
The book of Joshua was written to document the initial fulfilment of God's promises to Abraham, Issaac, and Jacob, as the people of God enter Canaan. It records the Israelite invasion of the Promised Land, the partitioning of the Promised Land and the settling down in the Promised Land. Joshua is full of military battles, specific towns, and places. The spiritual principles used in Joshua are the same principles to be used in the spiritual battles faced by all generations of God's followers. *See Hebrews 4:1-11*

Author
According to Jewish tradition and Joshua 24:26 the author was Joshua: "And Joshua recorded these things in the Book of the Law of God."

Date
Approximately 1350 BC. Joshua was probably written in the early days of the Judges of Israel.

Brief outline
1. Entering the land
1:1–5:12

2. Conquering the land
5:13–12:15

3. Distributing the land
13:1–21:45

4. Joshua's farewell
22:1-24:33

Christ in Joshua
- "The commander of the army of the Lord" *(5:14)*, was an appearance of Jesus.

Judges
Israel's twelve judges

"In those days Israel had no king; everyone did as he saw fit."
Judges 21:25
["... did what was right in his own eyes." New King James Version]

Major theme
The book of Judges is the link between Joshua bringing the Israelites into the Promised Land and Saul, David and the other kings of Israel. Through the book the Israelites fall into chaos and desert God – yet there is a loving God who disciplines them, loves them and refuses to give up on them.

Background and purpose
The twelve "judges" in this book were not only concerned with legal matters but were charismatic military leaders. The book is made up of six periods of oppression covering approximately 300 years. The following "sin-cycle" is repeated:
• A time of peace. God is ignored. Pagan gods replace God.
• A time of oppression. Israel is attacked.
• A time of repentance. Israel turns back to God.
• A time of deliverance. God sends a judge and delivers Israel.
• A time of peace. God is ignored again and the "sin-cycle" starts once more.
The apostasy illustrated in Judges shows why the people felt they needed a king and leads on to the books of Samuel and Kings.

Author
The book's author is not named. Samuel or one of his prophetic students may have written it. Another suggestion is that a prophet such as Nathan or Gad, who were linked to David's court, may have written it.

Date
Various dates have been suggested and an eleventh century or tenth century BC date is probable.

Brief outline

1. Conquest of Canaan retold *1:1–3:6*

2. Israel under the judges' oppression and deliverance *3:7–16:31*

3. The religious and moral failings under the judges *17:1–21:25*

Christ in Judges
• Jesus is seen as our Deliverer.

Ruth
Human loyalty

"But Ruth replied, 'Don't urge me to leave you or to turn back from you. Where you go I will go, and where you stay I will stay. Your people will be my people and your God my God.'"
Ruth 1:16

Major theme
Ruth, a Moabite widow, because of the love for her mother-in-law, Naomi, leaves her own country and travels back with Naomi to Bethlehem. There she meets Boaz, a relative of Naomi, who marries her.

Background and purpose
The book of Ruth singles out one family that lived in the time of the judges *(1:1)*. The book illustrates that the blesssings of God came to non-Jews as well as Jews. The genealogy at the end of the book shows that Ruth, a non-Jewish woman, became the grandmother of King David and an ancestor of Jesus. *See Matthew 1:5*

Author
The author is unknown. Samuel was the author according to a Talmudic tradition. But this is unlikely since David is mentioned *(4:17,22)*, and Samuel died before David's coronation *(1 Samuel 25:1)*.

Date
It seems likely that Ruth was written in the time of the kings of Israel and so an eleventh century or tenth century BC date is probable.

Brief outline

1. Ruth and Naomi return to Bethlehem *1:1-22*

2. Ruth meets Boaz *2:1–3:18*

3. Boaz marries Ruth *4:1-22*

11

Christ in Ruth
• Jesus is our Kinsman-redeemer.

1 & 2 Samuel
Israel's first kings

"'Does the Lord delight in burnt offerings and sacrifices
as much as in obeying the voice of the Lord?
To obey is better than sacrifice, and to heed is better than the fat of rams.'"
1 Samuel 15:22

"And David knew that the Lord had established him as king over Israel and had exalted his kingdom for the sake of his people Israel." *2 Samuel 5:12*

Major theme
1 and 2 Samuel are a single book in the Hebrew Bible. 1 Samuel continues the history of Israel from the time of the judges to the founding of the monarchy under Saul. 2 Samuel records David's successes and failures as king.

Background and purpose
1 Samuel records the birth, childhood and ministry of Samuel, the life of Saul and the first part of David's life.

2 Samuel records David as king at Hebron and then at Jerusalem and David's last days. Jerusalem becomes the religious capital of Israel.

Author
The author's name is not stated. The Talmudic tradition states that Samuel was the author, but since his death is recorded in 1 Samuel 25:1 he couldn't have written the whole book.

Date
The anonymous author must have lived after Solomon's death in 930 BC, and after the division of the kingdom since "Israel and Judah" are mentioned in 1 Samuel 11:8 and 2 Samuel 5:5. This means that the writing took place sometime between 930 BC and 722 BC

Brief outline

1 Samuel

1. Samuel judges Israel *1:1–8:22*

2. Saul as first King of Israel *9:1–15:35*

3. Saul and David *16:1–31:13*

2 Samuel

1. David reigns over Judah *1:1–6:23*

2. David expands the kingdom *7:1–10:19*

3. David's sins and their consequences *11:1–20:26*

4. The conclusion of the kingdom under David *21:1–24:25*

Christ in 1 & 2 Samuel
- **1 Samuel** Samuel is a type of Jesus.
- **2 Samuel** David is one of the main Old Testament portrayals of Jesus.

12

1 & 2 Kings
The kingdom is united and then divided

"So the Lord said to Solomon, 'Since this is your attitude and you have not kept my covenant and my decrees, which I commanded you, I will most certainly tear the kingdom away from you and give it to one of your subordinates.'" *1 Kings 11:11*

"So the people of Israel were taken from their homeland into exile in Assyria ..." *2 Kings 17:23*

Major theme
1 and 2 Kings was originally a single book, tracing the history of God's people from the death of David to their deportation to Babylon.

Background and purpose
In 1 Kings Israel is united, Solomon builds the temple and then the kingdom of Israel is divided.

2 Kings records the ministry of Elijah and Elisha and the capture of Israel and Judah.

The books depict the consequences of obedience and disobedience to God. The story of the two nations of Israel and Judah is presented in a systematic form. An account of the events in the life of a king of Israel is followed by an account of the events in the lives of all the kings of Judah who reigned at the same time. 1 Kings shows an illustrious beginning for the kingdom of Israel. 2 Kings shows the affect of a broken kingdom as seen in the spiritual hollowness in the lives of the people.

Author
The author is not known. Talmudic tradition refers to the prophet Jeremiah.

Date
It is possible for a single author living in exile to have used the source materials available to him and to have written 1 and 2 Kings around 560 BC.

Brief outline

1 Kings

1. David's death *1:1–2:11*

2. Solomon's reign *2:12–11:43*

3. Israel divided: Northern and Southern kingdoms *12:1–22:53*

2 Kings

1. The divided kingdom to Israel's fall *1:1–17:41*

2. Kings in the surviving nation of Judah *18:1–21:26*

Christ 1 & 2 Kings
• **1 Kings** Solomon is a "type" of Jesus. Jesus himself said, "'... one greater than Solomon is here'" *(Matthew 12:42)*.
• **2 Kings** Elisha is a "type" of Jesus, while Elijah is a "type" of John the Baptist.

13

1 & 2 Chronicles
David's reign and Israel's apostasy

"'I will set him [David] over my house and my kingdom for ever; his throne will be established for ever.'" *1 Chronicles 17:14*

"'... if my people, who are called by my name, will humble themselves and pray and seek my face and turn from their wicked ways, then will I hear from heaven and will forgive their sin and will heal their land.'" *2 Chronicles 7:14*

Major theme
1 and 2 Chronicles covers the same period of the history of God's people as that described in 2 Samuel through 2 Kings. Chronicles views these events from a spiritual perspective, whereas 2 Samuel and 1 and 2 Kings traces them from more of a political standpoint.

Background and purpose
1 and 2 Chronicles emphasize that God is still with his people. Although God's people were living in a secular environment and their nation had been nearly destroyed by war, God had brought them back to Jerusalem. 1 and 2 Chronicles explain why the history of God's people took the course it did and why it is still possible to have faith. God's people are told to learn from the mistakes of history.

Author
1 and 2 Chronicles is one book in the Hebrew Bible.
The author is not known, but according to an old Jewish tradition Ezra wrote the book. 1 and 2 Chronicles is a compilation drawn from many written sources.

Date
It is quite possible that the book was written, if not by Ezra himself, in Ezra's lifetime, in the last half of the fifth century BC.

Brief outline

1 Chronicles

1. Genealogies from Adam to Saul *1:1–9:44*

2. The death of Saul *10:1-14*

3. David's reign *11:1–29:30*

2 Chronicles

1. Solomon's reign *1:1–9:31*

2. The history of Judah *10:1–36:12*

3. The fall of Jerusalem *36:13-23*

Christ in 1 & 2 Chronicles
- **Jesus** is King of kings and Lord of lords.

Ezra
Return from Babylon

This is what Cyrus King of Persia says: "'may his God be with him, and let him go up to Jerusalem in Judah and build the temple of the Lord, the God of Israel, the God who is in Jerusalem.'" *Ezra 1:3*

Brief outline

1. Cyrus' decree to return to Jerusalem *1:1-11*

2. The first group of exiles return to Jerusalem *2:1-70*

3. The rebuilding of the temple *3:1–6:22*

4. Ezra returns to Jerusalem *7:1–10:44*

Major theme
Restoration: The return of the exiles from Babylon to Jerusalem.

Background and purpose
Ezra is a sequel to 1 and 2 Chronicles. It helps us to understand the background for the prophecies of Malachi. Chapters 1–6 show the providence of God as they describe how Cyrus' decree allows the exiles to return to Jerusalem under Zerubbabel, and the rebuilding of the temple. Chapters 7–10 describe the return under Ezra along with his moral and religious reforms which help to safeguard the spiritual heritage of Israel.

Author
The author is not named, but the Talmud attributes the book to Ezra. Some of the book is written in the first person from Ezra's point of view.

Date
The middle of the fifth century BC, approximately 440 BC.

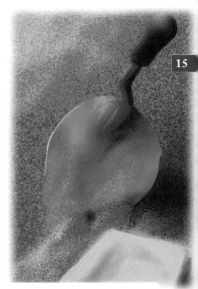

15

Christ in the book of Ezra
• **Jesus** is the Lord of heaven and earth.
• The book of Ezra typifies Jesus' work of restoration and forgiveness.

Nehemiah
Rebuilding Jerusalem's walls

"But we prayed to our God and posted a guard day and night to meet this threat." *Nehemiah 4:10*

Major theme
Chapters 1–7 describe Nehemiah's restoration of the walls of Jerusalem. Chapters 8–13 record Ezra's and Nehemiah's reforms. Nehemiah fully trusted in God as he prayed and planned for the rebuilding of the walls. Even facing opposition, his faith did not waver.

Background and purpose
The book of Nehemiah, which serves as a natural sequel to the book of Ezra, shows how God's providential hand re-established his people in their homeland after their exile. Without walls Jerusalem could not be thought of as a city at all. So Nehemiah's first priority was to rebuild the walls of Jerusalem. Nehemiah constantly reveals his dependence on God in his frequent prayers. The book of Nehemiah fills in the background to the three prophetic books of Haggai, Zechariah and Malachi.

Author
The book opens with the words, "The words of Nehemiah son of Hacaliah"

(1:1). The book of Nehemiah is the only Old Testament first-person narrative written by an important Jewish leader.

Date
The fifth century BC, approximately 430 BC, some time after the 32nd year of Artaterxes, king of Persia.

Brief outline
1. Nehemiah returns to Jerusalem *1:1–2:20*

2. Jerusalem's walls are rebuilt *3:1–7:73*

3. The Law is read and the covenant renewed *8:1–10:39*

4. Jerusalem is organized and revival spreads *11:1–13:31*

Christ in Nehemiah
• Nehemiah portrays Jesus in Jesus' work of restoration.

16

Esther

God rules behind the scenes

"'For if you remain silent at this time, relief and deliverance for the Jews will arise from another place, but you and your father's family will perish. And who knows but that you have come to royal position for such a time as this?'"
Esther 4:14

Major theme

Esther becomes queen to the Persian King, Xerxes. Driven by his hatred for Mordecai, Haman plots to exterminate the Jews. Esther cleverly persuades the king to reverse his decision against the Jews and Haman is hanged.

Background and purpose

The book of Esther explains the origin of the Feast of Purim, which the Jews celebrate between 13th and 15th Adar (February-March). *See 3:7; 9:20-32.* The book of Esther does not mention the name of God, although the name of a pagan king is mentioned over 150 times. God's power is apparent and is seen in his divine control and intervention.

Author

The author is not named. The contents of the book reveal that the author was Jewish and had first hand knowledge about Persian etiquette and customs. Esther or a younger

contemporary of Mordecai have been suggested as possible authors.

Date

The book is set in the reign of Ahasuerus, the Hebrew name, or Xerxes, the Greek name, of Khshayarsh, king of Persia in 486–464 BC. The book of Esther was probably written in the middle of the fifth century BC.

Brief outline

1. Esther becomes queen of Persia *1:1–2:23*

2. Haman's plot and Esther's intervention *3:1–5:14*

3. Haman is executed *6:1–7:10*

4. The Jews defend themselves; the Feast of Purim *8:1–10:3*

17

Christ in Esther

• Esther, like Jesus, put herself in the place of death for her people when she seeks the king's approval. Esther portrays Jesus' work as Advocate on our behalf.

Job
Why do the innocent suffer?

> "'But he knows the way I take;
> when he has tested me, I shall
> come forth as gold.'"
> *Job 23:10*

Major theme

Job was a "blameless and upright" man *(1:1)* who lost everything, which seems totally unjust. In three cycles of debate with his friends, they argue that God judges the wicked and conclude that Job must be wicked. Job challenges the reader with the difficult question, "If God is a God of mercy, why do the righteous suffer?"

Background and purpose

The book of Job does not explain the reason for innocent suffering but rather gives Job a glimpse of God's greatness, goodness and wisdom. *See 38:1–42:6.* In chapter 42 Job acknowledges God's majesty and sovereignty and stops demanding an answer to the "why?" of his situation.

Author

The author is not named. Although most of the book is made up of the words of Job and his "counselors", Job was probably not the author of the book. The unknown author of the book must have been a Jew, for he (but not Job and his friends) use Yahweh (NIV "the Lord") as the name for God. Some have credited Moses or Solomon as the author.

Date

No one knows for certain when the book was written. Some claim that it is the oldest book in the Bible with a date of 2000–1800 BC It is clearly possible that it could have been written at any time from King Solomon's reign to the exile. A date as early as the tenth century BC is sometimes favored.

Brief outline

1. Prologue: Job's test *1:1–2:13*

2. The false comfort of Job's friends *3:1–31:40*

3. Elihu's advice *32:1–37:24*

4. God's speaks to Job 38:1–42:6

5. Epilogue: Job's restoration *42:7-17*

Christ in Job

- Job acknowledges a Redeemer, *(19:25-27)*, and calls out for a Mediator *(9:33; 25:4; 33:23)*.

Psalms
The book of devotion and praise

"Come, let us sing for joy to the
Lord; let us shout aloud to the
Rock of our salvation."
Psalms 95:1

Major theme
The psalms reveal a loving
God who is not only the Savior
and Shepherd of his own
people, but also the Creator,
Sustainer, Judge and King of
the whole world.

Background and purpose
The name of the book of
Psalms comes from a Greek
word meaning "a song sung to
the accompaniment of a
plucked instrument." The
psalms were the hymn-book of
the Israelites. They were used
in the two temples as well as
for personal use. A large
number of themes are included
in the psalms but their
common theme is worship.
The intent of the psalms is to
kindle in the souls of men and
women a devotion and
affection for God, the Creator
and Lord.

Author
Most people automatically
think of David as being the
author of the psalms. From the
superscriptions at the head of
all but 34 of the psalms, it is
possible to conclude David
wrote 73 of the psalms, the

sons of Korah wrote ten of
them, Asaph wrote twelve of
them, Solomon wrote two of
them, "Moses the man of
prayer" wrote one *(Psalm 90)*,
and Heman and Ethan also
wrote one each. The book of
Psalms is "a collection of
collections," as the 150 psalms
are split up into five "books."

Date
The psalms cover a wide
period of time. Scholars date
some of them back as far as
Moses, with some written in
the times of Ezra and
Nehemiah. Most of the psalms
were written in the tenth
century BC.

Brief outline

1.	Book *1*	*1–41*
2.	Book *2*	*42–72*
3.	Book *3*	*73–89*
4.	Book *4*	*90–106*
5.	Book *5*	*107–150*

Christ in Psalms
Many psalms have direct or
typical references to Jesus:
- Jesus as King *(2; 45; 72; 110)*
- Jesus' sufferings *(22; 41)*
- Jesus' resurrection *(16)*
- Jesus' ascension *(68:18)*

Proverbs
Maxims to live by

"Trust in the Lord with all your
    heart
    and lean not on your own
    understanding;
in all your ways acknowledge him,
    and he will make your paths
    straight."
Proverbs 3:5-7

Major theme
The key theme in Proverbs is wisdom, which is mentioned one hundred and four times. Proverbs points out that this wisdom is available to everyone. Wise people are depicted as those who heed God's commands while the foolish ignore them.

Background and purpose
Proverbs is a collection of practical, ethical precepts about day-to-day living. They are arranged in balanced pairs of thoughts using contrasting parallelism. Teaching with the use of proverbs is one of the world's most ancient methods of instruction. Solomon's writing cover a broad range of topics, emphasizing correct moral and religious behavior that should be seen in God's people.

Author
Solomon wrote most of the proverbs in the book of Proverbs. Solomon "spoke three thousand proverbs and his songs numbered a thousand and five" *(1 Kings 4:32)*. Other authors in the book of Proverbs are "the sayings of the wise" *(22:17)*; Agur *(30)*; and King Lemuel *(31:1-9)*.

Date
Solomon's proverbs would have been written in the tenth century BC.

Brief outline

1. Facets of wisdom *1:1–9:18*

2. Proverbs of Solomon *10:1–22:16; 25:1–29:27*

3. Proverbs of wise men *22:17–24:34*

4. Proverbs of Agur *30:1-33*

5. Proverbs of King Lemuel *31:1-9*

6. The ideal wife *31:10-31*

Christ in Proverbs
- Jesus is the wisdom of God, *see 1 Corinthians 1:30*
- Jesus is "a friend who sticks closer than a brother" *(18:24)*.

Ecclesiastes

What is the meaning of life?

"Now all has been heard; here is the conclusion of the matter: Fear God and keep his commandments."
Ecclesiastes 12:13

Major theme

Ecclesiastes is the Bible's most philosophical book. Its perspective is human wisdom and thus has some verses which run counter to the general teaching of Scripture, such as, "A man can do nothing better than to eat and drink and find satisfaction in his work" *(2:24)*. The writer is pointing out the folly of human reasoning in order to focus on the only true satisfaction which is to be found in God.

Background and purpose

Ecclesiastes is sort of an Old Testament treatise for worldly people. It is as if the author is saying: "Let's see what life without God is like. Yes, life is indeed futile and miserable and meaningless, but life with God makes all the difference." Solomon shows the pointless-ness of things that people commonly look to for happiness: human learning, politics, sensual delight, honor, powers, riches and possessions.

Author

The author of the book of Ecclesiastes calls himself *qoheleth*, the preacher. He also calls himself, "son of David, king of Jerusalem" *(1:1)*. This would appear to make it plain that Solomon wrote Ecclesiastes and this is the prevailing view.

Date

Assuming that Solomon was the author places the date of Ecclesiastes in the tenth century BC.

Brief outline

1. The theme: the emptiness of godless living *1:1-3*

2. This theme is demonstrated *1:4–3:22*

3. The problems of human life *4:1–6:12*

4. Coping in this life *7:1–12:8*

5. Conclusion: Fear God and keep his commands *12:9-14*

Christ in Ecclesiastes

- God has "set eternity in the hearts of men" and only Jesus can provide ultimate satisfaction and wisdom.

21

Song of Songs
The most beautiful of all songs

"Many waters cannot quench
     love;
   rivers cannot wash it away."
Song of Songs 8:7

Major theme
No Bible book has been
interpreted in so many
different ways as the Song of
Songs. Most of the
interpretations fall into two
categories: literal or allegorical.

1. Allegorical
- The Jewish Talmud, the official
  teaching of Orthodox Jews,
  states that it is an allegory of
  God's love for Israel.
- Some Christian commentators
  extend this interpretation to say
  that it is an allegory of God's
  love for his people, the
  Christian Church.

2. Literal
- Theodore of Mopsuestia, 4th
  century, said that it was a love
  poem that Solomon wrote in
  honor of his marriage.
- Some Christian commentators
  extend this interpretation to
  say that it is a beautiful
  depiction of a married couple.

Background and purpose
The directly sensuous
language in this book has been
criticized. Some say this
represents the holy affections
that exist between God and his
people while others say that
this is a description of one of
God's gifts: the unashamed

appreciation of physical
attraction.

Author
Good arguments exist for
crediting Solomon as the
author of the Song of Songs as
the Talmud did. The book
opens with the words,
"Solomon's Song of Songs"
(1:1). Solomon is mentioned
seven times in the book.
"Look! It is Solomon's
carriage" *(3:7)*.

Date
Assuming that Solomon was
the author, the Song of Songs
was written in the 10th century
BC.

Brief outline

1. Affection between bride and
   bridegroom *1:1–3:5*

2. The bride accepts the
   bridegroom's invitation
   3:6–5:1

3. The bride's dream *5:2–6:3*

4. The bride and bridegroom
   express mutual love *6:4–8:14*

Christ in Song of Songs
- If the book is interpreted as a
  picture of the Christian church,
  the bridegroom is then taken to
  represent Jesus and the great
  love he has for every believer.

Isaiah
Salvation and the Servant

"For to us a child is born,
   to us a son is given,
   and the government will be
      on his shoulders.
And he will be called
   Wonderful Counselor, Mighty
   God, Everlasting Father,
   Prince of Peace."
Isaiah 9:6

Major theme
Isaiah has a two-fold message:
condemnation *(1–39)* and
consolation *(40–66)*.

Background and purpose
Isaiah's prophecies and visions
came during the reigns of four
kings: Uzziah, Jotham, Ahaz
and Hezekiah. When Isaiah
started his prophecies Israel
was in the final stages of
collapse. The northern
kingdom had been captured by
Assyria and the southern
kingdom of Judah was heading
for a similar end. Isaiah
pronounces God's judgment
on the sins of Judah and then
the surrounding nations. But
Isaiah goes on to console
God's people with his message
of future restoration and hope.

Author
The author of the prophecy of
Isaiah is stated in the opening
verse. "The vision concerning

Judah and Jerusalem that
Isaiah son of Amoz saw ..."
(1:1)

Date
Isaiah lived in Jerusalem in the
second half of the eighth
century BC. Since most of the
events described in chapters
1–39 took place in Isaiah's
ministry, Isaiah probably wrote
these chapters shortly after 701
BC following the destruction of
the Assyrian army. The rest of
the book was written later on
in his life.

23

Brief outline

1. Messages of rebuke and
   promise *1:1–6:13*

2. Judgment and blessings on
   Judah *7:1–12:6*

3. Judgment on the other nations
   13:1–23:18

4. The apocalypse of Isaiah
   24:1–27:13

5. Judgment and blessing on
   Judah, Israel and Assyria
   28:1–39:8

6. Future blessing and comfort on
   Judah *40:1–66:24*

Christ in Isaiah
• Jesus is the Servant about whom
   Isaiah prophecies. The best
   known prophecies describe
   Christ's virgin birth *(Isaiah
   7:14)* and his sufferings *(ch. 53)*.

Jeremiah
"The weeping prophet"

"'The time is coming,' declares the Lord, 'when I will make a new covenant with the house of Israel.' ... 'I will put my law in their minds and write it on their hearts. I will be their God, and they will be my people.'"
Jeremiah 31:31,33

Major theme
Jeremiah's main message is one of impending judgment on the people of Jerusalem.

Background and purpose
Jeremiah's prophecies are God's final words of warning to the people in the final years before the destruction of Jerusalem. Jeremiah directed his prophecies to the people of Judah from 627 BC until the time of the fall of Jerusalem to King Nebuchadnezzar of Babylon in 586 BC. Jeremiah consistently prophesied that this would happen to Jerusalem. His message was unheeded. As a result he was persecuted, put in stocks, and even thrown into a cistern. With foreign powers constantly threatening Jerusalem, it's hard to understand why the preaching of Jeremiah was viewed with such contempt by the people of that generation.

Author
The book of Jeremiah bears its author's name. Jeremiah is called "the weeping prophet" because of the intense despair and loneliness he felt as the people rejected God and his words.

Date
The book of Jeremiah was written in the sixth century BC. It covers the three parts of Jeremiah's ministry:
- From 627–605 BC when he prophesied while Judah was threatened by Assyria and Egypt.
- From 605–586 BC when he prophesied while Judah was besieged by Babylon.
- From 586–580 BC when he ministered in Jerusalem and Egypt after Judah's downfall.

Brief outline

1. Prophecies against Judah
1:1–25:38

2. Jeremiah's life *26:1–45:5*

3. Prophecies against foreign nations *46:1–51:64*

4. The fall of Jerusalem *52:1-34*

Christ in Jeremiah
- Jesus is the "Hope of Israel." *(14:8)*
- Jesus is our Potter *(18:6)*.
- Jesus is the "Shepherd" and "righteous Branch" *(23:3,5)*.

Lamentations
The book of tears

"They [the Lord's compassions]
    are new every morning;
    great is your faithfulness.
I say to myself, 'The Lord is my
    portion;
    therefore I will wait for him.'"
Lamentations 3:23-24

Major theme
The book is a sequel to the
book of Jeremiah. It is a series
of laments over the fallen
Jerusalem.

Background and purpose
Each chapter of this book
consists of one lamentation or
elegy written in a special poetic
form.

Each lamentation has 22
sections and each section
corresponds to a successive
letter of the Hebrew alphabet
(which has only 22 letters).

The Septuagint introduces
this book with the words:
"And it came to pass after
Israel was led into captivity
that Jeremiah sat weeping and
lamenting and lamented this
lamentation over Jerusalem."

The disastrous fall of
Jerusalem in 587 BC needs to
be explained. This book says
that although the visible signs
of God's presence in God's
city and God's temple have
been destroyed, God's people
will be purified as a result.

Author
The author is not named, but
tradition and the fact that
Jeremiah was an eyewitness of
the destruction of Jerusalem,
makes Jeremiah the most likely
author.

Date
Lamentations must have been
written after the fall of
Jerusalem in 586 BC, but
before it was rebuilt and
dedicated in 516 BC. The
graphic laments place the time
of writing close to the
destruction of Jerusalem.

Brief outline

1. Jerusalem's sorrows *1:1-22*

2. Jerusalem's punishment *2:1-22*

3. Judah's hope in God's mercy
   3:1-66

4. Jerusalem: past and present
   4:1-22

5. A prayer for mercy
   5:1-22

25

Christ in Lamentations
- Jesus is seen as "my portion"
  (3:24).

Ezekiel
The watchman's report

"'For I will take you out of the nations; I will gather you from all the countries and bring you back into your own land.'"
Ezekiel 36:24

Major theme

The book of Ezekiel shows God's faithfulness to Israel and all his holy people, and that God's purposes through judgment and blessing are the same: that his people may come to know that he is the Lord.

Background and purpose

Ezekiel the prophet was one of the Jewish exiles in Babylon during the last days of the kingdom of Judah. He was deported to Babylon in 597 BC along with King Jehoiachin and was relocated to the village of Tel Abib on the river Chebar. He announced God's judgment upon Judah and the surrounding countries. After the fall of Jerusalem he prophesied revival, restoration and a future for God's people.

Author

All that is known about the prophet Ezekiel comes from the prophecy which bears his name. More than any other prophet, he acted out the symbolism of his prophecies.

Date

The book of Ezekiel contains more dates than any other Old Testament prophetic book. Ezekiel received his call in July 593 BC, seven years before the destruction of Jerusalem. Ezekiel's last dated oracle came in April 571 BC, 15 years after the destruction of Jerusalem. It is assumed that Ezekiel wrote his prophecy around that time.

Brief outline

1. Ezekiel's call *1:1–3:27*

2. Prophecies of doom for Jerusalem *4:1–24:27*

3. God's judgment on the nations *25:1–32:32*

4. God's promise of renewal *33:1–37:28*

5. Prophecy against Gog *38:1–39:29*

6. Visions of the future temple and land *40:1–48:35*

Important events
Descriptions of:
- The departure of the glory of the Lord from the temple
- The fall of Jerusalem
- The return of God's glory

Christ in Ezekiel
- The caring, searching shepherd is a picture of Jesus. "'I will search for the lost and bring back the strays. I will bind up the injured and strengthen the weak ...'" *(34:16)*.

Daniel
The book of visions

"'In the time of those kings, the God of heaven will set up a kingdom that will never be destroyed, nor will it be left to another people. It will crush all those kingdoms and bring them to an end, but it will itself endure for ever.'" *Daniel 2:44*

Major theme
When God's people had little hope, Daniel provided encouragement by revealing God's power and his plans for the future.

Background and purpose
The book of Daniel records the experiences of Daniel and some of his fellow-exiles in Babylon and how their faith in God protected them. It has never been easy interpreting the visions about the rise and fall of several empires, in the second part of the book of Daniel. Jesus took seriously Daniel's prophecies about Antiochus Epiphanes, who ruled most of Asia Minor, Syria and Palestine from 175 BC until 164 BC. *See Matthew 24:15*

One helpful way of interpreting these prophecies is to see that they may have more than one point of fulfilment:
• In the time of Antiochus
• When the city of Jerusalem fell again in AD 70
• At the final End Time.

Author
Daniel is stated as the author of this book *(9:2)*. Jesus attributed the quotation from Daniel *(9:27)* to "the prophet Daniel" *(Matthew 24:15)*. Certain scholars do not accept Daniel as the author, nor do they accept prophetic predictions. Thus they date the book as late as 160 BC, which of course eliminates all the prophetic element of the book.

Date
Daniel prophesied in Babylon and probably completed his book just after Babylon was captured by Cyrus in 539 BC.

Brief outline
1. Daniel's life at the Babylonian court *1:1–2:49*

2. Daniel's early visions in Babylon *3:1–6:28*

3. Daniel's visions of world empires *7:1–8:27*

4. Daniel's prayer and vision of the 70 "sevens" *9:1-27*

5. Daniel's visions of Israel's future *10:1–12:13*

Important events
• Daniel's three friends survive being thrown into the fiery furnace
• Daniel in the lions' den

Christ in Daniel
• The "Ancient of Days" is Jesus *(7:13)*.

Hosea
The book for backsliders

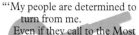

"'My people are determined to
    turn from me.
Even if they call to the Most
    High,
he will by no means exalt them.
'How can I give you up, Ephraim?
    How can I hand you over,
    Israel?'"
Hosea 11:7-8

Major themes
Apostasy from God is spiritual
adultery. The Lord loves Israel
despite her sin. The tone of the
book is filled with God's
mercy, loyalty, devotion and
unconditional love.

Background and purpose
Hosea had a tragic family life.
God told him to marry Gomer
but she proved unfaithful to
Hosea, ran away and became a
prostitute. Hosea continued to
love her, bought her back
(even though she was little
more than a slave) and
restored her to being his wife.

The prophet Hosea takes his
own marriage as a picture of
the relationship between God
and Israel. God loved Israel,
even when she was unfaithful
to him.

Author
Hosea was a prophet to the
northern kingdom of Israel for
about 50 years and the book
that bears his name is filled
with his prophecies.

Date
Hosea prophesied in the
middle of the eighth century
BC.

Brief outline

1. Hosea's family *1:1–3:5*

2. Israel's corruption *4:1–5:15*

3. God's love is rejected *6:1–8:6*

4. Judgment will come *8:7–10:15*

5. Repentance is possible
    11:1–14:9

Christ in Hosea
• Christ's loving, redemptive work
  on our behalf is mirrored in
  Hosea's love and restoration of
  Gomer.

28

Joel
Judgment and mercy

"'And afterwards,
  I will pour our my Spirit on all
    people.
Your sons and daughters will
    prophesy,
  your old men will dream
    dreams,
  your young men will see
    visions.'"
Joel 2:28

Major theme

The key theme in the book of Joel is the day of the Lord or the day of judgment when God directly intervenes in human history. Only a change of heart and a change of life will bring restoration and blessing.

Background and purpose

A recent plague of locusts is taken by Joel to signify divine judgment on Judah's sins. Judah was now surrounded by enemy nations who were like hordes of locusts. Judah's only hope of survival was to repent and seek God's mercy.

  The Spirit of God promised in *(2:28-31)* was fulfilled on the Day of Pentecost *(Acts 2:1-20)*.

Author

Joel, the son of Pethuel, was a prophet to the southern kingdom of Judah. Nothing is known about Joel outside his prophecy. There are twelve other people called Joel in the Old Testament, but the prophet Joel is linked to none of them.

Date

The book does not have any explicit time references in it and so cannot be precisely dated. Many conservative scholars suggest that Joel was written in the ninth or eighth century BC.

Brief outline

1. The plague of locusts
   1:1-20

2. Apocalyptic judgment
   threatened *2:1-27*

3. The outpouring of the Spirit
   2:28-32

4. The oppressor will be judged
   3:1-16

5. Restoration of God's people
   3:17-21

29

Christ in Joel

• Jesus is a "refuge for his people"
  (3:16).

Amos
Prophet to the affluent society

"Seek good, not evil,
   that you may live.
Then the Almighty will be with
   you,
   just as you say he is."
   Amos 5:14

Major theme
God is just. He
demands social
justice and must
judge sin.

Background and purpose
Amos accused Israel of
neglecting the worship of God
and indulging in extravagant
luxury. Rich merchants
oppressed the poor and
worshiped the pagan idols that
Jeroboam I had introduced.
Israel was enjoying great
prosperity and commanded a
strong political and military
position. But Amos warned
Israel of God's impending
judgment. The proportion of
teaching about God's
judgment compared to hope is
higher in Amos than in any
other prophet. However, Amos
ends his book on a note of
hope:
"'I will plant Israel in their own
   land,
   never again to be uprooted
   from the land I have given
      them,'
   says the Lord." *9:15*

Author
Amos was a sheep farmer from
"Tekoa" *(1:1)*, a small town
six miles south of Bethlehem,
in the southern kingdom of
   Judah, yet he prophesied to
      the northern kingdom of
      Israel. The only Old
      Testament appearance of
      the name "Amos" is in
      this book.

Date
   Amos prophesied "when
Uzziah was king of Judah
[792–740 BC] and Jeroboam
son of Jehoash was king of
Israel [793–753 BC]" *(1:1)*.
Amos probably prophesied
around 760–750 BC.

Brief outline

1. Prophecies against the nations
   1:3–2:16

2. The corrupt land *3:1–6:14*

3. Visions of doom *7:1–8:3*

4. Judgment day *8:4–9:10*

5. Promised restoration *9:11-15*

Christ in Amos
• Jesus is the Restorer of his
  people *(9:11-15)*.

Obadiah
God's judgment is certain

"Deliverers will go up on Mount
   Zion
   to govern the mountains of
   Esau.
   And the kingdom will be the
   Lord's."
Obadiah 21

Major theme
Sure retribution must overtake
merciless pride. God will
punish those who refuse to live
justly and righteously.

Background and purpose
Obadiah's prophecy is aimed
at the Edomites who are
judged by God for their
inhumanity to Israel in the day
of its suffering. "'Because of
the violence against your
brother Jacob, you will be
covered with shame; you will
be destroyed for ever'" *(10)*.
The Edomites refused to allow
Israel to travel through their
country *(Numbers 20:14-21)*,
and they rejoiced when
Jerusalem was captured *(Psalm
137:7)*. Edom's crimes are
listed in order of their
ascending horror *(11-14)*.
   Obadiah has one of the most
realistic descriptions of the
siege and attack of a city in the
whole of the Old Testament.

Author
Nothing is known about
Obadiah outside his prophecy.
We are not told the name of
his father or where he was
born. His name means
"servant of the Lord" and was
a common one in the Old
Testament.

Date
If verses 11-14 refer to the
Babylonian attacks on
Jerusalem in 605–586 BC that
would mean that Obadiah was
a contemporary of Jeremiah
and this gives a sixth century
BC date for the writing of
Obadiah.

Brief outline
1. Edom's fall is prophecied *1-9*
2. Edom's sins exposed *10-14*

Christ in Obadiah
• Jesus is the Judge of the nations
  (15-16), and the Savior of Israel
  (17-20).

Jonah
Can God bless the wicked?

"'Go to the great city of Nineveh and proclaim to it the message I give you.'"
Jonah 3:2

Major theme
Jonah reveals God's concern for all people as he shows the power of God over nature *(1–2)*, and the mercy of God in human affairs *(3–4)*.

32

Background and purpose
Some interpret the whole book of Jonah as a parable rather than as actual fact.

Arguments in favor of treating Jonah as an historical event are:
• Jonah is described as a real person.
• Jesus took Jonah and his adventures seriously and even compared his own resurrection to Jonah's experience inside the fish *(Matthew 12:39-41)*.

The Hebrew idiom about the time Jonah was inside the fish, "three days and three nights" *(1:17)* only requires a part of the first and third days.

Author
The book does not identify the author, but it is traditionally ascribed to Jonah.

Date
A wide range of dates for the writing of Jonah have been proposed, from the days of Elijah and Elisha in the ninth century BC to the third century when it has been reduced to an historical fiction by some commentators. If Jonah was a contemporary of Amos there are good reasons for suggesting that Jonah was written in the eighth century BC.

Brief outline

1. God commissions Jonah to preach against Nineveh, but Jonah takes a boat destined for "Tarshish" *(1:3)* in the opposite direction. The Lord saves pagan sailors from being shipwrecked *1:1-17*

2. The Lord rescues disobedient Jonah from drowning by the timely arrival of a huge fish *2:1-11*

3. The Lord saves repentant Nineveh *3:1-10*

4. Jonah learns to look beyond his own nation and to trust the Creator of all people *4:1-11*

Christ in Jonah
• Jonah's experience is a "type" of the death, burial, and resurrection of Jesus *(Matthew 12:39-41)*.
• The Bible does not mention a whale, but a "great fish" (King James Version), or a "huge fish" *(Matthew 12:40)*.

Micah
Judgment and hope

"He has showed you, O man,
    what is good.
    And what does the Lord
    require of you?
To act justly and to love mercy
    and to walk humbly with your
    God."
Micah 6:8

Major theme

The focus is on God's hatred of sin, but also his promise to rescue those who would change their hearts and actions. The Bethlehem-born Messiah will be humankind's deliverer.

Background and purpose

The book of Micah is a collection of speeches. Micah forecasts about God's impending judgment on Judah's sins *(chapters 1–3)*, and graphically describes both their sins and punishment. Micah goes on to prophesy a bright future after this judgment *(chapters 4–5)*. The concluding two chapters are in the form of the Lord's controversy with his people and the mercy he finally has on them.

Author

Micah was a prophet to the southern kingdom of Judah. He is mentioned in Jeremiah 26:18, "Micah of Moresheth [in southern Judah] prophesied in the days of Hezekiah king of Judah." Apart from that and what we learn about him from the book of Micah we know nothing about him.

Date

We ascertain from the opening verse of Micah that the prophet prophesied during the reigns of Jotham, Ahaz and Hezekiah. This makes Micah a contemporary of the prophet Isaiah. Micah must have prophesied between 750 BC and 686 BC.

Brief outline

1. Judgment against Israel and Judah *1:1–3:12*

2. Hope for Israel and Judah *4:1–5:15*

3. God's case against Israel *6:1-16*

4. Micah's sad poem and a hopeful future *7:1-20*

Christ in Micah

• Micah contains one of the clearest and most important prophecies about Jesus:
"'But you, Bethlehem Ephrathah, though you are small among the clans of Judah,
out of you will come for me one who will be ruler over Israel,
whose origins are from of old, from ancient times.'"
Micah 5:2

33

Nahum
The fall of Nineveh

"The Lord is good,
a refuge in times of trouble."
Nahum 1:7

Major theme
God is good, but God's judgment is to engulf wicked Nineveh.

Background and purpose
God's followers in Judah would be comforted to learn about God's judgment on the brutal Assyrians. Nahum announces that the Assyrians are doomed because of their excessive pride, idolatry and oppression. The book affirms God's active interest in all nations, not just Israel.

Author
Nahum is only mentioned in the opening verse of the prophecy which bears his name. "An oracle concerning Nineveh. The book of the vision of Nahum the Elkoshite" *(1:1)*. Even the location of Elkosh is not known.

Date
Nahum pictures the fall of Nineveh to the Babylonians in 612 BC as a future event. Nahum also refers to the fall of Thebes (663 BC) as an event that had already happened: "Are you better than Thebes ... Yet she was taken captive" *(3:8,10)*. As Nahum pictures the fall of Nineveh as an imminent event, it is likely that the book of Nahum was much closer to 612 BC than to 663 BC. This would make Nahum a contemporary of Zephaniah.

Brief outline

1. Nahum announces the coming of the divine avenger on Nineveh *1:1-15*

2. Nahum gives a detailed description of the sieges, fall and sacking of Nineveh *2:1-13*

3. Using horrific language, Nahum pronounces, "Woe to the city of blood" *3:1-19*

Christ in Nahum
• "... the feet of one who brings good news, who proclaims peace!' is applied to the message and ministry of Jesus. *See Isaiah 52:7* and *Romans 10:15*

Habakkuk
Can God use the wicked?

> "'See, he is puffed up;
> his desires are not upright–
> but the righteous will live by his
> faith– ...'"

Habakkuk 2:4

Major theme
Justification by faith is God's way of salvation. God is just and he is still in control.

Background and purpose
Habakkuk wrestles with a profound and perplexing theological problem: "How can God's patience with evil conform with his holiness?"

The answer provided by the book of Habakkuk is that God is sovereign and thus deals with the wicked in his own way, in his own time.

Paul quotes Habakkuk 2:4 in Romans 1. It was this verse that profoundly influenced Martin Luther and led to the Protestant reformation.

Author
All we know about Habakkuk is that he was a prophet.

Date
The only explicit time reference in Habakkuk is to the impending Babylonian invasion *(1:6; 2:1; 3:16)*. "I am raising up the Babylonians, that ruthless and impetuous people, who sweep across the whole earth to seize dwelling-places not their own" *(1:6)*. Since the Babylonians won a decisive victory at Carchemish in 605 BC, the prophecy of Habakkuk was probably at this time.

Brief outline
1. Habakkuk argues with God *1:2-4*

2. God replies *1:5-11*

3. Habakkuk protests *1:12-17*

4. God replies *2:1-20*

5. God's judgment and salvation *3:1-16*

6. The confidence of the godly *3:7-19*

35

Christ in Habakkuk
- "I will be joyful in God my Savior" *(3:18)*. Jesus, the root of whose name means "salvation", is "the Savior of the world" *(John 4:42)*.

Zephaniah
A warning of judgment

"Seek the Lord, all you humble of
   the land,
   you who do what he
      commands.
Seek righteousness, seek humility;
   perhaps you will be sheltered
   on the day of the Lord's anger."
      Zephaniah 2:3

Major theme
God's judgment must precede
kingdom blessing. Seek the
Lord now!

Background and purpose
Zephaniah prophesies a
universal judgment which will
begin with Judah, but ends
with a promise of restoration.
He states that their sins are the
reason for God's punishment
of their nation. He also makes
it clean that God will be
merciful toward the Israelites.

Author
According to the opening verse
of this prophecy Zephaniah
was the great, great, great
grandson of King Hezekiah, a
notable king of Judah. We are
not given any other information about Zephaniah's
background, but from his
prophecy we learn that he was
fully acquainted with the
current political issues and
with court circles.

Date
"The word of the Lord came to
Zephaniah son of Cushi, the son
of Gedaliah, the son of Amariah,
the son of Hezekiah, during the
reign of Josiah son of Amon king
of Judah." *1:1*

Since King Josiah reigned
640–609 BC, we know the
dates of Zephaniah's prophetic
ministry.

Brief outline

1. God's judgment is announced
   1:1-18

2. Judah is told to repent. *2:1-3*

3. God's judgment on other
   nations *2:4-15*

4. Judah will not escape God's
   judgment *3:1-8*

5. God promises to restore a
   remnant *3:9-20*

Christ in Zephaniah
• Jesus fulfils the promise of
  (3:17):
  "'The Lord your God is with
     you,
  he will quiet you with his love,
  he will rejoice over you with
     singing.'"

Haggai
Building for God

"This is what the Lord Almighty says: 'Give careful thought to your ways. Go up into the mountains and bring down timber and build the house, so that I may take pleasure in it and be honored,' says the Lord."
Haggai 1:7-8

Major theme
The Lord's temple and worship deserve top priority. God must have just place in a person's life.

Background and purpose
Haggai's prophecies help us to understand some of the problems of the returning Jews. Haggai rebukes them for their neglecting their work for God and concentrating their efforts on their own prosperity, rather than first rebuilding the temple and re-establishing the priestly offerings.

Author
Haggai was a prophet to the Jews who returned to Jerusalem from Babylonia.

Date
This book has five separate prophecies which are all dated. The first prophecy was "In the second year of King Darius, on the first day of the sixth month" *(1:1).* This can be related to our modern calendar and is August 19, 520 BC. All Haggai's prophecies come during a four-month period in 520 BC.

Brief outline

1. **First prophecy** Haggai urges that work be started on the rebuilding of the temple *1:1-11*

2. **Second prophecy** Haggai encourages the Jews in their work *1:12-15*

3. **Third prophecy** Another message of encouragement from Haggai *2:1-9*

4. **Fourth prophecy** Present blessings are promised *2:10-19*

5. **Fifth prophecy** Haggai gives a personal message to Zerubbabel *2:20-23*

Christ in Haggai
• Jesus is portrayed in Zerubbabel. "'I will take you, my servant Zerubbabel ... and I will make you like my signet ring, for I have chosen you ...'" *(2:23)*

Zechariah
Prepare for the Messiah

"'Therefore tell the people: This is what the Lord Almighty says: "Return to me," declares the Lord Almighty, "and I will return to you."'" *Zechariah 1:3*

Major theme
The Lord will remember his people Israel and will show the eventual holiness of Jerusalem and her people. The book gives the assurance that God is in control at all times.

Background and purpose
Zechariah, a contemporary of Haggai, tells the Jews who returned to Jerusalem from Babylonia to complete the rebuilding of the temple. The motivation Zechariah gives for this is that the temple has always been central to Israel's spiritual heritage and that it is closely linked to the coming of the Messiah.

The book of Zechariah contains a series of eight visions *(1–8)*, four messages *(7–8)*, and two burdens *(9–14)* which convey some of the clearest prophecies in Scripture about the coming Messiah.

Author
Zechariah was a priest as well as a prophet, being the son of Berekiah and grandson of Iddo *(1:1)*. He was born in Babylonia and brought to Palestine when the Jewish exiles returned under Zerubbabel and Joshua the high priest.

Date
Zechariah was a contemporary of Haggai the prophet, Zerubbabel the governor and Joshua the high priest. Haggai started preaching in 520 BC, but his final prophecy *(chapters 9–14)*, were probably not delivered until after 480 BC.

Brief outline

1. A call to repentance *1:1-6*

2. A series of eight night visions *1:7–6:8*

3. The crowning of Joshua *6:9-15*

4. The question of fasting *7:1-3*

5. Four messages of Zechariah *7:4–8:23*

6. Two burdens of Zechariah *9:1–14:21*

Christ in Zechariah
Jesus is seen as
- The Branch *(3:8)*.
- The priest on his throne (King-Priest) *(6:13)*.
- The Shepherd *(13:7)*.

Malachi
God's love for his faithless people

"'But for you who revere my name, the sun of righteousness will rise with healing in its wings. And you will go out and leap like calves released from the stall.'"
Malachi 4:2

Major theme
Let the wicked be warned about the certainty of judgment, but God will love and bless his people as they turn to him.

Background and purpose
The Lord is seen having a dialogue with his people. "But you ask," is contrasted with, "This is what the Almighty says."

Question, for which God has good answers
- "'How have you loved us?'" *1:2-5*
- "'How have we shown contempt for your name?'" *1:6-2:9*
- "'Why do we profane the covenant?'" *2:10-16*
- "'How have we wearied him?'" *2:17-3:6*
- "'How are we to return?'" *3:7-12*
- "'What have we said against you?'" *3:13-4:3*

Author
Malachi is only mentioned in the Old Testament in the opening verse of the prophecy which bears his name. The book of Malachi is traditionally attributed to him.

Date
Malachi's prophecies, like those of Haggai and Zechariah, were addressed to the restored community of Israel, around 450 BC and 425 BC. Malachi's prophecies are the last of the Old Testament prophecies in the Bible. After Malachi no prophetic voice was heard until the coming of John the Baptist.

Brief outline

1. The Lord's love for Israel *1:2-5*

2. The priests are rebuked *1:6-2:9*

3. Israel's faithlessness in worship and marriage *2:10-16*

4. The day of the Lord's justice *2:17-3:5*

5. The Lord's blessing on giving *3:6-12*

6. The righteous are vindicated in the day of the Lord *3:13-4:6*

39

Christ in Malachi
- Jesus is the messenger of God's covenant. "Then the Lord you are seeking will come to his temple; the messenger of the covenant, whom you desire, will come" *(3:1)*.
- Jesus is the "sun of righteousness" *(4:2)*.

Matthew
Jesus, the promised King

"'All authority in heaven and on earth has been given to me. Therefore go and make disciples of all nations, baptizing them in the name of the Father and of the Son and of the Holy Spirit, and teaching them to obey everything I have commanded you. And surely I am with you always, to the very end of the age.'"
Matthew 28:18-20

Major theme
Matthew wrote this account of Jesus' life to convince the Jews that Jesus was their Messiah.

Background and purpose
Matthew wrote his Gospel to show the links between the Old Testament and Jesus, to record the wealth of teaching Jesus gave to his disciples, to set out how Jesus expected his followers to behave, to answer some of the questions raised by members of the church, (such as the early life of Jesus and when he would return) and to say how the church should be run.

Author
Matthew. One of Jesus' twelve apostles, the former tax-collector, who was also known as Levi. When he became a follower of Jesus he abandoned everything and held a feast in his house for Jesus and other tax-collectors and "sinners".

Date
Probably written between AD 60–65 before the fall of the city of Jerusalem in AD 70.

Brief outline

1. Genealogy and birth of Jesus Christ *1:1–2:23*

2. John the Baptist's ministry *3:1-12*

3. Jesus' baptism and temptations *3:13–4:11*

4. Jesus' public ministry in Galilee *4:12–18:35*

5. From Galilee to Jerusalem *19:1–20:34*

6. Jesus' last week *21:1–27:66*

7. The resurrection and appearances of Jesus *28:1-20*

Keys to Matthew
- **Key word** Kingdom
- **Key chapter 12**, in which the Pharisees reject Jesus as Messiah of the nation of Israel.
- Matthew stresses Jesus' exhortations to his followers and so this book has always had a strong appeal to new Christians. 60% of Matthew's Gospel, that is 644 verses out of the total of 1,071 verses, contain the spoken words of Jesus.
- Matthew has 53 quotations from the Old Testament and 76 allusions from the Old Testament.

40

Mark
Jesus, the obedient Servant

"'For even the Son of Man did not come to be served, but to serve, and to give his life as a ransom for many.'" *Mark 10:45*

Major theme
Through the example of Jesus, Mark demonstrates the service and sacrifice of the Messiah that Jesus is continually serving and doing.

Background and purpose
Mark's Gospel is a short book. It does not give a full account of Christ's sermons but focuses on Christ's miracles. Mark presents the person and work of Jesus Christ to a primarily, non-Jewish audience, possibly those experiencing persecution in Rome.

Author
John Mark.
Mark and his cousin, Barnabas, accompanied Paul on his first missionary journey *(Acts 13:5)*. Mark deserted the missionaries at Perga, so Paul refused to take Mark on a second journey. Instead, Mark went with Barnabas to Cyprus. Later he was reconciled to Paul *(Colossians 4:10)* and was closely associated with Peter *(1 Peter 5:13)*.

Date
Between AD 55 and the early 60s. Tradition suggests Mark wrote this Gospel under the direction of Peter.

Brief outline

1. Jesus begins his public ministry *1:1-20*

2. Jesus' public ministry in Galilee *1:21–6:29*

3. Jesus withdraws from Galilee *6:30–9:50*

4. Jesus' ministry in Perea *10:1-52*

5. Jesus' last week *11:1–15:47*

6. Jesus comes back to life and his ascension *16:1-20*

Keys to Mark
- **Key word** The Greek word *euthus* (immediately or at once) occurs 42 times. Mark seems to hurry the reader on from one amazing story to the next.
- **Key chapter 8**, which shows a change of emphasis in Jesus' ministry. After Peter confesses, "You are the Christ" (*8:29*), Jesus teaches his disciples about his sacrificial death.
- 42% of Mark's Gospel, that is 285 verses out of the total of 678 verses, contain the spoken words of Jesus.
- Mark has 36 quotations from the Old Testament and 27 allusions from the Old Testament.

Luke
Jesus, the perfect Man

"Therefore, since I myself have carefully investigated everything from the beginning, it seemed good also to me to write an orderly account for you, most excellent Theophilus, so that you may know the certainty of the things you have been taught."
Luke 1:3-4

Major theme

Luke wanted to show that Jesus was Savior for all types of people and not just an elite group. Jesus is pictured showing more interest in children, women and social outcasts than in the other Gospels.

Background and purpose

Luke is the only Gospel writer to spell out at length why he wrote his Gospel. See *Luke 1:1-4*

Luke stresses the humanity of Jesus and so writes in detail about his ancestry and birth.

Author

Luke, a Greek-speaking doctor, was Paul's faithful friend. He was a Gentile and a traveling companion of Paul *(Philemon 24)*, who remained with the apostle even when he was imprisoned late in life *(2 Tim 4:11)* Luke also wrote Acts.

Date

Most scholars accept between AD 60 and 65.

Brief outline

1. Prologue *1:1-4*

2. Birth and childhood of John the Baptist and Jesus *1:5–2:52*

3. John the Baptist's ministry *3:1-20*

4. Jesus' baptism and temptations *3:21–4:13*

5. Jesus' public ministry in Galilee *4:14–9:50*

6. From Galilee to Jerusalem *9:51–19:27*

7. Jesus' last week *19:28–23:56*

8. Jesus' resurrection, appearances and ascension *24:1-53*

Keys to Luke

• **Key word** Seek.
• **Key chapter 15**, with its three parables illustrating that God through Jesus came to seek and to save the lost.
• **Key teaching** The parables of Jesus. Luke's portrait of Jesus uses more material than the other three Gospels.
• 16 of the 26 parables of Jesus recorded by Luke are found only in Luke's Gospel.
• 50% of Luke's Gospel, that is 586 verses out of the total of 1,151 verses, contain the spoken words of Jesus.
• Luke has 25 quotations from the Old Testament and 42 allusions from the Old Testament.

John
Jesus, the divine Son

"For God so loved the world that he gave his one and only Son, that whoever believes in him shall not perish but have eternal life."
John 3:16

Major theme
John's Gospel is no mere biography. It is a carefully-prepared Gospel treatise in which he selects evidence so his readers may believe that Jesus is the Christ.

Background and purpose
At the end of his Gospel, John tells his readers why he wrote it. See *John 20:30-31*

Much of John's teaching about Jesus is presented in the form of the different conversations people had with Jesus. John brings forward witness after witness who have had encounters with Jesus so that the reader has to make a decision about Jesus.

Author
The apostle John. John, a fisherman and son of Zebedee, was one Jesus' inner circle of three very close apostles; along with his brother, James. They were given the nickname the "sons of thunder". John, who leaned on Jesus at the Last Supper, was Jesus' closest friend. John never mentions himself by name in his Gospel,

but uses the words "the disciple Jesus loved" instead.

Date
Approximately AD 90, probably the last of the Gospels to have been written.

Brief outline

1. Prologue *1:1-18*

2. Jesus' ministry in Galilee *1:19–12:50*

3. Jesus and the Last Supper *13:1–14:31*

4. Jesus' discourses as he goes to Gethsemane *15:1–16:33*

5. Jesus' prayer for his own *17:1-26*

6. Jesus' arrest, trial and crucifixion *18:1–19:42*

7. Jesus' resurrection and appearances *20:1–21:25*

Keys to John
- **Key word** Believe, nearly 100 times.
- John stresses the deity of the incarnate Son of God with his: seven "I am" statements *(6:35; 8:12; 10:7; 10:11; 11:25; 14:6; 15:1)*
- Seven miraculous signs *(1–12)*
- Five witnesses *(5:30-40)*
- 50% of John's Gospel, that is 419 verses out of the total of 879 verses, contain the spoken words of Jesus.
- John has 20 quotations and 105 allusions from the Old Testament.

Acts
The witnessing Church

"'But you will receive power when the Holy Spirit comes on you; and you will be my witnesses in Jerusalem, and in all Judea and Samaria, and to the ends of the earth.'" *Acts 1:8*

Major theme

Acts is Luke's sequel to his gospel and is an accurate account of the spread of the early Church under the guidance and empowering of the Holy Spirit. Luke records the spread of the Gospel from the ascension of Jesus to Paul's imprisonment in Rome – the center of the Roman Empire.

Background and purpose

The book is written to Theophilus, the same person to whom Luke's Gospel is addressed and presumably for the same purpose: to present an orderly account of historical facts to Theophilus (*Luke 1:1-4*). Basically, the book is written to confirm the faith of believers. It is the history of the apostles and covers approximately the first 30 years of the early Church.

Author

Luke. Luke, the writer of the gospel which bears his name accompanied the apostle Paul on some of his journeys, and recorded what happened in the book of Acts. Luke sailed to Rome with Paul, staying with him while he was a prisoner in the imperial capital.

Date

This book was apparently written in a two-year period after Paul's imprisonment in Rome, about AD 63, but before Paul's death (Acts 28:30). No outcome of Paul's trial is mentioned by Luke; nor is there any mention of the destruction of Jerusalem in AD 70. Therefore, a date in the early 60s is probable.

Brief outline

1. Peter and the beginning of the church in Jerusalem *1:1–2:47*

2. The ministry of Peter, Stephen, Barnabas and others *3:1–8:40*

3. Paul's conversion *9:1-31*

4. Peter's continuing ministry and the non-Jewish church *10:1–12:24*

5. Paul's missionary journeys *12:25–21:26*

6. Paul's imprisonment, trip to Rome and defense *21:27–28:31*

Keys to Acts

Key word Witness, coming more than 30 times.

Key chapter Chapter 2, which records the life-changing events of the Day of Pentecost.

Key teaching Acts describes the work of the Holy Spirit in the lives of the apostles and how God brought the Gentiles into the early church.

Romans
The heart of the Gospel

"I am not ashamed of the gospel, because it is the power of God for the salvation of everyone who believes; first for the Jew, then for the Gentiles. For in the gospel a righteousness from God is revealed, a righteousness that is by faith from first to last, just as it is written: 'The righteous will live by faith.'" *Romans 1:16-17*

Major theme
Romans, the first great work of Christian theology, is the most influential of all Paul's letters. It shows how helpless humanity can be delivered in Jesus.

Background and purpose
Paul longed to visit the Christians in Rome, the capital of the known world. This letter prepares the way for his visit. It is probable that some people had been criticizing his teaching. This gave him the opportunity to put down a summary of the good news about Jesus in greater detail than anywhere else in the New Testament. Included in this discussion are statements on righteousness and how it is obtained, God's justification and what makes it possible, holiness and how God accomplishes it in the lives of his people, Israel's rejection of the Messiah and its meaning

for Jew and non-Jew. The last five chapters are an encouragement to live the Christian life.

Author
The apostle Paul. The great apostle and pioneering missionary, whose letters form a large part of the New Testament.

Date
Paul dictated this letter to his friend Tertius around AD 57 in Corinth:
"I, Tertius, who wrote down this letter, greet you in the Lord." *Romans 16:22*

Brief outline

1. Greetings *1:1-7*	
2. All the world is sinful *1:8–3:20*	
3. The fact of salvation *3:21–5:21*	
4. Salvation applied *6:1–8:39*	
5. What about the Jews? *9:1–11:36*	
6. Guidelines for the believer *12:1–15:33*	
7. Closing greetings *16:1-27*	

Keys to Romans
Key word Righteousness, used 62 times.
- When Christians rediscovered the book of Romans at the time of the Reformation the Christian Church was revitalized.

1 Corinthians
Dealing with a divided church

"Do you not know that your body is a temple of the Holy Spirit, who is in you, whom you have received from God? You are not your own; you were brought at a price. Therefore honor God with your body." *1 Corinthians 6:19-20*

Major theme
Paul writes this letter to the church he had founded in hope of resolving the many problems that had arisen among the new Christians at Corinth – problems of division and Christian conduct.

Background and purpose
1 Corinthians is like listening to only one end of telephone conversation. It answers the following questions:
- How should we view church leaders?
- How should church discipline be carried out?
- Is it right for a Christian to take a fellow Christian to court?
- What does it mean to be free as a Christian?
- What are the spiritual gifts and which are the most important ones?
- What happens after we die?

Author
The apostle Paul. Paul was probably at Ephesus *(16:8)*, when Stephanus and two friends arrived with a letter from the Christians at Corinth: "I was glad when Stephanus,

Fortunatus and Achaicus arrived, because they have supplied what was lacking from you" *(16:18)*. This letter apparently requested Paul's judgment on certain issues: "Now for the matters you wrote about ..." *(7:1)*. Paul penned this letter to answer these questions.

Date
c. AD 54–55

Brief outline

1. The scandal of a divided church *1:1–4:21*

2. The scandal of immorality *5:1–6:20*

3. Questions about marriage *7:1-40*

4. Christian freedom *8:1–11:1*

5. Order in church services *11:2–14:40*

6. The resurrection of Jesus and believers *15:1-58*

7. Closing greetings *16:1-24*

Key to 1 Corinthians
- Corinth was infamous for its paganism and immorality. The term *Korinthiazomai* (to act like a Corinthian) was synonymous with debauchery and prostitution. *See 5:1-2.*
- **Key teaching** The church, spiritual gifts, and evidence for and implications of Jesus' resurrection.

2 Corinthians
Paul reveals his minister's heart

"Therefore, if anyone is in Christ, he is a new creation; the old has gone, the new has come!"
2 Corinthians 5:17

Major theme
Paul wrote 2 Corinthians in response to strong attacks which some Christians at Corinth had made on his person, motive and character.

Background and purpose
False apostles had moved in among the Christians at Corinth *(11:12-15)*. These "super-apostles" *(11:5)*, taught a different gospel *(11:12-15)*, and defied Paul's authority. The Christians at Corinth had, or were on the verge of, changing their minds about Paul. Paul wrote 2 Corinthians to tell them just how much this change of mind meant to him.

His letter warns them not to be too harsh with his opponents *(2:5-11)*; not to be closely linked with unbelievers *(6:14)*; to give generously to the collection of money being made for the poor Christians in Jerusalem *(8–9)*; how to deal with false teachers *(11:1-6)*; and concludes with Paul's happiness that the Corinthians have stopped following false teachers *(11:12-15)*.

Author
The apostle Paul.

Date
We know the precise date that Paul was originally in Corinth. It was when Gallio was proconsul in Achaia: "Paul left Athens and went to Corinth. ... While Gallio was proconsul of Achaia, the Jews made a united attack on Paul and brought him into court" *(Acts 18:1,12)*. This was in AD 51 or 52. So his first letter to Corinth must have been written in about AD 54–55 and his second letter about one year later in AD 55–56.

Brief outline
1. Introduction *1:1-11*
2. Why Paul changed his plans *1:12–2:13*
3. Paul's ministry *2:14–6:10*
4. Paul's instructions *6:11–9:15*
5. Paul defends his apostleship *10:1–12:14*
6. Closing remarks and farewell greetings *12:20–13:13*

Keys to 2 Corinthians
- It is full of autobiographical material.
- It is one of Paul's most personal letters.
- It has many personal anecdotes into Paul's personal life.

Galatians
The true Gospel

"It is for freedom that Christ has set us free. Stand firm, then, and do not let yourselves be burdened again by a yoke of slavery."
Galatians 5:1

Major theme
To show that faith and faith alone is the only ground for justification and good living *(2:16,22)*.

Major theme
Some Jewish Christians arrived in Galatia and were undermining Paul's teaching. The letter to the Galatians was Paul's response that Jesus brings freedom from the law.

Background and purpose
Galatians has been called the "Magna Charter of Christian freedom," as it has freed countless Christians, notably Martin Luther, from various forms of outward observance which have endangered the freedom of the gospel.

Paul knew what it was to live under the law and he saw that the gospel of grace was at stake if the new Christians tried to fulfil the requirements of the Mosaic Law. So, with great passion, he wrote this, his most "severe" letter to the Christians at Galatia.

Paul's purpose is to counteract the false teaching that was blending Jewish rituals and the Christian faith. Paul urges the Galatians to remain in the freedom they have in Christ but also cautions against the abuse of this freedom.

Author
The apostle Paul.

Date
This is probably the earliest letter Paul wrote – approximately AD 48. Other scholars suggest a date of AD 56.

Brief outline

1. Introduction *1:1-5*

2. Paul's defense of his apostolic authority *1:6–2:14*

3. Justification by faith *2:15–4:31*

4. Christian freedom and responsibility *5:1–6:10*

5. Conclusion *6:10-18*

Keys to Galatians
- It is a fighting letter. Paul uses strong language to make his point. "If anyone is preaching to you a gospel other than what you accepted, let him be eternally condemned!" *1:9*
- It is a loving letter. It reveals the care and concern of a great pastor. *4:19-20*

Ephesians
The letter of fullness

"Praise be to the God and Father of our Lord Jesus Christ, who has blessed us in the heavenly realms with every spiritual blessing in Christ." *Ephesians 1:3*

Major theme
There are two primary themes: God's grace and the unity of the body, the Church.

Background and purpose
Chapters 1–3 list the believer's heavenly possessions: adoption, citizenship, grace, inheritance, life, power and redemption.

Chapters 4–6 have 35 directives which instruct the believer about living the Christian life.

Paul made at least three visits to Ephesus, and lived there for three years teaching the new Christians and laying a firm spiritual foundation. Perhaps that is why this book does not address any specific error or false doctrine. Rather, the letter to the Ephesians was intended to strengthen the Church and to make Christians more conscious of their unity in Christ.

Author
The apostle Paul. Paul wrote this letter while he was in prison in Rome. During his first imprisonment Paul wrote what have become known as the "prison letters": Ephesians, Philippians, Colossians and Philemon.

Date
Approximately AD 61–62 while Paul was still in a Roman prison.

Brief outline

1. Introduction *1:1-2*

2. Blessing of the Christian inheritance *1:3–2:22*

3. Paul's work and prayer *3:1-21*

4. The nature of the church *4:1-32*

5. Following Jesus *5:1-20*

6. Living with others *5:21–6:9*

7. Defeating the enemy *6:10-24*

Keys to Ephesians
Key thought Christians are to be aware of their position in Christ and draw on his spiritual resources in order to live "a life worthy of the calling you have received" *(4:1)*.

• The phrase "in Christ," or its equivalent, comes more frequently in this letter than any other New Testament book: 35 times.

Philippians
A letter of joy

"Your attitude should be the same as that of Christ Jesus."
Philippians 2:5

Major theme
Christians should not allow their lives to be shaped by outward circumstances but live out the life of Jesus in them. They should experience joy in the Lord, regardless of circumstances, opposition or persecution.

Background and purpose
Paul had been used by God to found the church at Philippi *(Acts 16:11-40)*, and his special love for that church is evident in this letter. They were more sensitive and responsive to his financial needs than any other church *(4:15-18)*. Paul tells them the latest news about his imprisonment *(1:12-20)*. He also takes the opportunity in chapter 3 to warn them about the legalists (Judaizers) and the antinomians (against all laws) who wanted to throw all restraints overboard.

Author
The apostle Paul. He writes this "thank you" letter from his imprisonment in Rome to his Christians friends at Philippi for the gift they had sent him.

Date
When Paul wrote this letter he was expecting imminent execution *(2:17)*. Paul was in fact released from prison shortly after writing this letter in about AD 62.

Brief outline
1. Joy in suffering *1:1-30*
2. Joy in serving Jesus *2:1-30*
3. Joy in Jesus himself *3:1-21*
4. Joy derived from contentment *4:1-23*

Key to Philippians
Key words Joy and rejoice.
- 2:5-11 is one of the most crucial passages about Jesus in all of Paul's writings. It contains profound insights in Jesus' pre-existence, incarnation, humiliation and exaltation.

Colossians
Jesus is pre-eminent

"For in Christ all the fullness of the Deity lives in bodily form, and you have been given fullness in Christ, who is the Head over every power and authority."
Colossians 2:9-10

Major theme

Paul writes to oppose a strange teaching that stressed the necessity of fasting, observing special "holy" days and worshiping angels.

Background and purpose

Paul wrote this letter because he heard that heresy was being taught in this church and he felt he had to correct it. One can only deduce the exact nature of the heresy from the way Paul refuted it in *(2:8-23)*. This false teaching held unchristian views on:
• Asceticism *(2:21)*.
• Angel worship *(2:18)*.
• Human wisdom and tradition *(2:4,8)*.
• Secret knowledge, which the Gnostics boasted about *(2:2-3,18)*.

Author

The apostle Paul. Paul was writing to a group of Christians he had never met. The Christian church at Colossae had been founded by Epaphras *(1:4-8; 2:1)*. Paul's large pastoral heart caused him to send this warning letter to "all who had not met me personally" *(2:1)*.

Date

Colossians is one of Paul's "prison letters" and was written from his prison in Rome in approximately AD 61–62.

Brief outline

1. Focus on doctrine – Jesus' deity and pre-eminence *1:1-24*

2. Focus on refuting arguments – the danger of being led astray by false teachers *2:1-23*

3. Focus on conduct – how Christian employers, employees and families should live *3:1-25*

4. Focus on prayer – so that Christians can give a reason for their Christian beliefs *4:1-18*

Keys to Colossians
Key word Fullness.
Key phrase With Christ.
Colossians is perhaps the most Christ-centered book in the Bible.

I Thessalonians
A letter to young Christians

"May the Lord make your love increase and overflow for each other and for everyone else, just as ours does for you. May he strengthen your hearts so that you will be blameless and holy in the presence of our God and Father when our Lord Jesus comes with all his holy ones."
1 Thessalonians 3:12-13

Major theme
1 Thessalonians is a simple follow-up letter to new converts. One major concern is the return of Christ.

Background and purpose
Paul and Silas founded the Christian church in the city of Thessalonica, the capital of Macedonia on Paul's second missionary journey. Paul is anxious to learn how these new Christians are progressing in their Christian lives. The apostle spares them complex doctrine and writes to encourage them. He speaks of the second coming of Jesus as:
- An inspiration for new Christians *(1:10)*.
- A stimulus for Christians to serve God *(2:19)*.
- A comfort for bereaved Christians *(4:18)*.
- An incentive for holy living *(5:23)*.

Author
Paul acknowledges himself as the author of 1 Thessalonians.

Date
Paul wrote this letter from Corinth shortly after leaving Thessalonica around AD 50, making it one of Paul's earliest letters.

Brief outline
1. Greetings and exhortations *1:1–2:20*
2. Paul rejoices over Timothy's report *3:1-13*
3. Exhortation to Christian conduct *4:1-12*
4. Teaching about Jesus' second coming *4:13–5:11*
5. Closing exhortations *5:12-28*

Keys to I Thessalonians
Key word Sanctified.
Key teaching God is at work in the life of those who have come to believe.
- The call of God *(1:4; 2:12; 4:7)*.
- The word of God *(1:6,8; 2:13); (4:15)*.
- The will of God *(4:3; 5:18)*.
- The peace of God *(5:23)*.
- The faithfulness of God *(5:24)*.
- Paul describes himself, in his ministry, as being a nurse *(2:7)*, a laborer *(2:9)*, and a father *(2:11)*.

52

2 Thessalonians

Jesus' second coming

"Concerning the coming of our Lord Jesus Christ and our being gathered to him, we ask you, brothers, not to become easily unsettled or alarmed by some prophecy, report or letter supposed to come from us, saying that the day of the Lord has already come."
2 Thessalonians 2:1-2

Major theme

False teachers were the plague of Paul's life. They had made inroads at Thessalonica. Some went so far as to say that the Day of the Lord had already happened.

Background and purpose

In this letter, Paul writes to encourage the Christians at Thessalonica to withstand persecution and not to give up earning a living. He also corrects some false notions they entertained about Jesus' return.

Paul dictated this letter wanting to make quite sure that any other letter purporting to be from him would not deceive anyone. So he ends by writing: "I, Paul, write this greeting in my own hand, which is the distinguishing mark in all my letters. This is how I write" *(3:18)*.

Author

The apostle Paul wrote his second letter to the Thessalonians from Corinth, probably within six months of his first letter to them, after Silas and Timothy had returned from delivering his first letter to them.

Date

Approximately AD 51.

Brief outline

1. Paul congratulates the Thessalonians on making progress in the Christian life and urges them to endure persecution *1:1-12*

2. Paul corrects false teaching about the day of the Lord *2:1-17*

3. Incorrect behavior caused by wrong beliefs about Jesus' return must be corrected *3:1-18*

Keys to 2 Thessalonians

- 1 and 2 Thessalonians, with Matthew 24–25 and the book of Revelation, are the major sections about prophecy in the New Testament.
- Jesus' return, mentioned 318 times in the New Testament, is the major theme of this letter.
- Paul teaches these new Christians that God is with them. See *1:5,11; 2:13,14; 3:3,16.*

53

1 Timothy
Advice to ministers

"But you, man of God, flee from all this, and pursue righteousness, godliness, faith, love, endurance and gentleness. Fight the good fight of the faith. Take hold of eternal life to which you were called when you made your good confession in the presence of many witnesses."
1 Timothy 6:11-12

Major theme
Paul, the elderly and experienced apostle, writes to the young timid pastor, Timothy, who faces the great responsibility of caring for the Christians at Ephesus.

Background and purpose
During his fourth missionary journey Paul had "urged" Timothy to "stay there in Ephesus so that" he might "command certain men not to teach false doctrines any longer" *(1:3)*. Paul feared that he might be "delayed" in visiting Timothy and so wrote "these instructions" *(3:14-15)* to help him silence false teachers *(1:3-7; 4:1-8; 6:3-5, 20-21)*, and to organize church worship and the appointment of the right sort of church leaders *(3:1-13; 5:17-25)*.

Author
The apostle Paul. Paul was released from his house arrest in Rome, which is described at the end of the book of Acts, in approx. AD 62–63. He then continued his missionary endeavors for two years or so before being arrested again in approximately AD 64–65, and executed in approximately AD 65–67.

Date
Sometime between Paul's two imprisonments he wrote 1 Timothy and Titus. 1 Timothy was written probably in AD 63–64.

Brief outline

1. Correct teaching *1:1-20*	
2. Public worship *2:1–3:16*	
3. False teaching *4:1-16*	
4. Church discipline *5:1-25*	
5. A pastor's motives *6:1-21*	

Keys to 1 Timothy
- The three letters, 1 and 2 Timothy and Titus, were first referred to as the "Pastoral Epistles" in the 18th century. This is an appropriate name as they focus on the oversight of church life.
- The phrase "God my Savior" is found only in the Pastoral letters *(1 Timothy 1:1; 2:3; 4:10; Titus 1:3; 2:10, 13; 3:4)*.
- 1 Timothy is now regarded as a manual for church leaders.

54

2 Timothy
Paul's last will and testament

"Do your best to present yourself to God as one approved, a workman who does not need to be ashamed and who correctly handles the word of truth."
2 Timothy 2:15

Major theme
Paul's final instructions to his young friend and co-worker, Timothy, is the focus for this book. Paul's unwavering faith and his love for Timothy permeate this letter.

Background and purpose
Paul is facing martyrdom. This letter is made up mostly of personal advice to Timothy. Timothy is told to endure and continue as a faithful witness to Jesus and to keep a good grip on the teaching of the Gospel and of the Old Testament. He is to work as a teacher and an evangelist despite all opposition.

Author
The apostle Paul. When Paul writes his letter he is on his own *(4:10-12)*, awaiting execution, but his case has been postponed *(4:16-17)*.

Date
Paul was arrested and imprisoned under Emperor Nero in AD 65–66. From his cold prison cell Paul wrote this his last letter, AD 66–67.

55

Brief outline

1. Advice from a father to a son
1:1-18

2. Advice for all Christian workers
2:1-26

3. A look at the last days *3:1-17*

4. Paul's last words *4:1-22*

Keys to 2 Timothy
Key word Endure.
  Although Paul is facing execution he is very interested in other people. There are 23 references to individuals in this letter.
• Timothy is especially warned to keep clear of "godless chatter" which spreads "like gangrene" *(2:16-17)*.

Titus
How to live as a Christian

"But when the kindness and love of God our Savior appeared, he saved us, not because of righteous things we have done, but because of his mercy. He saved us through the washing of rebirth and renewal by the Holy Spirit ..."
Titus 3:4-5

Major theme
The young pastor, Titus, has been left by Paul to organize the new Christians and the local churches on the island of Crete. Paul's letter is full of practical wisdom on church organization and administration.

Background and purpose
This letter was probably written at the same time and from the same place as 1 Timothy. Titus became a follower of Jesus through Paul, so Paul starts this letter: "To Titus, my true son in our common faith" *(1:4)*. Paul had left Titus in Crete to "straighten out what was left unfinished and appoint elders in every town" *(1:5)*. Paul's letter is crammed with practical advice and warnings about how to deal with false teachers.

Author
The apostle Paul. Paul must have found out that Zenas and Apollos were about to travel through Crete *(3:13)*, thus he took this opportunity of sending a letter by them to Titus.

Date
This letter was written after Paul's first imprisonment in Rome in AD 63–64.

Brief outline

1. Appointment of elders *1:1-16*

2. Advice for different groups of people: older men, older women, young men, young women and servants *2:1-15*

3. Keep going with good deeds, not profitless arguments *3:1-15*

Keys to Titus
Key word Renewal.
   Titus 2:11-14 and 3:4-7 are two of the most comprehensive statements about the Gospel in the New Testament.
• 2:13 refutes the accusation that Paul forgot about Jesus' return towards the end of his life.

56

Philemon
Take back your runaway slave

"Perhaps the reason he was separated from you for a little while was that you might have him back for good – no longer as a slave, but better than a slave, as a dear brother." *Philemon 15-16*

Major theme

Paul's shortest letter is a model of tact and concern for the forgiveness of one who might otherwise face harsh punishment, if not death.

Background and purpose

When Tychicus arrived in Colossae he came with a letter to the Christians there, as well as with this letter to Philemon, who lived in Colossae. Tychicus also brought Onesimus with him. "Tychicus will tell you all the news about me. ... He is coming with Onesimus, our faithful and dear brother, who is one of you." *Colossians 4:7, 9*

Onesimus was a runaway slave. He found Paul in prison and became a Christian, probably with the help of Paul, as Paul calls him "my son Onesimus" in v.10. Now Paul is sending Onesimus back to his owner, Philemon. Paul hopes that this letter will enable Philemon to receive Onesimus back, "no longer as a slave, but better than a slave, as a dear brother" (*16*).

Author

The apostle Paul. Paul was in prison, most probably in Rome, when he wrote this letter.

Date

Approximately AD 61.

Brief outline

1. Paul gives thanks for Philemon *1-7*

2. Pleads for his runaway slave Onesimus *8-16*

3. Paul reminds Philemon that he owes his own Christian life to him *17-25*

57

Keys to Philemon
Key word Welcome.

Hebrews
Good news about better things

"Therefore, since we are surrounded by such a great cloud of witnesses, let us throw off everything that hinders and the sin that so easily entangles, and let us run with perseverance the race marked out for us." *Hebrews 12:1*

Major theme
The basic theme of Hebrews is found in the use of the word "better/superior" *(1:4; 6:9; 7:7, 19, 22; 8:6; 9:23; 10:34; 11:16, 35, 40; 12:24).* Jesus is shown to be superior to Judaism.

Background and purpose
The book was addressed to Jewish Christians who were facing persecution and were being tempted to compromise their faith and return to the practices of Judaism. The author warns them against regarding Christianity as merely an offshoot of Judaism and encourages them to persevere in their faith.

Author
The authorship of Hebrews remains a mystery inasmuch as no direct identification is possible within the book. Traditionally, Paul has been credited as the author. Other suggested authors are Luke, Barnabas and Apollos.

Date
Because the fall of Jerusalem and the ending of the Old Testament sacrificial system is not mentioned in this letter it is assumed that it was written before AD 70. If the persecution mentioned *(chapter 10)* was caused by Nero, then this letter must be dated after the fire of Rome, approximately AD 64.

Brief outline

1. The superiority of the Son over the prophets and angels *1:1–2:18*

2. The superiority of the Son over Moses and Joshua *3:1–4:16*

3. The superiority of Jesus' priesthood over the Jewish priesthood *5:1–8:5*

4. The superiority of the new covenant over the old covenant *8:6–10:39*

5. The importance of faith *11:1–13:25*

Keys to Hebrews
Key words Heaven/heavenly, used 18 times, to show that Christianity is spiritual. Once/once for all, used nine times, to show the finality of God's revelation in Jesus.
Key chapter Chapter 11, the Bible's hall of fame of those who lived by faith in God in Old Testament times, even if it meant suffering or martyrdom.
• Jesus is depicted as our eternal High Priest according to the order of Melchizedek. *7:1-28*

James
Practical Christianity

"As the body without the spirit is dead, so faith without deeds is dead." James 2:26

Major theme

James writes as a pastor, rebuking and encouraging Christians. He stresses the importance of putting faith into practical action.

Background and purpose

James is full of practical advice about Christian conduct.
- For Christians under pressure (*see 1:2-4*)
- For wealthy Christians (*see 1:9-11, 5:1-6*)
- As church members (*see 2:1-9*)

The letter emphasizes practical Christianity and often echoes Jesus' teaching in the Sermon on the Mount (*Matthew 5–7*).

Author

James, the half-brother of Jesus. During Jesus' lifetime this James was not a believer (*John 7:2-5*), but he saw Jesus after the resurrection (*1 Corinthians 15:7*), and was present on the day of Pentecost (*Acts 1:14*). He became leader of the church in Jerusalem (*Acts 12:17; 15:13*). He was martyred about AD 62.

Date

Before AD 62. Because of its strong Jewish feel, a date of AD 48–49 or even earlier is often suggested for its writing. This date would make it one of the earliest New Testament letters.

Brief outline

1. Living faith is tested by trial *1:1-27*

2. Living faith is proved by deeds *2:1-26*

3. Living faith is revealed in behavior *3:1–4:17*

4. Living faith is exercised by persecution *5:1-20*

Keys to James

- James describes God as the One who comes close to us (*4:6-8*), a perfect description of Jesus.
- James has been called the "Proverbs of the New Testament" because it is similar in style and content to the wisdom books of the Old Testament, especially Proverbs.
- James has also been called the "Amos of the New Testament" because of his hard-hitting teaching against social injustice.
- James differs from all other New Testament letters in that:
- It only mentions Jesus twice, *1:1, 2:1*.
- It is the most Jewish book in the New Testament with many Old Testament references.
- It has many allusions to the Sermon on the Mount (*1:2,4,5,20,22; 2:10,13; 3:18; 4:4,10,11,12; 5:2,3,10,12*), and other teachings of Jesus.
- It is packed full of punchy proverbs.

1 Peter
A message for suffering Christians

"Dear friends, do not be surprised at the painful trial you are suffering, as though something strange were happening to you. But rejoice that you participate in the sufferings of Christ, so that you may be overjoyed when his glory is revealed."
1 Peter 4:12-13

Major theme
Peter wrote this letter to encourage those Christians who were downhearted because of the persecution they were suffering.

Background and purpose
Peter gives his readers practical advice about how to react as they endure undeserved suffering. They are to stand firm. Peter bases his teaching on the example set by Jesus towards such suffering. Peter wanted to overcome any attitude of bitterness and anxiety with an attitude of dependence on and confidence in God. Peter's words are to remind Christians of their conversion, the privileges they have in Christ, and the holy lives they are to live.

Author
Peter the apostle. Peter wrote from "Babylon" *(5:13)*, a code name for Rome.

Date
This letter was written in AD 63–64 as the most vicious persecutions under Emperor Nero were gathering steam, shortly before Peter himself suffered martyrdom under that regime.

Brief outline

1. Christian salvation *1:1–2:10*

2. Christian relationships, in pagan society, political life, at work, in the family and when treated unfairly *2:11–3:12*

3. Christian suffering *3:13–4:19*

4. Christians in the community *5:1-14*

Keys to 1 Peter
Key word Suffer, used 15 times.
Key phrase Strangers in the world.
- Peter writes as one who is always thinking about his days as Jesus' disciple.
- Peter recalls the death of Jesus *(2:22-25)*.
- Peter appears to be reflecting on his encounter with Jesus after the resurrection *(5:2, see John 21:15-23)*.

60

2 Peter
No passive journey

"For prophecy never had its
origin in the will of man, but
men spoke from God as they
were carried along by the
Holy Spirit."
2 Peter 1:21

Major theme

The need for growth in
the grace and knowledge
of Jesus. The need to stay
diligent.

Background and purpose

This letter has been called
Peter's "swan song", as he
left this letter to guide those
who would carry on after his
death:
"I think it right to refresh your
memory as long as I live in the
tent of this body, because I know
that I will soon put it aside ..."
(1:13-14).
Peter writes to help with three
great problems facing his
readers:
• the temptation to become
  complacent and sit back;
• vicious false teaching from
  people who were "like brute
  beasts, creatures of instinct"
  (2:12)
• cynicism about the delay in
  Jesus' return.

Author

The apostle Peter. The writer
of this letter calls himself
"Simon Peter" in the opening
verse and claims to have been
an eyewitness to the
transfiguration of Jesus, which
we know was only seen by
Peter, Andrew and John.
"We were eyewitnesses of his
majesty. ... We ourselves heard
this voice that came from heaven
when we were with him on the
sacred mountain." *(1:16,18)*

Date

Peter wrote this letter after he
wrote 1 Peter, "this is now my
second letter to you" *(3:1)*,
and before AD 68, as he was
martyred in Nero's reign of
terror. It was written shortly
before Peter's death, "I know
that I will soon put it [the tent
of this body] aside, as our Lord
Jesus Christ has made clear to
me" *(1:14)*, in AD 65–66.

Brief outline

1. Cultivate a Christian character
   1:1-21

2. False teachers are condemned
   2:1-22

3. Have confidence that Jesus will
   return *3:1-18*

Keys to 2 Peter

Key word Knowledge (of God),
used 16 times, in its various
forms.

Key thought The best antidote
to false teaching is correct
understanding of the truth.

1, 2, & 3 John
Knowing and being sure

"I write these things to you who believe in the name of the Son of God so that you may know that you have eternal life." *1 John 5:13*
"And this is love: that we walk in obedience to his commands. As you have heard from the beginning, his command is that you walk in love." *2 John 6*
"I have no greater joy than to hear that my children are walking in the truth." *3 John 4*

Major theme

- 1 **John**'s theme is assurance; the tests for discovering false teaching.
- 2 **John** has a warning against denying the incarnation and emphasizes the necessity of obeying God's command of love.
- 3 **John** is about how to be witnesses to the truth.

Background and purpose

The elderly John wrote these fatherly letters out of loving concern for his "children," whose steadfastness in the truth was being threatened by the lure of worldliness and the guile of false teachers.

Author

The apostle John. None of these letters name an author, but their style and range of ideas indicate a single author. The author claims to have been an eyewitness of Jesus' life *(1 John 1:1-3)*. The letters have many words and thought forms which are the same as John's Gospel. Compare John 5:24 with 1 John 3:14 and John 1:14,18; 3:16 with 1 John 4:9.

Date

It is not possible to place the writings of these three letters to a precise year, but it is most probable that they were written towards the end of John's life, around AD 85–95.

Brief outline

1 John

1. The basis of fellowship *1:1–2:27*

2. The characteristics of fellowship *2:28–5:3*

3. The consequences of fellowship *5:4-21*

2 John

1. Abide in God's commandments *1-6*

2. Avoid false teachers *7-13*

3 John

1. Gaius' commendation *1-8*

2. Diotrephes' condemnation *9-14*

Keys to 1, 2, & 3 John

Key words Fellowship, in 1 John; love, in 2 John; and truth, in 3 John.

62

Jude
Coping with heresy

"Dear friends, although I was very eager to write to you about the salvation we share, I felt I had to write and urge you to contend for the faith that was once for all entrusted to the saints."
Jude verse 3

Major theme

Jude had intended to write a letter about salvation *(3)*, but because of the threats against his readers he turns his attention instead to those who were seeking to destroy the gospel.

Background and purpose

Jude warned his readers against the evil people who were trying to use the gospel for their own ends. Jude told them that it was important that they defended the gospel. Jude ends his letter with a series of practical exhortations aimed to strengthen their Christian lives.

Author

Jude. Jude identifies himself as "a brother of James" *(1)*. This would make Jude a brother, or, to be more accurate, half-brother of Jesus. He was clearly a humble man as he also calls himself a "servant of Jesus Christ" in the opening verse.

Date

If Peter made use of Jude in his second letter, as seems probable, then Jude must be dated before 2 Peter, that is AD 64–65.

Brief outline

1. Jude's concern about the influence of false teachers *1-4*

2. Jude's description of the false teachers *5-16*

3. Jude's defense against false teachers *17-23*

4. Jude's powerful doxology *24-25*

63

Keys to Jude

• **Key word** Keep.
• Jude quotes two books that are not in the Bible.
The Book of Enoch, see *14-15*, was a popular religious book in those days.
The Assumption of Moses, see verse *9*.
Jude does not quote these books as if they had equal authority as books of the Bible, but as a preacher today might use a quotation from Shakespeare to illustrate what he was saying.

Revelation
A glimpse into the future

"'Write, therefore, what you have seen, what is now and what will take place later.'"
Revelation 1:19

Major theme
The book of Revelation is called an "apocalyptic" book as it unveils and reveals truth in a vivid and poetic way. It is an encouragement to withstand persecution and centers round Jesus who alone has authority to judge the earth and to rule it in righteousness.

Background and purpose
There are four main approaches to interpreting this book.
• **The preterist view** focuses on the events that happened when the book was written, which would have all been known by the first readers. There is no need to look for any detailed revelation in this book about our own times.
• **The historic view** sees Revelation as one long outline of history, from the first century to today.
• **The futurist view** ignores all possible historical allusions and teaches that the book refers only to the end times.
• **The symbolic view** sees symbols in every passage. They can be interpreted without any reference to world history.
Perhaps the best way to interpret the book of

Revelation is to combine these four approaches. Then, for example, the prophecies in the book can be taken as referring to the time of dreadful persecution under Domitian in the first century *and* to events of the end time.

Author
The apostle John. The author is named as "John" four times *(1:1,4,9; 22:8)*.

Date
The first major persecution took place under Nero and seems to be reflected in Revelation. The second, even fiercer persecution, under Emperor Domitian, lasted from AD 91–95 which is the most likely time for the writing of Revelation.

Brief outline

1. **Chapter 1:** "What you have seen" *(1:19)*

2. **Chapter 2–3** "What is now" *(1:19)*

3. **Chapters 4–22:** "What will take place later" *(1:19)*
• John's view of heaven *4:1–5:14*
• Times of tribulation *6:1–19:21*
• The thousand years and final judgment *20:1-15*
• The new heaven and new earth *21:1–22:21*

Bible
Study
made
easy

Bible Study made easy introduces you to the world of Bible study. If you want to learn how to study the Bible on your own, this is the place to start.

Bible Study made easy also has dozens of profitable ideas to increase your understanding about different facets of the Bible. It explains how you can:

• Do your own microscopic Bible studies
• Do your own telescopic Bible studies
• Do your own biographical Bible studies
• Do your own year-long Bible studies
• Do your own study of the life of Jesus
• Do your own Bible studies as a spiritual exercise

Bible Study made easy will help you to focus on the main purpose of Bible study:

"The main purpose of Bible study is to help deepen our relationship with the Lord and to be more and more transformed into the likeness of Christ."

John R. Kohlenberger III

Contents

Which Bible version should I use?

Use a Bible
Beg, borrow or buy a Bible.
You can borrow a Bible from a library.
You will need to use your Bible as you follow through each study in this book.

Which Bible version should I use?
There are scores of different Bible versions to choose from in bookstores. They fall into two categories:
- **Translations.** Great attention is paid to translating the exact meaning of each Greek or Hebrew word or phrase.
- **Paraphrases.** These may add or omit words in order to communicate the original meaning in the most helpful and arresting way.

J.B. Phillips' version of Romans 12:2 is a good example of an excellent paraphrase:
> "Don't let the world around you squeeze you into its own mould, but let God re-make you so that your whole attitude of mind is changed."

Six versions of John 3:16 compared

King James Version	New Revised Standard Version	Today's English Version
For God so loved the world, that he gave his only begotten Son, that whosoever believeth in him should not perish, but have everlasting life.	For God so loved the world that he gave his only Son, that whoever believes in him should not perish but have eternal life.	For God loved the world so much he gave his only Son, so that everyone who believes in him may not die but have eternal life.

Inclusive language

Some Bibles published in the 1990s now have "inclusive" language editions. Direct translations of the Bible may appear sexist to modern readers, with references to "man" or to "brothers." Inclusive language editions use the words "human beings" and "brothers and sisters."

Bible reference	Traditional translation	NRSV inclusive language
Matthew 4:19	"I will make you fishers of men."	"I will make you fishers of men and women."
1 Thessalonians 5:25-26	"Brothers, pray for us. Greet all the brothers with a holy kiss."	"Brothers and sisters, pray for us. Greet all God's people with a holy kiss."

The choice is yours

There has never been a wider variety of good translations from which to choose.

New Living (translation)
For God loved the world so much that he gave his only Son so that anyone who believes in him shall not perish but have eternal life.

The Message (paraphrase)
For God loved the world so much that he gave his only Son, so that everyone who believes in him should not be lost, but should have eternal life.

New International Version
For God so loved the world that he gave his one and only Son, that whoever believes in him shall not perish but have everlasting life.

Making a start

Mastering Bible references

Breaking down what is meant by the code **1 John 3:16** is easy.
• **1** means John's first letter (John wrote three letters).
• **John** is the name of the Bible book.
• The first figure after the name of the Bible book, in this case **3**, is the chapter number.
• The figure after the colon, in this case **16**, is the verse number.
So **1 John 3:16** is John's first letter, chapter 3, verse 16.

Finding Bible books

But where exactly does John's first letter come in the Bible? The easiest way to find any Bible book is to go to the front of the Bible. Here books are listed, often both in Bible order and in alphabetical order, with the page number next to the Bible book.

To get the most out of Bible study, look up all the Bible references in this book. Think of it as an exciting way to explore your Bible for yourself.

Give it a try

Try looking up John 3:16 and 1 John 3:16. This is not a catch! John 3:16 is not one of John's letters, but his gospel, known to us as John's Gospel. But 1 John 3:16, as we've just seen, is from John's first letter. Look up both verses, and you'll see that amazingly, they have a common theme.

How's your memory?

Try memorizing John 3:16. Bring it to mind during the day. See if you can remember it at the end of the day. Then do the same for 1 John 3:16.

You will now have done what you are told to do in Psalm 119:11!

Pray before you start

A version of Psalm 119:18 is used as a prayer by many people as they start to read the Bible.

> "Open my eyes [that is, my spiritual understanding] that I may see wonderful things in your law. Amen."

Remember, the main point of Bible study is not to acquire knowledge, but to get acquainted with God and his purpose for you.

6

Think

Praying and turning things over in our minds are complementary activities. We are meant to use our God-given faculties to the fullest when we read the Bible.

How to cope with difficult passages

Don't be put off by parts that are hard to understand. This is the best way to deal with them. Always ask God to send his Holy Spirit to illuminate the passage for you. Write down the Bible reference, and jot down your question. Then ask an experienced Christian, or read a reference book about the passage. When you do find the answer, be sure to write it down next to your question. Over the course of a year, you'll be very pleasantly surprised at how many of your questions have been answered!

Boredom

Many people give up reading and studying the Bible through sheer boredom. This is because they are reading the Bible as an abstract exercise. Look at your Bible reading as an adventure – an opportunity to know God, and his Son Jesus Christ. Each time you read your Bible, ask God to show you how to take action on what you have read – then do it. Help to counteract boredom by giving yourself plenty of variety, in reading different parts of the Bible.

See also:
• *Questions to ask*, page 10
• *15 ways to enhance your Bible study*, page 64.

Nine ways NOT to study the Bible

The Bible is the most wonderful book in the world.
But sadly, it has often been misused and misquoted.

The mistake	The solution
Taking a text out of its context. An example of this is comes in Genesis 4:9: "Am I my brother's keeper?" Some have quoted these words to mean that we should not be concerned with other people's welfare.	**A text out of context is a pretext.** The words in Genesis 4:9 are words spoken by Cain, who has just murdered his brother Abel! Cain lies to God, saying he does not know where Abel is. The point is that we are meant to be our "brother's keeper."
Interpreting a poetic image in a literal way. This has led to dreadful persecution, as Galileo would tell you! For example, take Psalm 93:1, which says: "The world is firmly established; it cannot be moved." For hundreds of years some Christians thought that anyone who did not believe that the earth was fixed, and the sun went round it, was a heretic.	**Interpret poetic language as poetry.** The first half of Psalm 93:1 states: "The Lord reigns, he is robed in majesty; the Lord is robed in majesty and is armed with strength." The psalm is about God's majesty and power: it is not meant to teach us about astronomy. Look out of your window. Doesn't the earth seem solid and fixed? The psalmist is saying that God is strong in the same way.
Misquoting a verse. One of the most frequently misquoted verses is 1 Timothy 6:10, which comes out as: "Money is the root of all evil." (This has been taken to mean that money in itself is evil, and that Christians should have nothing to do with it.)	**Make accurate quotations.** 1 Timothy 6:10 actually says, "For the love of money is a root of all kinds of evil." It is the love of money, not money itself which is the problem, as the second half of the verse amplifies: "Some people, eager for money, have wandered away from the faith and pierced themselves with many griefs."
Quoting half a verse. Matthew 22:21, "Give to Caesar what is Caesar's..." is frequently quoted in isolation from the second half of the verse. It emphasizes only a Christian's duty to the State.	**Quote the whole verse.** The second half of Matthew 22:21 reads, "... and to God what is God's." Jesus is saying that we have a dual responsibility: to the State and to God.

Studying only the "nice" verses. Some parts of the Bible make very disturbing reading. Psalm 137:8-9 reads, "Happy is he … who seizes your infants and dashes them against the rocks."	**Face the tough verses head-on.** There may be some verses in the Bible that you do not understand. Do not let these stop you from appreciating the rest that you do understand. When the psalmist cried out for immediate vengeance against evil people, he had no idea of Christ's sacrificial death for sin, or of the future final judgment.
Getting submerged in the Old Testament. Some long passages in the Old Testament might not make much sense to you, and discourage you from reading the Bible. When the British pop star Cliff Richard began to read the Bible, he started at Genesis but gave up when he reached Leviticus because he did not understand what all the sacrifices were about.	**Move from the familiar to the unfamiliar.** If you haven't read the Bible before, start with some of the following key Old Testament passages. • The creation. *Genesis 1:1-2:7* • The fall of man. *Genesis 3:6-24* • The call of Abraham. *Genesis 12:1-9* • The story of Joseph. *Genesis 37-38* • The Ten Commandments. *Exodus 20:1-17* • The shepherd's psalm. *Psalm 23*
Starting with the most difficult New Testament books. If you are not familiar with the New Testament, it is best not to start with the Book of Revelation and the Letter to the Hebrews.	**Start with an overview of the New Testament.** Here are some key New Testament passages. • The birth of Jesus. *Luke 1:26–2:40* • The Sermon on the Mount. *Matthew 5–7* • The prodigal son. *Luke 15:11-32* • The Last Supper. *Matthew 26:20-25* • The death and resurrection of Jesus. *John 19–20* • The conversion of Paul. *Acts 9:1-31* • The life of joy. *Paul's Letter to the Philippians*
Not acting on the Bible's commands	**Obedience is crucial** "Be doers of the word, and not hearers only." *James 1:22 (NRSV)*
Using the Bible as a battleground for fruitless arguments	**Avoid arguing over unimportant things** *See Titus 3:9*

9

Questions to ask

When Jesus met people, he often asked them questions.
When we read the Bible, one of the best ways to increase our
understanding about a passage is to ask questions about it.

General questions

There are some general questions which are well worth asking
of any Bible passage. Some people find it helpful to have a
notepad in which they write down all their questions, and the
answers they discover.

• What have I learned about God the Father?
• What have I learned about Jesus?
• What have I learned about the Holy Spirit?
• Did I find a good example to follow?
• Is there a promise to believe in the passage?
• Is there a command to obey?

Looking at a specific Bible passage

You will need to ask different questions about different
passages. Here are some questions to ask about the opening
verses of a Bible book which some people find very hard to
understand – the Book of Revelation.

Bible passage

(1) The revelation of Jesus Christ, which God gave him to show his servants what must soon take place. He made it known by sending his angel to his servant John, (2) who testifies to everything he saw – that is, the word of God and the testimony of Jesus Christ. (3) Blessed is the one who reads the words of this prophecy, and blessed are those who hear it and take to heart what is written in it, because the time is near.
(4) John,
To the seven churches in the province of Asia: Grace and peace to you from him who is, and who was, and who is to come, and from the seven spirits before his throne, (5) and from Jesus Christ, who is the faithful witness, the firstborn from the dead, and the ruler of the kings of the earth.
To him who loves us and has freed us from our sins by his blood, (6) and has made us to be a kingdom and priests to serve his God and Father – to him be glory and power for ever and ever!
Amen.
Revelation 1:1-6

se who believed in him,
hing, you are really my
know the truth, and the
se."
descendants of Abraham,"
nd we have never been any-
t do you mean, then, by

Question	Answer
1 Who wrote this book?	See verses 1, 4. See also Revelation 1:9.
2 To whom did John write this book?	See verse 4. Also see Revelation chapters 2-3.
3 What is the theme of the book?	See verse 1.
4 What type of book is this?	See verse 3.
5 What does John want his readers to receive?	See verse 4.
6 In which three ways is Jesus described?	See verse 5. Also see Revelation 1:8.
7 Which three things has Jesus done for us?	See verses 5-6.
8 What directions are we given about how to read this book?	See verse 3. Also see Revelation 22:18-19.
9 What response should we give to God the Father?	See verse 6. See also Revelation 4:6-11.

What are commentaries, concordances, Bible dictionaries, New Testament interlinears?

While there is no substitute for reading the words of the Bible itself, there are many different books to help you in your study of the Bible.

Commentaries

These are books which give systematic comments, observations, and sometimes personal application notes, on different passages of the Bible.

• There are some excellent one-volume Bible commentaries which look at each book of the Bible, from Genesis to Revelation.

• There are commentaries on individual books of the Bible, examining each verse in detail.

Concordances

These are books which enable you to look up almost any word found in the Bible.

• If you were studying the Holy Spirit, you would find dozens of references if you looked up the words **"Spirit"** and **"Holy"** in a Bible concordance.

• If you wanted to find a passage in the Bible about the Good Samaritan, you would look up **"Samaritan"** and find: "But a Samaritan, as he traveled, came where." *Luke 10:33*

• You could see how words are linked together in the Bible. By looking up the occurrence of the word **"grace"** in the New Testament, you would discover that it was most often linked with "peace." *(See Romans 1:7;*

1 Corinthians 1:3; 2 Corinthians 1:2; Galatians 1:3; Ephesians 1:2; Philippians 1:2; Colossians 1:2; 2 Thessalonians 1:2; Titus 1:4; Philemon 3; 1 Peter 1:2; 2 Peter 1:2 and Revelation 1:4.) "Grace and peace to you" was the normal way of starting a letter!

• Other information may be gleaned from the references. For example, you could find out who gives grace, and what the purpose of receiving grace is.

• Bible concordances are linked to a particular translation of the Bible. So if you buy one, make sure that it is based on the Bible version you like using.

Bible dictionaries are ideal books for looking up individual Bible words, Bible people and Bible themes.

- **Samaria and the Samaritans**
  For example, if you look up the entry under "Samaria," it will not only tell you about the origin of the country of Samaria (the northern kingdom of Israel), but also about Samaritans. In Jesus' time, Samaritans were people of mixed race who were despised by the Jews. When Jesus told the story of the Good Samaritan, he asked his listeners who, in the story, had acted as a neighbor? The man who answered could not even bring himself to say the word "Samaritan," so replied, "The one who had mercy."

You need to know just a little Greek to benefit from an interlinear Bible. New Testament interlinears set the complete New Testament in Greek, with the literal English translation for each word underneath each line of Greek text. This means that you can see which Greek word is used in a particular verse.

These books are excellent for giving you background information about the Bible, along with a summary of each Bible book. They cover such topics as archeology, minerals, animals and insects, plants and herbs, trades, travel, warfare, money, marriage, childhood, disease and music.

Bible atlases are ideal for increasing our understanding of the Bible.

- **From Dan to Beersheba**
  This phrase means from the north to the south. "Then all the Israelites from Dan to Beersheba came." *Judges 20:1.* An atlas shows that Dan was the northernmost city in Israel, while Beersheba was the southernmost city in Israel.

- **Jonah fled to Tarshish**
  God told Jonah to go to Nineveh but he headed for Tarshish. *Jonah 1:1-3.* A Bible atlas reveals Jonah's great disobedience, as Tarshish was hundreds of miles from Nineveh and in the opposite direction.

Looking through a microscope

Opening observations

Thinking about one person, theme, event or word is a most helpful way of studying the Bible.

This study puts the key word "faith" under the microscope.

It is possible to make such a study by tracking down the places where the word comes in the Bible.

A study of the word "faith"

The table on page 15 sets out where the word "faith" occurs frequently in the Bible. The Bible book is followed by the relevant chapter. The verse number refers to the first occurrence of the word in that chapter. You will have to find how many other occurrences exist in the chapter.

By looking up these Bible references, you will have a good overview of the Bible's teaching on faith.

List the various aspects of faith mentioned and the different people who have faith. Note the Bible reference under each topic or person, as you proceed with this study.

> "Faith is being sure of what we hope for and certain of what we do not see." *Hebrews 11:1*

> "I live by faith in the Son of God, who loved me and gave himself for me." *Galatians 2:20*

N.B. Some Bible versions use the words "believe" or "convert" in place of the word "faith."

Book of Bible	Chapter and verse of first occurrence of "faith"	Number of times "faith" comes in this chapter
Hebrews	11:1	
James	2:5	
Romans	4:3	
Galatians	3:6	
1 Timothy	1:2	
Mark	9:23	
Romans	3:22	
1 Timothy	6:10	
Romans	14:1	
1 Thessalonians	3:2	
1 Peter	1:5	
Matthew	18:6	
Romans	1:8	
Romans	10:6	
Luke	17:5	
1 Corinthians	13:2	
Galatians	2:16	
Colossians	2:5	
1 Timothy	3:6	
1 Timothy	4:1	
2 Timothy	1:5	
2 Timothy	3:8	
Titus	1:1	
Hebrews	4:2	
2 Peter	1:1	

Concluding thought

- At the end of some study Bibles, complete lists of key words are set noted, providing material for hundreds of Bible studies.
- See also: *The telescopic approach to Bible study*, page 16.

The telescopic approach to Bible study

Opening observation

To gain an overview of a long and involved Bible book, it is sometimes best to read it in one sitting. John's Gospel can be read in about an hour.

The purpose of John's Gospel

John tells us why he wrote his gospel:

"Jesus did many other miraculous signs in the presence of his disciples, which are not recorded in this book. But these are written that you may believe that Jesus is the Christ, the Son of God, and that by believing you may have life in his name." *John 20:30-31*

Themes in John's Gospel

It's useful to keep the major themes in mind, as you read John.

Eternal life	John links eternal life with the "new birth" and with the "second birth."	*John 1:4, 12-13; 3:3-7, 16, 36; 5:21, 24-29; 6:27, 40, 47, 54, 57-58, 68; 10:28; 11:25; 12:25, 50; 17:2-3*
The Holy Spirit	John talks more about the Holy Spirit than the other three gospel writers. The Holy Spirit is spoken of as the one who takes the place of Jesus, after Jesus returns to the Father.	*John 1:32-33; 3:5-6, 8, 34; 4:23-24; 6:63; 7:37-39; 14:16-17, 25-26; 16:7-15; 20:22*
Jesus died for sinners	John concentrates on why Jesus had to die, and on the great love which motivated him in this.	*John 1:29, 36; 2:19-22; 3:14-17; 6:51, 53-56; 8:28; 10:11, 15, 18; 11:50-52; 12:24, 27, 32-34; 15:13*

Outline of John's Gospel

17

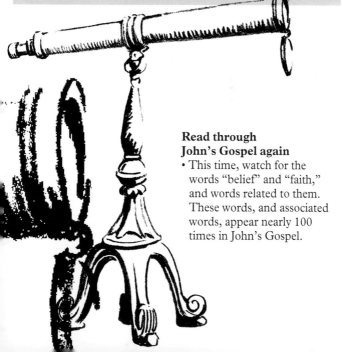

**Read through
John's Gospel again**
• This time, watch for the
words "belief" and "faith,"
and words related to them.
These words, and associated
words, appear nearly 100
times in John's Gospel.

Linking the Old and New Testaments

Jesus' temptation

During Jesus' time of temptation in the desert, he countered the Devil three times with quotations from the Book of Deuteronomy.

The devil's attack	Jesus' defense
"If you are the Son of God, tell these stones to become bread." *Matthew 4:3*	"It is written: 'Man does not live on bread alone, but on every word that comes from the mouth of God.' " *Matthew 4:4, quoting Deuteronomy 8:3*
"If you are the Son of God … throw yourself down [from the highest point of the Temple]." *Matthew 4:6*	"It is also written: 'Do not put the Lord your God to the test.' " *Matthew 4:7, quoting Deuteronomy 6:16*
"All [the kingdoms of the world] I will give you … if you will bow down and worship me." *Matthew 4:9*	"Away from me, Satan! For it is written: 'Worship the Lord your God, and serve him only.' " *Matthew 4:10, quoting Deuteronomy 6:13*

Jesus quotes the two greatest commandments in the Old Testament

In Matthew 22:37-40, Jesus quotes from Deuteronomy 6:5:

"Love the Lord your God with all your heart and with all your soul and with all your mind."

In Matthew 22:39, Jesus quotes from Leviticus 19:18:

"Love your neighbor as yourself."

Jesus quotes from the Old Testament to explain his ministry

Jesus was in the synagogue of his home town, Nazareth, when he read from part of the Isaiah scroll (Isaiah 61:1-2).

"Jesus went to Nazareth, where he had been brought up, and on the Sabbath day he went into the synagogue, as was his custom. And he stood up to read. The scroll of the prophet Isaiah was handed to him. Unrolling it, he found the place where it is written:

'The Spirit of the Lord is on me, because he has anointed me to preach good news to the poor. He has sent me to proclaim freedom for the prisoners and recovery of sight for the blind, to release the oppressed, to proclaim the year of the Lord's favor.'

Then he rolled up the scroll, gave it back to the attendant and sat down. The eyes of everyone in the synagogue were fastened on him, and he began by saying to them, 'Today this scripture is fulfilled in your hearing.' "

Luke 4:16-21

Jesus predicts that his disciples will fall away

Jesus dramatically quotes Zechariah 13:7 in Matthew 26:31, to say that his followers will desert him:

"I will strike the shepherd, and the sheep of the flock will be scattered."

Jesus' words on the cross

As Jesus is dying, he quotes two highly significant passages from the Old Testament.

19

• Jesus quotes Psalm 22:1 after the three hours of darkness:

"Eloi, Eloi, lama sabachthani?" – which means, "My God, my God, why have you forsaken me?"

Matthew 27:46

• As Jesus prepares to say his final words, he calls out:

"I am thirsty." *John 19:28.*

Commenting on this, John writes:

"So that the Scripture would be fulfilled, Jesus said, 'I am thirsty.' "

Jesus was fulfilling the scriptures as he said these words. This is clear from Psalm 69:21:

"They … gave me vinegar for my thirst."

To ponder

• The risen Lord Jesus continued to use the Old Testament scriptures to explain his death and resurrection to his disciples. Read Luke 24:25-27. Also read Luke 24:45.

It's all Greek to me!

All 27 books of the New Testament are written in Greek. But you don't have to learn Greek to understand it, because there are so many excellent Bible translations. Just a little knowledge of Greek enhances our understanding of various passages and words.

Jesus on the cross

"It is finished," Jesus said from the cross. *John 19:30* In Greek, this is just one word of triumph: *"Tetelestai!"* It was a cry of victory, not a cry of despair.

Alpha and omega

Jesus is called the "alpha" and the "omega" three times in the Book of Revelation.

Alpha is the first letter of the Greek alphabet, and omega is the last. Jesus was saying that he is the beginning and end of everything.

"I am the alpha and the omega." *Revelation 1:8; 21:6; 22:13*

Eutheos!

Mark 1:12 reads, "At once the Spirit sent [Jesus] out into the desert."

The Greek word for "at once" is *eutheos*. It is used over forty times in Mark's Gospel – over half the occurrences in the whole of the New Testament. Its frequent usage reveals the dynamic pace of Mark's Gospel, as Jesus moves from one amazing act to another.

Dynamite!

Sometimes we become so familiar with our translation of the Bible that we forget the force of a particular word. In Romans 1:16, Paul talks about the power of the gospel. The Greek word for "power" is *dunamis*, from which we derive our word "dynamite." Paul is saying, "The gospel is dynamic or dynamite!"

Hypocrite

In the New Testament, the word "hypocrite" appears in the gospels of Matthew (thirteen times), Mark (one time), and Luke (three times). The word is used by Jesus only and it appears nowhere else in the New Testament.

"When you fast, do not look somber as the hypocrites do, for they display their faces to show men they are fasting."
Matthew 6:16

"Hypocrite" is simply the Greek word *hupokrites* written in English. It originally meant "actor." In Matthew 6:16, it is clear that the hypocrites were performing to an audience. The aim of this play-acting was to win human praise.

Love

Most Bibles translate the Greek words *philia* and *agape* by the word "love."
Philia means brotherly love, the love we have for our family and friends. Paul writes to his Christian friends at Thessalonica, "Now about brotherly love we do not need to write to you."
1 Thessalonians 4:9

When the writers of the New Testament describe God's great love towards us, they want to make it clear that it is different and superior to the love humans have for each other. They use the word *agape*. John writes, "This is how God showed his love (*agape*) among us... God is love (*agape*)." *1 John 4:9, 16*

Something to do
• Consider learning New Testament Greek. That may sound difficult, but it is not impossible. Courses, some of which are correspondence courses, can teach you.

God speaks through every Old Testament book

God has two purposes:
- To tell us about God.
- To show how God brings us his salvation.

From your reading of each Old Testament book, note one thing you discover about God (with a Bible reference).

The historical books of the Old Testament

Genesis 1:1	God is creator
Exodus 6:6	God is redeemer
Leviticus 20:7-8	God is holy
Numbers 14:22-23	God punishes those who reject him
Deuteronomy 10:12-13	What God requires of us
Joshua 1:8	God's recipe for success
Judges 2:20-21	God's warnings are clear
Ruth 4:17-22	God's plan for the redemption of the world
1 Samuel 15:22	God places great importance on obedience
2 Samuel 7:12-13	God's kingdom will last for ever
1 Kings 9:4-5	God requires integrity of heart
2 Kings 2:6	God is alive
1 Chronicles 29:11	The whole world belongs to God
2 Chronicles 16:9	God sees everything, especially those who are loyal to him
Ezra 1:1	God moves the hearts of rulers for his purposes
Nehemiah 6:15-16	God works through the efforts of godly people
Esther 4:14	God's special care for his people, revealing his will through things that happen. (Esther is the only Bible book in which God is not mentioned or directly referred to.)

> "Yours, O Lord, is the greatness and the power
> and the glory and the majesty and the splendor,
> for everything in heaven and earth is yours.
> Yours, O Lord, is the kingdom;
> you are exalted as head over all."
> *1 Chronicles 29:11*

Poetic books

Job 19:25	God commands the lives
Psalm 103:2	God is to be worshipped
Proverbs 1:7	We are to revere God
Ecclesiastes 12:13-14	God will judge our actions
Song of Solomon 8:7	God positively endorses married love

> "The fear of the Lord is the beginning of knowledge,
> but fools despise wisdom and discipline."
> *Proverbs 1:7*

Prophetic books

Isaiah 53:6	God has taken our sin upon himself
Jeremiah 31:33	God promises his new covenant
Lamentations 3:22-25	God is a God of mercy
Ezekiel 36:24-26	God promises to give us new hearts
Daniel 2:44	God rules over the nations
Hosea 14:4	God heals our turning away from him
Joel 2:28-29	The pouring out of the Holy Spirit is promised
Amos 5:12-14	God is against social injustice
Obadiah 21	God is to be king
Jonah 2:8-9	God brings salvation
Micah 6:8	God wants us to walk humbly before him
Nahum 1:7	God protects his followers
Habakkuk 3:17-19	God's strength is to be our strength
Zephaniah 3:15	God's presence is promised
Haggai 2:23	God chooses people to do his will
Zechariah 9:9	God appears in humility
Malachi 3:1	God is almighty

> "I will heal their waywardness
> and love them freely."
> *Hosea 14:4*

Following a chain from Genesis to Revelation

Many key words in the Bible can be traced from Genesis to Revelation. The references which link up in this way are sometimes referred to as "chain" references.

The word "sin" – rebellion against God, and the concept of sinning against God, can be studied in this way.

Sin chain

Genesis 2:17	The fatal choice.
Genesis 13:13	Sin spreads.
Exodus 12:5-7	The blood of the killed lamb protects the people from death.
Exodus 32:7	The sin of making the golden calf.
Leviticus 16:6	Aaron makes a sin offering.
Numbers 14:18	The Lord forgives sin.
Numbers 32:23	Your sin will find you out.
Deuteronomy 20:18	Worshiping other gods is sin.
Joshua 22:17	Sin needs to be cleansed.
Judges 3:7	Forgetting God is sin.
1 Samuel 2:17	Showing contempt for God is sin.
2 Samuel 12:13	David confesses his sin.
1 Kings 15:26	Not being fully devoted to God is sin.
2 Kings 8:18	Doing evil in God's sight is sin.
1 Chronicles 9:1	Unfaithfulness to God is sin.
2 Chronicles 7:14	"If my people, who are called by my name, will humble themselves and pray and seek my face and turn from their wicked ways, then I will hear from heaven and forgive their sin and heal their land."
Ezra 6:17	As the Temple is dedicated, a sin offering is offered.
Nehemiah 1:6	Nehemiah identifies himself with the sin of Israel.
Job 1:5	Job shows his concern for any sins of his children.
Psalm 51:3	"My sin is always before me."
Proverbs 5:22	"The cords of his sin hold him fast."
Ecclesiastes 5:6	"Do not let your mouth lead you into sin."
Isaiah 6:5	"Woe is me ... for I am a man of unclean lips, and I live among a people of unclean lips."
Jeremiah 14:7	Backsliding is sin.
Lamentations 1:5	Sin brings grief.

Ezekiel 18:4	"The soul who sins is the one who will die."
Daniel 4:27	"Renounce your sin by doing what is right."
Hosea 14:1	"Your sins have been your downfall."
Amos 5:12	"For I know how many are your offences and how great are your sins. You oppress the righteous and take bribes and you deprive the poor of justice in the courts."
Micah 6:7	Sin cannot be covered up by empty outward actions.
Zechariah 1:4	"Turn from your evil ways."
Matthew 5:27-28	Inward sins are not hidden from God.
Mark 7:20-23	Thirteen deadly sins.
Luke 18:11-14	The Pharisee and the tax-collector.
John 16:8-9	The Holy Spirit convicts us of sin.
Acts 2:36-41	God offers forgiveness for sin.
Romans 7:7-25	The "I" of self (sin) comes 32 times in Romans 7.
1 Corinthians 15:21	"Death came through a man."
Galatians 1:3-4	"The Lord Jesus Christ ... gave himself for our sins."
Ephesians 1:7	"In him ... we have forgiveness of sins."
Philippians 2:15	"A crooked and depraved generation ..."
Colossians 2:11	"Putting off the sinful nature..."
1 Thessalonians 2:16	"They always heap up their sins to the limit."
2 Thessalonians 2:12	Some people delight in wickedness.
1 Timothy 5:20	"Those who sin are to be rebuked publicly."
2 Timothy 3:6	"Loaded down with sins ..."
Titus 3:11	Divisive people are "warped and sinful."
Hebrews 12:1	"Let us throw off ... the sin which so easily entangles."
James 1:15	"Sin, when it is full grown, gives birth to death."
1 Peter 2:24	"He himself bore our sins in his body on the tree, so that we might die to sins and live for righteousness."
2 Peter 1:9	A reminder about being cleansed from sin.
1 John 1:7	"The blood of Jesus cleanses us from all sin."
Revelation 1:5	"... [He] has freed us from our sins."

25

Something to do

• Use a reference or chain reference Bible to do some more chain studies. Suggested topics: love, holiness, vine.

See also:
Looking through a microscope, page 14.
A year's worth of Bible studies, page 62.

The names of God

The names and titles given to God have special meanings. They tell us just how great he is.

Hebrew name	Meaning	Bible reference
Elohim	The All-Powerful One	*Genesis 1:1*
El (singular)	The Strong One	*Exodus 6:3*
El-Elyon	The Most High God	*Genesis 14:18-22*
El-Shaddai	The All-Sufficient One	*Genesis 17:1*
El-Olam	The Everlasting God	*Genesis 21:33*
Jehovah (Yahweh)	The Self-Existent One	*Exodus 3:14*
Jehovah-Elohim	Lord God, as Creator	*Genesis 1:26*
Jehovah-Jireh	Jehovah Will Provide	*Genesis 22:13-14*
Jehovah-Rapha	Jehovah Who Heals	*Exodus 15:25*
Jehovah-Nissi	Jehovah Is My Banner	*Exodus 17:15*
Jehovah-Shalom	Jehovah Is Peace	*Judges 6:24*
Jehovah-Shammah	Jehovah Is There	*Ezekiel 48:35*
Jehovah-Tsidkenu	Jehovah Our Righteousness	*Jeremiah 33:16*

Name in the Psalms	Meaning	Bible reference
Jehovah-Raah	The Lord Is My Shepherd	*Psalm 23:1*
Jehovah-Sabaoth	The Lord Of Hosts (God's power in time of trouble)	*Psalm 46:7*
The Living God	God gives strength	*Psalm 42:2*
King	God rules	*Psalm 44:4*
Strength	God gives us power	*Psalm 59:9*
Redeemer	The God who saves	*Psalm 78:35*
The One of Sinai	The God who gives the Law	*Psalm 68:8*

Other titles	Meaning	Bible reference
Rock	God's strength	*Deuteronomy 32:15*
Savior	God rescues	*Deuteronomy 32:15*
The Ancient of Days	God's global authority	*Daniel 7:9*
Father	God loves his family	*Ephesians 3:14*
God of gods, Lord of lords	The great, mighty God	*Deuteronomy 10:17*

Attributes	Example	Bible reference
God is compassionate	"compassionate and gracious"	*Exodus 34:6*
God is merciful	"his mercy is very great"	*1 Chronicles 21:13*
God is holy	"I am holy"	*Leviticus 11:44*
God is love	"God so loved the world"	*John 3:16*
God is Spirit	"God is Spirit"	*John 4:24*

Something to do

• Look up the above references to each name, title or attribute of God. Read the surrounding verses to understand more fully the significance of the name and why God was called by it.

Hopping about from book to book

Opening observation
One of the best ways of understanding the Bible is to compare one passage with another.

Genesis 1-3 and Revelation 20-22
The last three chapters of the Bible are understood more clearly in the light of the first three chapters of the Bible.

Read through Genesis 1-3 and Revelation 1-3. Work through the table on page 29, looking up the Bible references, then read the books again and see how your understanding has been increased.

Compare Revelation with Revelation
Sometimes one part of a Bible book sheds light on another part of the same book.

Read the descriptions of Jesus in chapters two and three of the Book of Revelation. You will find a short descriptive passage at the start of each of the seven letters. The verses to note are:

• *Revelation 2:1*	Seven stars…seven gold lampstands
• *Revelation 2:8*	The First and the Last
• *Revelation 2:12*	Sharp, double-edged sword
• *Revelation 2:18*	Eyes like blazing fire…feet like burnished bronze
• *Revelation 3:1*	Holding seven spirits of God and the seven stars
• *Revelation 3:7*	The keys of David
• *Revelation 3:14*	The Amen, the faithful and true witness

Now read the key to understanding these descriptions in Revelation 1:5-20, where John has his vision of Jesus. You will find that all the features described in chapters two and three refer to the picture of Jesus that John saw in chapter one.

Genesis chapters 1-3	Revelation chapters 20–22
In the beginning. *Genesis 1:1*	A new heaven and a new earth. *Revelation 21:1*
Darkness. *Genesis 1:5*	No night. *Revelation 21:25*
God made the sun and the moon. *Genesis 1:16*	No need for the sun or moon. *Revelation 21:23*
Death. *Genesis 2:17*	No more death. *Revelation 21:4*
Satan appears to deceive humankind. *Genesis 3:1*	Satan disappears forever. *Revelation 20:10*
A garden which become defiled. *Genesis 3:6-7*	A city with nothing shameful in it. *Revelation 21:27*
God's walk with us interrupted. *Genesis 3:8-10*	God's presence with us resumed. *Revelation 21:3*
The initial victory of the serpent. *Genesis 3:13*	The ultimate triumph of the Lamb. *Revelation 20:10; 22:3*
Sorrow is increased. *Genesis 3:16*	No more crying or pain. *Revelation 21:4*
The ground is cursed. *Genesis 3:17*	No longer will there be any curse. *Revelation 22:3*
The first paradise is closed. *Genesis 3:23*	The new paradise is opened. *Revelation 21:25*
Access to the tree of life is barred. *Genesis 3:24*	Access to the tree of life is reinstated. *Revelation 22:14*
They were driven out of the garden. *Genesis 3:24*	They will see his face. *Revelation 22:4*

29

Concluding thought

• Many of the symbols used in the Book of Revelation are explained in previous books of the Bible. You can see this as you look up the Bible references in the following table.

Symbol in Revelation	Reference in Revelation	Helpful Bible reference
Iron sceptre	*Revelation 2:27*	*Psalm 2:9*
Morning star	*Revelation 2:28*	*Daniel 12:3*
Key of David	*Revelation 3:7*	*Isaiah 22:22*
Lion, ox, man, eagle	*Revelation 4:7*	*Ezekiel 1:10; 10:14*
Lamb	*Revelation 5:8*	*John 1:29*

Study, if you dare, about God's wrath!

This is such a formidable and frightening subject that we are inclined to skip the study of God's wrath.

Who taught about heaven and hell?

It may come as a surprise to realize that the person who taught more about heaven and hell than anyone else, was Jesus himself.

Hell

It is hard to escape the conclusion that Jesus believed there was a counterpart to heaven, for those who were condemned before God.

The New Testament has a great deal of teaching on the subject of hell. It was Jesus who spoke about:

- People being in danger of "the fire of hell." *Matthew 5:22*
- A body to "be thrown into hell." *Matthew 5:29*
- The "soul and body [being destroyed] in hell." *Matthew 10:28*
- And who asked the Pharisees the question, "How will you escape being condemned to hell?" *Matthew 23:33*

God's wrath

- God's wrath is not to be confused with human anger or irritability.
- God is perfectly holy and righteous and can have nothing to do with evil.
- God's wrath is God's response to sin.
- People who refuse God's grace in Jesus are under God's wrath. *Romans 1:18; 2:5; Ephesians 2:3; Colossians 3:6*

Descriptions of hell in the New Testament

Words used	Meaning	Bible references
Abaddon	Destruction	*Revelation 9:11*
Abyss	Valley of Hinnom. The rubbish dump outside Jerusalem. Child sacrifice by fire used to take place there. The place of final punishment in the New Testament.	*Matthew 5:22, 29-30* *Matthew 23:15-33* *Mark 9:43-47* *Luke 12:5* *James 3:6*
Hades	The place of the dead. From the name of the Greek god Hades. The word used in the New Testament for the Old Testament word *sheol*.	*Matthew 16:18* *Revelation 1:18; 6:8;* *20:13; Matthew* *11:23; Luke 10:15;* *Acts 2:27, 31;* *1 Corinthians 15:55*
Lake of fire	John's symbol for "the second death."	*Revelation 19:20;* *20:10, 14-15; 21:8*
Tartaros	Gloomy dungeon. In Greek mythology this was the place of eternal punishment.	*2 Peter 2:4*

An illustration of God's wrath

A good example of God's wrath in action is Jesus' reaction to the traders in the Temple, described by John:

When it was almost time for the Jewish Passover, Jesus went up to Jerusalem. In the Temple courts he found men selling cattle, sheep and doves, and others sitting at tables exchanging money.
So he made a whip out of cords, and drove all from the Temple area, both sheep and cattle; he scattered the coins of the money changers and overturned their tables. To those who sold doves he said, "Get these out of here! How dare you turn my Father's house into a market!"

His disciples remembered that it is written, "Zeal for your house will consume me."
John 2:13-17

Hundreds of years of Bible history in 20 verses

The long history books of the Old Testament may seem incomprehensible. One way to approach them is to read summaries.

Stephen's summary

Before Stephen was stoned, he summarized God's actions in the history of God's people.

Read the speech Stephen made before the Sanhedrin, and then read the fuller account from the Old Testament references.

(2) Brothers and fathers, listen to me! The God of glory appeared to our father Abraham while he was still in Mesopotamia, before he lived in Haran. (3) "Leave your country and your people," God said, "and go to the land I will show you."

(4) So he left the land of the Chaldeans and settled in Haran. After the death of his father, God sent him to this land where you are now living. (5) He gave him no inheritance here, not even a foot of ground. But God promised him that he and his descendants after him would possess the land, even though at that time Abraham had no child. (6) God spoke to him in this way: "Your descendants will be strangers in a country not their own, and they will be enslaved and ill-treated for four hundred years. (7) But I will punish the nation they serve as slaves," God said, "and afterwards they will come out of that country and worship me in this place."

(8) Then he gave Abraham the covenant of circumcision. And Abraham became the father of Isaac and circumcised him eight days after his birth. Later Isaac became the father of Jacob, and Jacob became the father of the twelve patriarchs.

(9) Because the patriarchs were jealous of Joseph, they sold him as a slave into Egypt. But God was with him (10) and rescued him from all his troubles. He gave Joseph wisdom and enabled him to gain the goodwill of Pharaoh king of Egypt; so he made him ruler over Egypt and all his palace.

(11) Then a famine struck all Egypt and Canaan, bringing great suffering, and our fathers could not find food. (12) When Jacob heard that there was grain in Egypt, he sent our fathers on their first visit. (13) On their second visit, Joseph told his brothers who he was, and Pharaoh learned about Joseph's family. (14) After this, Joseph sent for his father

Jacob and his whole family, seventy-five in all. (15) Then Jacob went down to Egypt, where he and our fathers died. (16) Their bodies were brought back to Shechem and placed in the tomb that Abraham had bought from the sons of Hamor at Shechem for a certain sum of money.

(17) As the time drew near for God to fulfil his promise to Abraham, the number of our people in Egypt greatly increased. (18) Then another king, who knew nothing about Joseph, became ruler of Egypt. (19) He dealt treacherously with our people and oppressed our forefathers by forcing them to throw out their newborn babies so that they would die.

(20) At that time Moses was born, and he was no ordinary child. For three months he was cared for in his father's house. (21) When he was placed outside, Pharaoh's daughter took him and brought him up as her own son.
Acts 7:2-21

Stephen's speech – Old Testament references

Acts 7:2-8. The experience of Abraham
Acts 7:2   Read with Genesis 11:31; 15:7.
Acts 7:3   Read with Genesis 12:1.
Acts 7:4   Read with Genesis 12:5.
Acts 7:5   Read with Genesis 12:7; 17:8; 26:3.
Acts 7:6   Read with Exodus 1:8-11; 12:40.
Acts 7:7   Read with Genesis 15:13-14; Exodus 3:12.
Acts 7:8   Read with Genesis 17:9-14; 21:2-4; 25:26; 29:31-35; 30:5-13, 17-24; 35:16-18, 22-26.

Acts 7:9-16. The experience of Joseph
Acts 7:9a   Read with Genesis 37:4, 11.
Acts 7:9b   Read with Genesis 37:28; Psalm 105:17.
Acts 7:9c   Read with Genesis 39:2, 21, 23; Haggai 2:4.
Acts 7:10   Read with Genesis 41:37-43; Psalm 105:20-22.
Acts 7:11   Read with Genesis 41:54.
Acts 7:12   Read with Genesis 42:1-2.
Acts 7:13   Read with Genesis 45:1-4; 45:16.
Acts 7:14   Read with Genesis 45:9-10; 46:26-27; Exodus 1:5; Deuteronomy 10:22.
Acts 7:15   Read with Genesis 46:5-7; 49:33; Exodus 1:6.
Acts 7:16   Read with Genesis 23:16-20; 33:18-19; 50:13; Joshua 24:32.

Acts 7:17-21. The experience of Moses
Acts 7:17   Read with Exodus 1:7; Psalm 105:24.
Acts 7:18   Read with Exodus 1:8.
Acts 7:19   Read with Exodus 1:10-22.
Acts 7:20   Read with Exodus 2:2.
Acts 7:21   Read with Exodus 2:3-10.

A biography – the life of Daniel

Opening observations

Nothing bad or negative is recorded about Daniel.
This is in striking contrast to people such as:
• David (a liar, adulterer and murderer).
• Jonah (who deliberately disobeyed God).
• Elijah (who expressed the wish to commit suicide).

Build up a picture about Daniel's circumstances

Find out about Daniel's background:
• Daniel was a prisoner of war. *Daniel 1:1-2*
• Daniel's family. *Daniel 1:3*
• The seven things mentioned about him. *Daniel 1:5*
• The gifts God gave him. *Daniel 1:17*

Compile a character profile of Daniel

• He shares problems with his friends. *Daniel 2:17*
• He takes his problems to God in prayer. *Daniel 2:18*
• He remembers to thank God for answered prayer. *Daniel 2:19-23*
• He makes it clear that his gifts are given him by God. *Daniel 2:27-28*
• He does not let honors go to his head. *Daniel 2:48-49; 5:29*
• He tells the truth, even if it means he might suffer for speaking up. *Daniel 5:1-31*

• He trusts God, even if it means he might be killed. *Daniel 6*

Daniel in the lions' den

Read chapter six, no matter how well you know the story. Note the following points.
• Even the best of God's followers are persecuted: see what Daniel was accused of. *Verses 1-9*
• Daniel deliberately goes against the king's decree. Why? *Verses 10-12*
• Daniel's faithfulness has quite an effect on the king. *Verses 13-18*
• How does Daniel give God the glory for what happened? *Verses 19-23*

Daniel's friends

Study chapter three, where Daniel's friends are thrown into the fiery furnace. In what ways do the men show their faith in God?

Concluding thought
• Daniel was about eighty years old when he was put in the
  lions' den. But he stayed faithful to God in his old age:
  "My God sent his angel, and he shut the mouths of the lions."
  Daniel 6:22

Making study
a spiritual exercise

We read and study the Bible primarily for our spiritual lives.
A good prayer before reading the Bible is:

> Lord Jesus Christ,
> May I love you more dearly,
> Follow you more nearly,
> See you more clearly,
> Day by day. Amen.

Making comparisons
See how many links you can
make between Isaiah 53 and
what you know about Jesus'
death.

Making a spiritual response
To prevent Bible study from
being little more than an
intellectual exercise,
remember this, as you think
about Jesus' death: "All this
you have done for me, what
will I do for you?"

Something to do
• Memorize Isaiah 53.
• Try learning one verse a day,
  or one a week. Repeat it to
  yourself during the day, and
  before you go to sleep.

See also:
• *15 ways to enhance your Bible
  study,* page 64.

Who has believed our message
and to whom has the arm of the
Lord been revealed?
He grew up before him like a
tender shoot,
and like a root out of dry ground.
He had no beauty or majesty to
attract us to him,
nothing in his appearance that we
should desire him.
He was despised and rejected by
men, a man of sorrows, and
familiar with suffering.
Like one from whom men hide
their faces
he was despised, and we esteemed
him not.
Surely he took up our infirmities
and carried our sorrows,
yet we considered him stricken by
God,
smitten by him, and afflicted.
But he was pierced for our
transgressions,
he was crushed for our iniquities;
the punishment that brought us
peace was upon him,
and by his wounds we are healed.

We all, like sheep, have gone
    astray,
each of us has turned to his own
    way;
and the Lord has laid on him
the iniquity of us all.
He was oppressed and afflicted
yet he did not open his mouth;
he was led like a lamb to the
    slaughter,
and as a sheep before her shearers
    is silent,
so he did not open his mouth.
By oppression and judgment he
    was taken away.
And who can speak of his
    descendants?
For he was cut off from the land
    of the living;
for the transgression of my people
    he was stricken.
He was assigned a grave with the
    wicked,
and with the rich in his death,
though he had done no violence,
nor was any deceit in his mouth.

Yet it was the Lord's will to crush
    him and cause him to suffer,
and though the Lord makes his
    life a guilt offering,
he will see his offspring and
    prolong his days,
and the will of the Lord will
    prosper in his hand.
After the suffering of his soul,
he will see the light of life and be
    satisfied;
by his knowledge my righteous
    servant will justify many,
and he will bear their iniquities.
Therefore I will give him a portion
    among the great,
and he will divide the spoils with
    the strong,
because he poured out his life
    unto death,
and was numbered with the
    transgressors.
For he bore the sin of many,
and made intercession for the
    transgressors.

Isaiah 53

Three men with a common desire – a death wish

Elijah, Jonah and Job all expressed the desire to die before their lives naturally ended. They are among some of God's greatest, strongest, and most faithful followers who at times felt like committing suicide.

ELIJAH the discouraged prophet

Elijah's death-wish

"Elijah was afraid and ran for his life. When he came to Beersheba in Judah, he left his servant there, while he himself went a day's journey into the desert. He came to a broom tree, sat down under it and prayed that he might die. 'I have had enough, Lord,' he said. 'Take my life; I am no better than my anscestors.' " *1 Kings 19:3-4*
• Read *1 Kings 19:5-9* to see how God comforted Elijah.

A bird's-eye view of Elijah's life
• He predicts famine in Israel. *1 Kings 17:1*
• He is fed by ravens. *1 Kings 17:2-6*
• He defeats the prophets of Baal. *1 Kings 18:16-46*
• He is taken to heaven in a whirlwind. *2 Kings 2:11-12*

JONAH – the man who wanted to avoid doing God's will

Jonah's death-wish

"When the sun rose, God provided a scorching east wind, and the sun blazed on Jonah's head so that he grew faint. He wanted to die, and said, 'It would be better for me to die than to live.' "
Jonah 4:8
• Read *Jonah 4:9-11* to see how God helped Jonah.

A bird's-eye view of Jonah's life

• He tries to run away from God. *Jonah 1*
• He prays inside a fish. *Jonah 2*
• He preaches to Nineveh. *Jonah 3*
• He is rebuked by God. *Jonah 4*

JOB – the man who suffered

Job's death-wish

"After this, Job opened his mouth and cursed the day of his birth. He said: 'Why did I not perish at birth, and die as I came from the womb?' "
Job 3:1-2, 11
• Read *Job 40:1-42:3* to see how God brought Job to worship him.

A bird's-eye view of Job's life

• His righteousness is tested by disaster. *Job 1*
• He keeps on saying that he is innocent. *Job 3-41*
• He worships God and is restored. *Job 42*

39

To ponder
•"Carry each other's burdens." *Galatians 6:2*

What's so fishy about Jonah?

Opening observations

People who describe the fish as a whale are incorrect. The correct translation is "great fish" or "large fish" (*Jonah 1:17*). Jesus calls it a "huge fish" (*Matthew 12:40*). The biological identification of the fish is not the important point of the story.

Read through the four chapters of Jonah

As you do this, bear in mind that the whole story hinges on Jonah's refusal to obey God, and his reluctant decision to go to the wicked town of Nineveh and speak out against it.

- **Chapter 1.** As you read chapter one, reflect on how the Lord saves pagan sailors from drowning at sea.

- **Chapter 2.** As you read chapter two, reflect on how the Lord also saves Jonah from drowning.

- **Chapter 3.** As you read chapter three, reflect on how the Lord saves the people of Nineveh from judgment.

- **Chapter 4.** As you read chapter four, reflect on how the Lord saves Jonah from his wrong ideas.

Questions to ask

What do we learn about Jonah?

- He runs away from God – at least he does his level best to! *Jonah 1:3, 10.* (Tarshish was in the opposite direction to Nineveh. Imagine Jonah was in London, and God told him to travel to New York, but he boarded the plane for Beijing, China.)
- When God is merciful, Jonah is angry. *Jonah 4:1-3, 9.* (Jonah was more concerned about a plant than about the people. *Read Jonah 4:10-11.*)
- Jonah prays to God. *Jonah 1:9; 2:1-9*

What do we learn about God?

- Throughout the Book of Jonah, it is assumed that God is fair and just and that he will punish wrong. *Jonah 1:2; 3:2, 9-10*
- God is in control of his world, which includes the weather, animals and plants. The great fish was God's way of rescuing Jonah. *Jonah 1:4, 9, 17; 2:10; 4:6-8*
- God shows how merciful and kind he is – to animals as well as to humans. *Jonah 2:8-9; 3:9-10; 4:2, 10-11*

Concluding thought

- What spiritual lesson did Jesus draw from Jonah? *Read Matthew 12:38-41; 16:4.* (Jonah, God's servant, was miraculously rescued by God. In the same way, Jesus' claims will be seen to be true through his resurrection. *Read Romans 1:3-4.*)

The great women of the Bible

Opening observations

Jesus surprised people by the way he cared for, talked to, and respected women.

John's Gospel says that Jesus' disciples were once "greatly surprised" to find Jesus talking to a woman, for religious teachers did not speak to women in public in those days. *John 4:27*

Look up the Bible references given for each woman.
Write down her good points.

Ten great women of the Old Testament

Deborah	The only judge (ruler) who gave Israel twenty years of peace.	*Judges 4-5*
Eve	The first woman.	*Genesis 2:18-4:2; 4:25*
Esther	Heroine of the Book of Esther.	*Esther*
Miriam	Moses' sister.	*Exodus 2:4, 7-8; 15:20-21; Numbers 12; 20:1*
Naomi	Ruth's mother-in-law.	*Ruth*
Rachel	Laban's daughter.	*Genesis 29-30; 35:18-20*
Rahab	Prostitute who lived in Jericho.	*Joshua 2; 6:22-25; Matthew 1:5; James 2:25*
Rebekah	Isaac's wife.	*Genesis 24; 25:19-26:16, 27*
Ruth	Heroine of the Book of Ruth.	*Ruth*
Sarah	Abraham's wife.	*Genesis 11-12; 16-18:15; 20-21*

Seven great women of the New Testament

Anna	An old prophetess, who practically lived in the Temple.	*Luke 2:36-38*
Dorcas (also called Tabitha)	Dorcas was renowned for caring for the poor.	*Acts 9:36-41*
Elizabeth	Related to Mary, the mother of Jesus.	*Luke 1*
Lydia	A successful businesswoman who became a follower of Jesus.	*Acts 16:14-15, 40*
Martha and Mary	Sisters of Lazarus.	*Luke 10:38-42; John 11, 12:1-9*
Mary	The mother of Jesus.	*Matthew 1:18-25; 2:11; 13:55; Luke 1-2; John 2:1-11; 19:25-27; Acts 1:14*

Mary's song

My soul praises the Lord
and my spirit rejoices in God my Savior,
for he has been mindful
of the humble estate of his servant.
From now on all generations will call me blessed,
for the Mighty One has done great things for me –
holy is his name,
His mercy extends to those who fear him,
from generation to generation.
He has performed mighty deeds with his arm;
he has scattered those who are proud in their inmost thoughts.
He has brought down rulers from their
     thrones
but has lifted up the humble.
He has filled the hungry with good things
but he has sent the rich away empty.
He has helped his servant Israel,
remembering to be merciful
to Abraham and his descendants for ever,
even as he said to our fathers.
Luke 1:46-55

Concluding thought
•In an age when women were despised and marginalized, the apostle Paul's statement in Galatians 3:28 was revolutionary.

Coming to grips with the Bible's longest chapter

Opening observation
The 176 verses of Psalm 119 make it, by far, the longest chapter in the Bible.

Working out the theme of Psalm 119 is not hard
Psalm 119 is about God's revelation to Israel. Nearly all of its 176 verses refer to the same thing. They focus on God's words and his law (verse 160) as statements about what to believe (doctrine) and how to behave (ethics).

Eight synonyms
The poetic writer of Psalm 119 uses eight words to celebrate God's revelation. You'll find one of the following words in just about every verse:

44

1 Precepts (verse 4).
2 Law ("the law of the Lord" verse 1).
3 Statutes (verse 24).
4 Decrees (verse 5).
5 Commands (verse 6).
6 Word or words (verse 17).
7 Laws (verse 13).
8 Promises (verse 41).

There is another word which also comes up often: "ways" (verse 3). This means a pattern of life based on God's will.

Eight definitions
As you read through this hymn of praise to God's revelation, match these definitions to the above eight synonyms.

1 Detailed rules for life.
2 Divinely revealed teaching.
3 Details about God's covenant which his people are to observe.
4 Written down rulings which are always to be observed.
5 A word that expresses the will of a personal God, who is Israel's Lord.
6 Communication of God's will to his people.
7 Verdicts of the divine judge about a wide range of topics.
8 Communication of God's will, specifically through his promises.

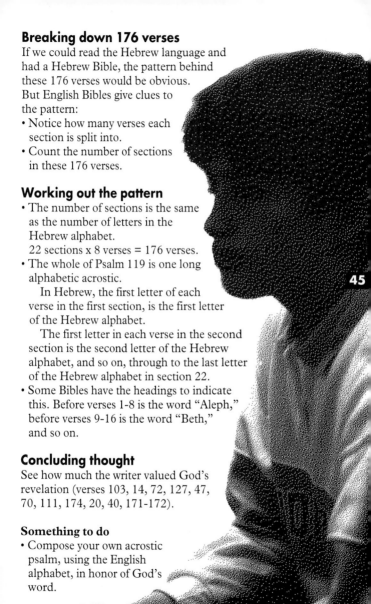

Breaking down 176 verses

If we could read the Hebrew language and
had a Hebrew Bible, the pattern behind
these 176 verses would be obvious.
But English Bibles give clues to
the pattern:

• Notice how many verses each
  section is split into.
• Count the number of sections
  in these 176 verses.

Working out the pattern

• The number of sections is the same
  as the number of letters in the
  Hebrew alphabet.
  22 sections x 8 verses = 176 verses.
• The whole of Psalm 119 is one long
  alphabetic acrostic.

  In Hebrew, the first letter of each
verse in the first section, is the first letter
of the Hebrew alphabet.
  The first letter in each verse in the second
section is the second letter of the Hebrew
alphabet, and so on, through to the last letter
of the Hebrew alphabet in section 22.
• Some Bibles have the headings to indicate
  this. Before verses 1-8 is the word "Aleph,"
  before verses 9-16 is the word "Beth,"
  and so on.

Concluding thought

See how much the writer valued God's
revelation (verses 103, 14, 72, 127, 47,
70, 111, 174, 20, 40, 171-172).

Something to do

• Compose your own acrostic
  psalm, using the English
  alphabet, in honor of God's
  word.

The names and titles of Jesus

The name "Jesus" is the Greek form of the word "Joshua," meaning "Yahweh is salvation." This is made clear in Matthew 1:21: "You are to give him the name Jesus, because he will save his people from their sins."

Titles used for Jesus in the Old Testament

There are six names which refer to Jesus in the Book of Isaiah.
• Immanuel, God with us. *Isaiah 7:14*
• Wonderful Counselor, Mighty God, Everlasting Father, Prince of Peace. *Isaiah 9:6*
• Root of Jesse. *Isaiah 11:10*
• Branch. *Zechariah 6:12*

Titles used for Jesus in the gospels

Every title, or name used to refer to Jesus, reveals his character.

Title used	Significance	Bible reference
Teacher/Rabbi and **The Teacher**	Jesus taught people about God	*Mark 5:35*
Prophet	He spoke the word of God	*Luke 24:19*
Christ (Greek for Anointed One/Messiah.)	Sent to establish God's kingdom on earth	*John 1:41*
I Am	Jesus existed before his human life on earth	*John 8:58*
The Lamb of God	Jesus would be a sacrifice for sin	*John 1:29*
Jesus the Nazarene	To distinguish him from other people called Jesus	*Matthew 2:23*
Son of David	Descended from David. Fulfilled all the promises made to King David.	*Matthew 15:22*
Son of God	Jesus was uniquely related to God	*Mark 1:1*
Son of Man	Showing his human identity	*Matthew 8:20*
Word	How Jesus revealed God	*John 1:1*
Rabboni	My dear Master	*John 20:16*
Lord	A title showing respect	*Luke 11:1*

Titles for Jesus in the rest of the New Testament

Title	Significance	Bible reference
Alpha and Omega	The beginning and the end	*Revelation 1:8*
Author of life	The one who gives life	*Acts 3:15*
The bright Morning Star	The one who brings light	*Revelation 22:16*
Head of the Church	The overseer of all Christians	*Ephesians 5:23*
Holy and Righteous One	Jesus was both holy and righteous	*Acts 3:14*
King of kings and Lord of lords	Ruler of all	*Revelation 19:16*
Lamb	Lamb killed as a sacrifice for sin	*Revelation 5:6-13*
Lion of the tribe of Judah	A title of the Messiah from the family of David	*Revelation 5:5*
Root of David	A title of the Messiah from the family of David	*Revelation 5:5*
Savior	One who saves from sin	*1 John 4:14*
Word of God	Gives voice to God's truth	*Revelation 19:13*

47

- In the seven "I ams" described in John's Gospel, Jesus uses seven figurative descriptions of himself. See: *What's so special about John's Gospel?* page 54.

Studying the life of Jesus

Opening observations
- Nearly everything we know about Jesus comes from the four gospels: Matthew, Mark, Luke and John.
- Many people have strong views about Jesus, but few people have taken the time to read the gospels.

Twelve highlights of Jesus' life
Questions to ask as you read through the highlights
- Why do you think the writer included this particular story in his gospel?
- What does this event tell us about who Jesus was?

1	His birth	*Luke 2:1-7*
2	The visit of the shepherds	*Luke 2:8-20*
3	The wise men and their gifts	*Matthew 2:1-12*
4	The twelve-year-old Jesus visits the Temple	*Luke 2:41-50*
5	Jesus' baptism	*Matthew 3:13-17*
6	Jesus is tempted	*Matthew 4:1-11*
7	A top religious leader talks to Jesus	*John 3:1-21*
8	Jesus speaks to a despised female half-caste	*John 4:1-42*
9	Jesus chooses his team	*Matthew 10:1-4*
10	Peter gets it right	*Matthew 16:13-20*
11	The transfiguration of Jesus	*Matthew 17:1-13*
12	The ascension of Jesus	*Luke 24:50-53*

Getting to know and to love the gospels
Here is a simple way to read through the gospels in less than thirteen weeks.
- Read a chapter a day of Mark's Gospel (16 days).
- Read a chapter a day of Matthew's Gospel (28 days).
- Read a chapter a day of Luke's Gospel (24 days).
- Read a chapter a day of John's Gospel (21 days).

It's a fact
The shortest verse in the Bible is John 11:35. It has two words, one in Greek.

What did Jesus say?

Occasion	Bible reference	Theme
Sermon on the Mount	*Matthew 5-7*	The way to be happy
The upper room	*John 13-17*	How to live the Jesus way
The Mount of Olives	*Matthew 24-25*	The shape of the future

What did Jesus do?

Miracle	Bible reference	Spiritual truth demonstrated
Paralytic healed	*Luke 5*	The forgiveness of sins
5,000 people fed	*John 6*	Jesus is the bread of life
Various miracles	*Matthew 8*	Jesus' authority over disease

How did people respond to Jesus?

People	Response	Reasons
Leaders	Few believed	They rejected Jesus because: • He said he was God. *John 5:18* • They disapproved of the company he kept. *Mark 2:16* • He challenged their traditions. *Mark 7:1-13*
Crowds	Many believed	Examples of those who welcomed Jesus: • Many Samaritans. *John 4:39* • Many Jews. *John 11:45* • Crowds listened to Jesus with delight. *Mark 12:37* • People rejected by society. *Luke 15:1*

Concluding thought
• As you read the four gospels, compile your own biography of Jesus. Use the four headings on this page, and write down what happened, with its reference in the gospels.

See also: *A year's worth of Bible studies*, page 62.

How do Matthew, Mark and Luke differ?

In one sense, the four gospels are similar, as they are all portraits of the life, death and resurrection of Jesus. But each gospel also contains a special message. One way to unlock the special message is to work out what is different about each gospel.

Matthew's Gospel

Jesus' words
Two-thirds of Matthew's Gospel, 1,071 verses, records the spoken words of Jesus.

Jesus is king
Matthew presents Jesus as Israel's promised messianic king. Look up the following Bible references, which clearly reveal a portrait of Jesus as a ruler or king. *1:23; 2:2; 2:6; 3:17; 4:15-17; 21:5; 21:9; 22:44-45; 26:64; 27:11; 27:27-37*

Mark's Gospel

Mark's message
It's not too hard to see what Mark's main message is. From reading Mark 1:1, it is clear that this gospel is all about Jesus, the Son of God.

The humanity of Jesus
Mark emphasizes the humanity and kindness of Jesus.
• Jesus is "deeply distressed." *3:5*
• Jesus has "compassion" for a large crowd. *6:34*

Luke's Gospel

Luke was a Gentile, not a Jew. He wrote his gospel for the Gentiles. Luke took great pains to stress that Jesus was for everyone, not just the Jews.
In his gospel, Luke presents Jesus as the savior of the world, and shows that Jesus came:
• For women as well as men.
• For slaves as well as for free men.
• For the poor as well as for the rich.
• For people who had not been brought up as Jews.

Father God

Matthew's favorite way of describing God is to refer to him as "heavenly Father" or "Father in heaven." What do we learn from the following verses about God our Father? 5:16; 5:45; 5:48; 6:1; 6:9; 7:11; 7:21; 10:32-3; 12:50; 16:17; 18:10; 18:14; 18:19

A gospel for Jews

Matthew quotes from the Old Testament more often than the other three gospels.

- Matthew shows his Jewish readers, through these quotes, that Jesus really was the Messiah prophesied in the Old Testament.
- Matthew indicates that Jesus came from the Jews.
- Matthew demonstrates that many events in Jesus' life – birth, early childhood, teachings, miracles, arrest, death and resurrection – fulfilled prophesies about him written hundreds of years before in the Old Testament.

- Jesus is deeply distressed and "troubled." 14:33
- The gospel's favorite title for Jesus is "Son of Man," used fourteen times. This title appears in Daniel 7:13-14, where it is used of the Messiah. It is a title that is never used by anyone but Jesus. 10:45

Jesus is the Son of God

Mark shows how Jesus is the Son of God.

- Read about the many times Mark refers to Jesus as the "Son of

God." 1:1, 11; 3:11; 9:7; 12:6; 13:32; 14:36, 61

- Mark shows that Jesus acted with divine authority. In his conflicts with the Pharisees, Jesus acts and speaks as God. 2:1-12, 15-17, 18-22, 23-38; 3:1-6

Discipleship

Mark concentrates on the death of Jesus on the cross, and the need for Jesus' disciples to follow him in a life of self-renunciation. 8:34-9:1; 9:35-10:31; 10:42-45

51

Key themes in Luke

There are six themes to look for. List the themes, and write down the related Bible references, as you come across them.

- Prayer
- Money
- The Holy Spirit
- Forgiveness
- Praise and joy
- Women and children

Incidents recorded only by Luke

Many events only appear in Luke's Gospel. See how they fit in with

the six key themes mentioned above.

- Zechariah's vision and Elizabeth's conception. 1:5-25
- Gabriel's visit to Mary. 1:26-38
- Mary's visit to Elizabeth. 1:39-56
- Birth of John the Baptist and Zechariah's song. 1:57-80
- The decree of Caesar Augustus. 2:1-3
- Jesus' birth in Bethlehem. 2:4-7
- The shepherds. 2:8-20
- Jesus' circumcision. 2:21
- Jesus is presented in the Temple; Simeon and Anna. 2:22-40

Choose a topic and make a Bible study

Profitable Bible studies can been made by studying words, themes, teachings, people and events in the Bible. You will need a Bible concordance or Bible dictionary to examine the places where your specific topic of study is found.

Baptism

Let's see if we can discover some of the meanings for this rather controversial subject. The word "baptism" or "baptize" is an interesting word to study because the word was never translated into English from the Greek *baptisma* or *baptizo*. To stay away from current controversies surrounding baptism, the translators left the word untranslated.

The best approach for discovering the meaning of baptism, is to look at all the Bible verses where this word occurs.

John the Baptist

The first occurrence of the word and its variations is in Matthew chapter three.

• Why was John called John the Baptist?	Because he was baptizing people. *Matthew 3:6*
• What substance did John use for baptism?	Water in the River Jordan. *Matthew 3:6, 11, 13*
• What did the people normally do prior to baptism?	They confessed their sins. *Matthew 3:6*
• Why did John baptize at a certain area in the River Jordan?	Because there was plenty of water there. *John 3:23*

Summarize what you have learned so far about baptism.

Jesus' baptism

• Where was Jesus baptized?	In the River Jordan: he went up out of the water. *Matthew 3:13, 16*
• Why was Jesus baptized?	To fulfill all righteousness. *Matthew 3:14-15*
• What were the last words of Jesus before he ascended to heaven?	To go and make disciples of all nations, baptizing them into the name of the Father, Son and Holy Spirit. *Matthew 28:19-20*

Baptism in Acts

In Acts chapter two, we find the first occurrence of baptism as the Church begins on the Day of Pentecost. If you look up each of the following passages from Acts, you will discover that a believer in Christ always submitted immediately to baptism.

Acts 2:38-41	*Acts 9:17-18*	*Acts 16:31-33*
Acts 8:12-13	*Acts 10:47-48*	*Acts 19:3-5*
Acts 8:36, 38	*Acts 16:14-15*	*Acts 22:16*

Finding out about baptism

Romans 6:3-5	*1 Corinthians 12:13*	*Ephesians 4:5*
1 Corinthians 1:13-16	*Galatians 3:27*	*Colossians 2:12*

In other passages throughout the New Testament, the term "baptism" also occurs. As you look up these passages, see if you can determine more fully the meaning and the importance of baptism.

There are some preliminary observations that we can make as we assemble all the information about baptism.

• It involves water (probably much).
• It involves confession of sin.
• It is important – it is something that God wants us to submit to.
• It was important enough for Jesus to submit to.

• As believers, we are told to baptize the disciples we make.
• It is the one thing in the Christian life that we are told to do only once.
• It involves us in a unique relationship with Jesus.

Concluding thought

• So now it is up to you to study and make up your own mind as to what baptism means to you. Look up each verse. Jot down some notes. Then come to your own conclusions.

What's so special about John's Gospel?

Opening observations

Matthew, Mark and Luke are similar to each other, but John is quite different.

Many of the incidents mentioned in John's Gospel, such as Jesus' washing of the disciples' feet (John 13:1-17), are not in Matthew, Mark or Luke.

Signs

One distinctive characteristic of John's Gospel is the fact that he does not talk about miracles, but signs.

Start by reading John 20:31, as John states why he recorded these miraculous signs. As you look up each sign, consider how it helped to reinforce who Jesus was.

The seven signs

1 Jesus changes water into wine	*John 2:1-10*
2 Jesus heals a royal official's son	*John 4:46-54*
3 Jesus heals an invalid	*John 5:1-9*
4 Jesus feeds 5,000	*John 6:1-14*
5 Jesus walks on the water	*John 6:16-21*
6 Jesus heals a blind man	*John 9:1-41*
7 Jesus brings Lazarus back to life	*John 11:1-44*

"I am"

John loved the number seven. As well as recording seven miraculous signs, he lists the seven "I am" sayings of Jesus.

The seven "I am" sayings

"I am the bread of life"	*John 6:35-40*
"I am the light of the world"	*John 8:12-13*
"I am the gate"	*John 10:7-10*
"I am the good shepherd"	*John 10:11-18*
"I am the resurrection and the life"	*John 11:17-27*
"I am the way, truth and life"	*John 14:1-7*
"I am the true vine"	*John 15:1-11*

Links

Did you know that some of the signs link up with the "I ams"? For example, the seventh sign links with the fifth "I am." You can link up others as well. Link the first sign and the seventh "I am," the fourth sign and the first "I am," the sixth sign and the second "I am."

Concluding thought

- In his gospel, John used a thematic approach rather than the chronological approach favored by Matthew, Mark and Luke.
- See how many of the following key word concepts you can find as you read John's Gospel: truth, light, darkness, word, knowledge, remain, love, world, judgment, belief and witness.

Studying a single word: humility

For a good Bible definition of humility, see Romans 12:3.
Another word for humility could be honesty.

One of the most famous Old Testament figures is called a humble person (in fact he was called "a very humble" man)	*Numbers 12:3*
Humility is not false modesty	*Colossians 2:23.*
Humility is linked to receiving God's salvation	*Psalm 149:4*
Humility is linked to receiving grace from God	*Proverbs 3:34*
In the Bible we are commanded to be humble	*Micah 6:8*
Humility is commended by Jesus	*Matthew 18:4*
Humility brings rewards	*Proverbs 15:33; 1 Peter 5:6.*
• The humble person is guided by God	*Psalm 25:9*
• The humble person enjoys God's help	*James 4:6*
• The humble person is promised rest of heart and mind	*Matthew 11:28-30*
• The humble person will be lifted up	*Matthew 23:12*
Humility is one of God's characteristics	
• God's humility is seen in his creation of and care for the world	*Psalm 113:5-9*
• God's humility is seen in his being prepared to live with lowly people	*Isaiah 57:15*
• God's humility is seen in his lowly birth in a manger	*Luke 1:32-35*
• God's humility is seen in his death	*Philippians 2:5-8*
Humility was one of Jesus' most obvious qualities	*Matthew 11:29 and John 8:50.*

Learning from Jesus' humility.   *2 Corinthians 10:1*
When the apostle Paul wanted to emphasize
the lesson about humility, he appealed to
Jesus' own humility

Humility is linked with
  • Wisdom   *James 3:13*
  • Compassion, kindness, gentleness
    and patience   *Colossians 3:12*
  • Righteousness   *Zephaniah 2:3*

Concluding thought
• We are expected to get dressed each day in a set of humble
  clothes, according to 1 Peter 5:5.

The death of Jesus

Opening observation

The four gospel writers give more space to Jesus' death than to any other event in his life.

The order of the events linked to Jesus' crucifixion

1	Arrival at Golgotha (Calvary)	*Matthew 27:33; Mark 15:22; Luke 23:33; John 19:7*
2	Offer of a numbing drink	*Matthew 27:34*
3	The crucifixion	*Matthew 27:35*
4	"Father forgive ..." (First "word" from the cross)	*Luke 23:34*
5	Gambling for Jesus' clothes	*Matthew 27:35*
6	Jesus is mocked.	*Matthew 27:39-44; Mark 15:29*
7	The thieves speak against Jesus, but one believes	*Matthew 27:44*
8	"Today you will be with me ..." (Second "word" from the cross)	*Luke 23:43*
9	"Dear woman, here is your son ..." (Third "word" from the cross)	*John 19:26-27*
10	The darkness	*Matthew 27:45; Mark 15:33*
11	"My God, my God ..." (Fourth "word" from the cross)	*Matthew 27:46-47; Mark 15:34-36*
12	"I am thirsty." (Fifth "word" from the cross)	*John 19:28*
13	"It is finished." (Sixth "word" from the cross)	*John 19:30*
14	"Father, into your hands ..." (Seventh "word" from the cross)	*Luke 23:46 (See also Matthew 27:50 and Mark 15:37, where Jesus dismisses his spirit.)*

What to look for in the events listed
- Look at the impact of each event on the people around Jesus.
- Notice where a gospel writer is the only one to record a particular event. Why do you think he included it? What does it add?
- Note that Jesus "said" seven things when he was on the cross (sometimes called his "seven words" from the cross). What does each reveal about Jesus?
- See how these events shed light on the words of Mark 10:45.

Concluding thought
- Some people say that at end of Jesus' life came as a result of "circumstances" (the Romans and the Jews), and as a consequence he was killed. But read Mark 8:31-9:1 and Mark 10:32-34, which show that Jesus foretold the details of his death.

59

See also: *Making study a spiritual exercise,* page 36.

"But the Bible's full of contradictions!"

It is no use pretending that there are no difficulties with the Bible. Some of the apparent contradictions are solved when we know more about the Bible; others may not be resolved in our lifetime.

The main purpose of the Bible is to teach us about God's love for us in his plan of salvation. It is not to satisfy other questions that we may have in our minds. The best way to cope with supposed contradictions in the Bible, is for us to know how to interpret them correctly in the first place.

Interpreting the Bible
What is the natural sense of the passage?

Christians believe that, "God is light; in him there is no darkness at all." (1 John 1:5.) So God reveals himself in the Bible in ways we can understand.

Sometimes this means that the correct way to interpret a Bible passage is in a figurative way, not in a literal way. This applies to certain types of literature, such as apocalyptic literature which reveals hidden truths, for example the Book of Revelation. There we read, "These ... have come out of the great tribulation; they have washed their robes and made them white in the blood of the Lamb." (Revelation 7:14.) It is impossible for robes which have been washed in "blood" to come out "white." John did not expect his readers to visualize this image, but to see it as a symbol.

Symbol	Interpretation
White robes	The righteousness of God's people.
The blood of the Lamb	The death of Jesus, which is totally responsible for bringing about the righteousness of God's people.
Washing robes	To wash a robe meant to put trust in Jesus.

When deciding how to interpret a passage in the Bible, ask yourself what the natural sense of the passage is – is it literal or figurative?

What is the general sense of the passage?
The Bible is in harmony with itself. When reading a verse or passage, we have to ask:
- How does it fit in with other teachings on the same subject in the Bible?
- What is its immediate context? (What is the subject matter of the paragraph, chapter and Bible book it is in?)

Do we have to believe that God literally wrote the Ten Commandments with his finger? Exodus 31:18 says, "When the Lord finished speaking to Moses on Mount Sinai, he gave him the two tablets of the Testimony, the tablets of stone inscribed by the finger of God."

What is the general teaching in the Bible about the finger of God?

People who talked about "the finger of God"	What they said
David	"When I consider your heavens, the work of your fingers." *Psalm 8:3*
Egyptian magicians referring (to the plague of gnats)	"The magicians said to Pharaoh, 'This is the finger of God.' " *Exodus 8:19*
Jesus (after he cast out demons)	"But if I drive out demons by the finger of God..." *Luke 11:20*

From these examples, we can conclude that the expression "the finger of God" is used in a special way in the Bible. It is a figure of speech meaning God's direct intervention.

Four interventions
- Intervention in creation: the heavens. *Psalm 8:3*
- Intervention in judgment: the plagues. *Exodus 8:19*
- Intervention in salvation: the exorcism of the demons. *Luke 11:20*
- Intervention in revelation: the giving of the law. *Exodus 31:18*

A year's worth of Bible studies

Opening observations
- Nearly everything we know about Jesus comes from the four gospels.
- Many people have set views about Jesus, but few of them have ever read the gospels.
- Spend an hour a week over the next year studying the life of Jesus in the four gospels.

Follow the life of Jesus in the table. Start by reading down one of the columns (Matthew, Mark, Luke and John), and looking up the Bible references. Complete Matthew before moving on to Mark, and so on.

A harmony of the four gospels

Topic	Matthew	Mark	Luke	John
Jesus' birth and childhood				
Jesus' family tree	1:1-17		3:23-38	
His birth	2:1-12		2:1-39	
Temple visit and childhood			2:40-52	
Preparing for public ministry				
Jesus' baptism	3:13-17	1:9-11	3:21-22	
Jesus' temptations	4:1-11	1:12-13	4:1-13	
Jesus starts his ministry				
John points to Jesus				1:19-34
Jesus' first "sign" (miracle)				2:1-12
Jesus meets Nicodemus				3:1-21
Jesus' work in Galilee				
Jesus' arrival in Galilee	4:12-17	1:14	4:14	4:43-45
Call of the twelve apostles	4:18-22	1:16-20	5:1-11	
The Sermon on the Mount	5:1–7:29		6:20-49	
Some of Jesus' parables	13:1-53	4:1-34	8:4-18	
Some of Jesus' miracles	8:23–9:8	4:35–5:43	8:22-56	
Jesus walks on the sea	14:22-33	6:45-52		6:16-21
Said to be the Christ	16:13-20	8:27–9:1	9:18-27	
Jesus' transfiguration	17:1-13	9:2-13	9:28-36	

Note what each gospel writer includes and leaves out.
• Ask yourself why a gospel writer tells a particular story in his gospel.
• What do the events tell us about who Jesus was?
• Note any differences between the gospel writers' accounts of the same incidents, and consider what these differences emphasize.

Topic	Matthew	Mark	Luke	John
Jesus' work in Judea				
Journey to Jerusalem	19:1-2	10:1	9:51-62	7:10
Jesus in Mary and Martha's home			10:38-42	
Jesus teaches a prayer			11:1-13	
Jesus brings Lazarus back to life				11:1-44
Jesus' journey towards Jerusalem				
The rich young ruler	19:16–20:16	10:17-31	18:18-30	
Jesus predicts his death	20:17-19	10:32-34	18:31-34	
Jesus arrives at Bethany				11:55–12:11
Jesus' last week				
Jesus enters Jerusalem	21:1-9	11:1-10	19:29-40	12:12-19
Jesus cleanses the Temple	21:12-16	11:15-19	19:45-48	
The widow's offering		12:41-44	21:1-4	
Teaching about the end	24–25	13:1-37	21:5-38	
The Passover meal	26:17-29	14:12-25	22:7-30	13:1-30
Peter's denial predicted	26:31-35	14:27-31	22:31-38	13:31-38
Jesus' final teachings				14:1–17:26
Jesus in Gethsemane	26:36-46	14:32-42	22:39-46	18:1
Good Friday	27:11-60	15:2-46	23:1-54	18:28–19:42
Resurrection appearances	28:9-20	[16:9-18]	24:1-49	20:1–21:23
Jesus' ascension		[16:19-20]	24:50-53	

15 ways to enhance your Bible study

Read to make you "wise for salvation"

Remember what the main purpose of the Bible is. It is not to acquire knowledge. According to 2 Timothy 3:15, Bible reading is *"to make us wise for salvation through faith in Christ Jesus."*

Don't be afraid to study the Bible

- Don't forget that you will get nowhere without relying on the Holy Spirit as you read, think, and study.
- Read through a different Bible book each month.
- Read one psalm every day.

Things to do

1 Compile your own biography. Find all the references you can to Peter in the New Testament. Make a list of the references. Write down one thing you learn about Peter's character next to each reference.

2 Read from a version of the Bible you have never used before.

3 Read one chapter from the New Testament in as many different Bible versions as possible.

4 Memorize verses. Memorize one Bible verse that has really helped you each week or month. Make a list of these verses and note down why you like them.

5 Read an Old Testament book you are unfamiliar with.

6 Watch a video about the Holy Land.

7 From the Book of Proverbs, compile a list of topics that are mentioned.

8 Use a computer. There are numerous software programs available. Your local Christian bookstore should be able to help you.

9 Buy a study Bible. These help you to understand the Bible better and better.

10 Join in with other people. Many churches and Christian organizations have Bible study groups, which can be very useful places for learning more about the Bible.

11 Read everything written in the New Testament by John. Start with John's Gospel, then his three letters, and finally the Book of Revelation.

12 Read John chapter ten alongside Psalm 23.

13 Each Christmas, ask for a present to help your Bible study.

14 Read a promise from the Bible before you go to sleep.

15 Listen to Handel's *Messiah*.

See also: *Making study a spiritual exercise*, page 36.

Key
Bible
Words
made easy

What do the following words found
in the Bible mean?

- Atonement
- Righteousness
- Kingdom of heaven
- Sanctification
- Predestination

And then, what does the Bible actually
teach about:

- Assurance
- Holiness
- Election
- Pride
- Eternal life?

Key Bible Words made easy gives you the basic
Bible teaching on more than 60 of the most
important words used in the Bible. As you learn
each word's meaning and see how it is used in
key passages, your understanding of the word,
and of the whole Bible, will be increased.

Contents

Creator, creation

MEANING The Bible teaches that a personal God created the heavens and the earth and all living things.

General Bible teaching

1. The Father as Creator
The Bible says that each person of the Trinity was active in the work of creation. The title of Creator is given to God the Father in several places in the Bible. **"The Lord is the everlasting God, the Creator of the ends of the earth."** *Isaiah 40:28.* See also *Ecclesiastes 12:1; Romans 1:25.*

2. The Son as Creator
"Through him [Jesus] all things were made; without him nothing was made that has been made." *John 1:3.* See also *John 1:10; Colossians 1:16; Hebrews 1:1,2.*

3. The Holy Spirit as Creator
"The Spirit of God has made me." *Job 33:4.* See also *Genesis 1:2; Job 26:13.*

What else does the supernatural creative activity tell us about God?

The creation shows God's glory
"The heavens declare the glory of God; the skies proclaim the work of his hands." *Psalm 19:1*

The creation reveals God's power
"For since the creation of the world God's invisible qualities – his eternal power and divine nature – have been clearly seen, being understood from what has been made." *Romans 1:20*

"In the beginning God created the heavens and the earth." *Genesis 1:2*

Quote TO PONDER
"When considering the creation, the how and the when does not matter so much as the why and the wherefore."
R. de Campoamor

God

MEANING In the Old Testament the three main names of God speak about the nature of God and about his link with humankind.

1. *El, Eloah, Elohim* are translated as "God." *El* conveys the basic idea of God and means "strong" or "powerful." **"The Israelites groaned in their slavery and cried out, and their cry for help ... went up to God [Elohim]."** *Exodus 2:23.* The word most often appears as an adjective as in *El Elyon*: "God most high."

2. *Adonai* is translated as "Lord." This refers to the One who rules over everything. **"The One enthroned in heaven laughs."** *Psalm 2:4*

3. *Yahweh,* translated as LORD, with small capital letters, in the NIV, is God's personal name for himself, and appears nearly 6,000 times in the Bible. When God told Moses this name at the burning bush, he said, **"I AM WHO I AM."** *Exodus 3:14.*

These different names for God all show that he is superhumanly strong and a transcendent being, and yet he pervades his creation. See *Acts 17:28.*

General Bible teaching

1. God is Spirit
"God is spirit, and his worshipers must worship in spirit and in truth." *John 4:24.* So God does not have a body or a physical presence and cannot be seen or heard. See *1 Timothy 1:17; John 1:18.*

2. God is love
"Whoever does not love does not know God, because God is love." *1 John 4:8.* See also *Matthew 5:45; 1 Timothy 6:17; Deuteronomy 7:7; 1 John 3:2; Romans 8:15.*

5

Jesus
If we want to know who God is like, the Bible tells us to look at Jesus. Jesus **"is the image of the invisible God."** *Colossians 1:15.* See also *2 Corinthians 4:4.*

"But the LORD is the true God; he is the living God, the eternal King." *Jeremiah 10:10*

Quote TO PONDER
"Before I had children of my own, I used to think, 'God will not forget me.' But when I became a father I learned something more – God cannot forget me." *Martin Luther*

The Fall

MEANING In Christian teaching "The Fall" refers to the events described in *Genesis 3* when Adam and Eve disobeyed God and fell from grace.

> "When the woman [Eve] saw that the fruit of the tree was good for food and pleasing to the eye, and also desirable for gaining wisdom, she took some and ate it. She also gave some to her husband [Adam], who was with her, and he ate it." *Genesis 3:6*

General Bible teaching
on the results of the Fall

1. The Fall affects our relationship to God
Adam and Eve "died" spiritually when they turned against God and since then all of us are fallen human beings. We are not totally corrupt in every way, but God's image in us has become tarnished. See *Genesis 1:27; 1 Corinthians 11:7; James 3:9.* Now we all have a fatal flaw, a bias towards evil actions and sin. **"Therefore, just as sin entered the world through one man, and death through sin, and in this way death came to all men, because all sinned. ..."** *Romans 5:12.* See also *Romans 5:13-21; Ephesians 2:1-3; Romans 1:18-32; 3:9-18.*

2. The Fall affected creation
God cursed the ground so that it produced thorns and thistles, see *Genesis 3:17,18.* Hence Paul looks forward to the day when **"the creation will be liberated from its bondage to decay."** *Romans 8:21*

Jesus and the Fall
Jesus came to reverse the effects of the Fall. A believer can now be "in Christ" and "a new creation." See *2 Corinthians 5:17.* Our friendship with God can be restored. See *1 Peter 3:18.*

Quote TO PONDER
"To the question, 'What is meant by the fall?' I could answer with complete sincerity, 'That whatever I am, I am not myself.'"
G.K. Chesterton

Satan and the devil

MEANING "Satan" means "adversary." "Devil" *diabolos* means "slanderer."

General Bible teaching

1. The adversarial nature of Satan is seen in the Old Testament when he:
- opposed God's servants, like Job (*Job 1:6-12*), and David (*1 Chronicles 21:1*);
- attacked the human race through the serpent in the Garden of Eden (*Genesis 3:1*).

2. In the New Testament Satan is mentioned by name 36 times and referred to as the devil 33 times.

3. Jesus came into the world to destroy Satan: **"The reason the Son of God appeared was to destroy the devil's work."** *1 John 3:8.* The Bible leaves us in no doubt at all about Satan's final defeat. **"The God of peace will soon crush Satan under your feet."** *Romans 16:20.*

Jesus and Satan

Unquestionably, Jesus believed in Satan, in demons, and in demon possession. Jesus called Satan:
- the evil one: *Matthew 13:19*
- a murderer ... a liar ... the father of lies: *John 8:44*
- the prince of this world: *John 12:31.*

Quote TO PONDER
"Don't doubt for a moment the existence of the devil!"
Billy Graham

"Your enemy the devil prowls around like a roaring lion looking for someone to devour." *1 Peter 5:8*

Death

MEANING In the Bible the word "death" is used to refer to the end of biological life as well as the spiritual state of being cut off from God.

General Bible teaching

1. Physical death
Everyone now dies. So we should live like the psalmist taught: **"Teach us to number our days aright, that we may gain a heart of wisdom."** *Psalm 90:1,2*

2. Spiritual death
The Bible repeatedly contrasts spiritual life and spiritual death. **"He who has the Son has life; he who does not have the Son of God does not have life."** *1 John 5:12*

3. Eternal death
The New Testament speaks of a third kind of death, eternal death, which is God's final punishment for those who reject him, see *2 Thessalonians 1:8,9*. This is referred to as the "second death" in *Revelation 20:6,14; 21:8*.

"Those who walk uprightly enter into peace; they find rest as they lie in death." *Isaiah 57:2*

Jesus and death
Jesus deals with all three kinds of death:

1. Physical death
Jesus **"has destroyed death and has brought life and immortality."** *2 Timothy 1:10.* Because of Jesus' resurrection Christians need not fear death. See *1 Thessalonians 4:13,14*.

2. Spiritual death
Jesus came to bring us spiritual life. See *John 10:10; 17:3*.

3. Eternal death
Christians will be "with Christ" (*Philippians 1:23*) and share in his eternal immortality.

Quote TO PONDER
"It is not darkness you are going to, for God is Light.
It is not lonely, for Christ is with you.
It is not unknown country, for Christ is there."
Charles Kingsley

8

Prophet

MEANING In the Bible a prophet was someone who communicated or interpreted messages from God.

General Bible teaching
Moses displayed the characteristics of a true prophet.

1. God revealed himself to Moses
See *Exodus 3:1-9.*

2. Moses was called and commissioned by God
True prophets did not choose their vocation. They were chosen by God to be prophets. See *Isaiah 6; Jeremiah 1:4-19; Ezekiel 1–3; Amos 7:14,15.*

3. Moses was a man with a message from God
Prophets delivered their messages in the name of the Lord. See *Exodus 3:13-15; Deuteronomy 18:19,20.*

4. Moses prophesied about the future
Many of the messages the prophets passed on were like sermons calling God's people to be faithful. See the books of *Amos* and *Hosea.* However, prophecy also included foretelling the future. See *Exodus 3:16-22; 2 Samuel 12:10-12; Isaiah 9:53.*

New Testament prophets
Some Christians were given a special gift of prophecy in the New Testament. See *1 Corinthians 14:22-25,29-32.* Prophecies were made by Zechariah (John the Baptist's father), Mary, Anna, Simeon, and John the Baptist. See *Luke 1:46-55,67-79; 2:26-38.* Jesus, the ultimate prophet, fulfilled all Old Testament prophecies. See *John 1:1-18.*

"The Lord said to me [Moses]: ... 'I will raise up for them a prophet like you from among their brothers; I will put my words in his mouth, and he will tell them everything I command him.'" *Deuteronomy 18:17,18*

Quote TO PONDER
"Not everyone who speaks in a spirit is a prophet; he is only a prophet if he walks in the ways of the Lord." *Didache, 1st or 2nd-century manual on Christian morals and church practice*

Angel

MEANING The New Testament word for "angel" is *angelos* and means messenger, and it is used in that way in *Luke 7:24*. The word most often refers to a specially-created order of heavenly beings.

General Bible teaching

1. The nature of angels
Angels are spiritual beings. "In speaking of angels he [God] says, 'He makes his angels winds, his servants flames of fire.'" *Hebrews 1:7*

Angels appear to have free will. Satan is a fallen, rebellious angel. See *Isaiah 14:12-17; Matthew 25:41; 2 Peter 2:4; Revelation 12:9*.

"Are not all angels ministering spirits sent to serve those who will inherit salvation?" *Hebrews 1:14*

2. The work of angels
Angels serve God and carry out his wishes. See *Genesis 3:24; Isaiah 6:1-4*.

Angels minister to human beings. The phrase "Guardian Angel" refers to the watchful care angels take over God's people. See *Matthew 18:10; Hebrews 1:13,14*. See also:
- Hagar: *Genesis 16:7-14*
- Elijah: *1 Kings 19:1-8*
- Joseph: *Matthew 2:13*
- Peter: *Acts 12:7*
- Paul: *Acts 27:23*

Jesus and angels
Jesus was superior to angels (*Hebrews 1*) but was also cared for by them. See:
- Jesus' temptations: *Matthew 4:11*
- Jesus' agony in the garden: *Luke 22:43*
- Jesus' resurrection: *Matthew 28:1-8*

Quote TO PONDER
"An angel is a spiritual being created by God without a body, for the service of Christendom and the church." *Martin Luther*

Covenant

MEANING The Greek word *diatheke* is sometimes translated as "covenant" in the NIV and as "testament" in older Bible translations. The word appears 33 times in the New Testament, and occurs most often in the book of Hebrews (17 times). It means "agreement." But in the Bible it is not an agreement between equals, but between a superior (God) and an inferior (humans).

A Bible covenant is similar to a will in that the person (God) making the will chooses what he will bequeath and no part of the will can be changed. See *Hebrews 9:16,17.*

> "Then God said to Noah and to his sons with him: 'I now establish my covenant with you and with your descendants after you and with every living creature that is with you.'"
> *Genesis 9:8,9*

Quote TO PONDER
"It is a new heart-righteousness which the prophets foresaw as one of the blessings of the Messianic age. 'I will put my law in their minds and write it on their hearts,' God had promised through Jeremiah, in Jeremiah 31:33. How would he do it? He told Ezekiel, in Ezekiel 36:27: 'I will put my Spirit in you and move you to follow my decrees and be careful to keep my laws.'"
John Stott

Covenants in the Bible

The eternal covenant	See *Hebrews 13:20.* This is a covenant about our **redemption**.
The first covenant	See *Genesis 1:26-28.* This is the covenant about our **creation**.
The covenant with Noah	See *Genesis 8:20–9:6*
The covenant with Abraham	See *Genesis 12:1-3*
The covenant with Moses	See *Exodus 10:1–31:18*
The new covenant	See *Jeremiah 31:31-33; Matthew 26:28; Hebrews 8:8-12*

Evil

MEANING Evil embraces everything that is naturally and morally bad rather than good. It includes our rebellion against God and the harm we do to each other.

"But the things that come out of the mouth come from the heart, and these make a man 'unclean.' For out of the heart come evil thoughts, murder, adultery, sexual immorality, theft, false testimony, slander." *Matthew 15:18,19*

General Bible teaching

It is all too easy to point out evil in society: criminal acts, terrorism, injustice, indifference to other people's suffering. Paul teaches the following about evil and sinful people: **"You followed the ways of the world and the ruler of the kingdom of the air [Satan], the spirit who is now at work in those who are disobedient."** Paul continues to describe this evil way of living as follows: **"All of us also lived among them at one time, gratifying the cravings of our sinful nature and following its desires and thoughts."** *Ephesians 2:2,3*

God and evil

The Bible says that God relates to evil in a variety of ways.
1. God has given us standards of right and wrong. See *Deuteronomy 30:15*.
2. God has provided governments to restrain evil. See *Romans 13*.
3. God punishes individuals and nations who indulge in evil. See *Isaiah 45:7; Jeremiah 18:11; Amos 3:6*.
4. God will punish evil people who spurn his offer of salvation. See *2 Thessalonians 1:3-10; Revelation 20:11-15*.

Quote TO PONDER

"He who passively accepts evil is as much involved in it as he who helps to perpetuate it."
Martin Luther King, Jr

Pride

MEANING The Bible speaks of pride in two basic ways. Positively, pride means taking delight in one's own or other people's accomplishments. See *2 Corinthians 7:4*.

Negatively, pride means arrogance, an unwillingness to submit to God, and a total disregard for other people. Pride is the basic human sin.

General Bible teaching

God hates pride: see *Proverbs 16:5*.
Pride stops people from seeking after God: see *Psalm 10:4*.
Pride makes our good deeds unacceptable to God as a way of salvation: see *Ephesians 2:8-10*.
Pride comes from our hearts: see *Proverbs 16:5*.
Pride is seen in:
• our looks: see *Proverbs 6:17*
• our words: see *Psalm 12:3*
• our deeds: see *Psalm 31:21*.
Pride leads to:
• cruelty: see *Zephaniah 2:10*
• deceit: see *Psalm 31:18*
• strife: see *Psalm 140:5*.

Quote TO PONDER
"Pride comes from a deeply buried root – it comes from the devil himself. Where pride is fostered a person will be insincere, harsh, bitter, cutting, disdainful." *François Fénelon*

13

"But after Uzziah became powerful, his pride led to his downfall. He was unfaithful to the LORD his God." *2 Chronicles 26:16*

Sabbath

MEANING The word "Sabbath" comes from the Hebrew word *shabbat*, which means to "desist" or "cease." *Genesis 2:3* says that God finished his work of creation on the seventh day and he "rested" or "ceased" from work.

Old Testament teaching
1. The Sabbath was a day of rest from: farming, *Exodus 24*; work in the home, *Exodus 35:1-3*; making demands on other people, *Exodus 20:10*; and collecting manna, *Exodus 16:22-30*.
2. The Sabbath was a day that belonged to the Lord. See *Isaiah 56:4-6; 58:13*.

Jesus and the Sabbath
Jesus observed the Sabbath (*Luke 4:16*) but insisted that acts of mercy, such as healing someone, and acts of necessity, such as getting food, were allowed on the Sabbath. See *Matthew 12:1-13*.

First Christians
Many of the early Christians did not observe the Sabbath on the seventh day of the week, that is Saturday, but on the first day of the week, that is Sunday. Celebrating Jesus' resurrection, which took place on Sunday, they used Sunday for worship, Christian service, and fellowship. **"On the seventh day of the week we came together to break bread."** *Acts 20:7*

"Remember the Sabbath day by keeping it holy." *Exodus 20:8*

The Sabbath today
Today, many Christians, following Augustine who argued that with the coming of Jesus, the shadow (that is the Sabbath) had been replaced by the reality (that is Jesus), believe that the Christian Sunday does not include observing the Jewish laws about the Sabbath.

Quote TO PONDER
"The conscientious keeping of the Sabbath is the Mother of all Religion." *Lewis Bayly*

Sacrifice

MEANING The Old Testament sacrifices were God-given rituals in which animals (or other possessions of the worshiper) were presented to God to deal with the worshiper's sin, or as a way of giving thanks to God.

The Old Testament and sacrifices

The idea of animals being used as sacrifices goes back to the time of Cain and Abel. See *Genesis 4:4*. See also Noah (*Genesis 8:20,21*) and Abraham and other patriarchs (*Genesis 12:8; 13:4; 26:15*).

The person making the sacrifice identified with the killed animal to which the person's sin was symbolically transferred. This is taught in *Leviticus 17:11*: **"The life of a creature is in the blood, and I have given it to you to make atonement ... for one's life."**

> **"The sacrifices of God are a broken spirit; a broken and contrite heart, O God, you will not despise."**
> *Psalm 51:17*

Quote TO PONDER
"I never made a sacrifice. We ought not to talk of 'sacrifice' when we remember the great sacrifice which he made who left his Father's throne on high to give himself for us." *David Livingstone*

Jesus and his sacrifice

The book of Hebrews explains in great detail how the Old Testament sacrifices portray and should be applied symbolically to Jesus' own sacrificial death:

- Jesus' death was **perfect**, in a way no animal sacrifice could be, as Jesus was sinless. See *Hebrews 9:11-18*.
- Jesus' sacrificial death was both a **once-for-all** sacrifice, and an **eternal** sacrifice. So, unlike the Old Testament sacrifices, it never needs repeating. See *Hebrews 7:27; 10:1-13*.

Christians and sacrificial service

The word "sacrifice" is applied to Christians who are meant to be **"living sacrifices, holy and pleasing to God."** *Romans 12:1*

Sin

MEANING The basic idea behind the word "sin" is our rebellion against and disobedience towards God, who is both holy and righteous.

"Sin" in the singular is our state or condition, while "sins" in the plural refer to individual evil actions.

General Bible teaching

The Bible uses a number of words to describe our wrongdoing against God.

1. Sin is falling short

The image here is an arrow falling short of its target. For example, we all fall short of God's Ten Commandments. Paul teaches that this falling short extends to us all. **"All have sinned and fall short of the glory of God."** *Romans 3:23*

2. Sin is iniquity

"Iniquity" means "out of line" or "unequal," and conjures up a picture of deviation from the correct path. It is failure in following God's path. **"We all like sheep, have gone astray, each of us has turned to his own say; and the Lord has laid on him the iniquity of us all."** *Isaiah 53:6*

3. Sin is lawlessness

When we sin we break God's law. **"Everyone who sins breaks the law; in fact, sin is lawlessness."** *1 John 3:4*

Jesus and sin

Jesus came in the world to deal with our sin. See *2 Corinthians 5:21; 1 John 1:7; Hebrews 2:14,15; Ephesians 2:18; 1 Peter 3:18; Galatians 2:28.*

Quote TO PONDER

"Custom of sinning takes away the sense of it; the course of the world takes away the shame of it; and the love of it makes people greedy in the pursuit of it."
John Owen

16

Law

17

MEANING In the Old Testament, *torah* "law" means the divine instruction God gave to the Israelites so they knew how to live in a way that pleased him.

In the New Testament, *nomos* ("law") also refers to God's specific commands. Paul contrasts the law, the Mosaic system of earning favor with God, with grace. **"For sin shall not be your master, because you are not under law, but under grace."** *Romans 6:14*

"Love does no harm to its neighbor. Therefore love is the fulfillment of the law." *Romans 13:10*

Why was the law given?

1. The law was given to provide us with a standard of righteousness.

2. The law was given to expose sin: **"Through the law we become conscious of sin."** *Romans 3:20*

3. The law was given to reveal the state of the human heart: **"The heart is deceitful above all things and beyond cure. Who can understand it? 'I the LORD search the heart and examine the mind.'"** *Jeremiah 17:9,10*

Jesus and the law

Jesus did not come to destroy the law, but to fulfill it, and emphasize its inner and spiritual meaning. See *Matthew 5:17*. The law is described by Paul as being like a schoolteacher who leads us to Jesus. **"So the law was put in charge to lead us to Christ."** *Galatians 3:24*

Quote TO PONDER

"The Law is a kind of mirror. When we look in the mirror we notice any dirty marks on our faces, so in the Law we are made aware first of our helplessness, then of our sin and finally the judgment." *John Calvin*

Faith

MEANING The New Testament word for faith, *pistis*, is the hallmark of Christians, and the first followers of Jesus were called *hoi pistueontes*, "the believers." They not only possessed faith in God intellectually but also actively placed their trust in Jesus.

General Bible teaching

1. Paul
Paul often contrasts the law with faith. See *Romans 3:27*. God is described as **"... the one who justifies those who have faith in Jesus."** *Romans 3:26*

2. Peter
According to Peter faith in the crucified and risen Jesus is the only hope for humankind. See *1 Peter 1:3,4.* **"You ... through faith are shielded by God's power until the coming of the salvation ..."** *1 Peter 1:4-5*

Jesus and faith
In the Gospels the faith Jesus looked for was confident trust that God is able, through his Messiah, to do what he had promised in the prophets. **"'Have faith in God,' Jesus answered. 'I tell you the truth, if anyone says to this mountain, "Go, throw yourself into the sea," and does not doubt in his heart but believes that what he says will happen, it will be done for him.'"** *Mark 11:22,23*

Quote TO PONDER
"When we have an atom of faith in our hearts, we can see God's face, gentle, serene, and approving." *John Calvin*

Faith in Hebrews 11

Old Testament examples of faith

"Now faith is being sure of what we hope for and certain of what we do not see."
Hebrews 11:1

Hebrews 11 is the greatest chapter in the Bible about the faith of God's Old Testament followers. In it we read about:

1. Abel's *justifying* faith: this illustrates *worship* (*Hebrews 11:4*)

2. Enoch's *sanctifying* faith: this illustrates our *walk* with God. **"By faith Enoch was taken from this life, so that he did not experience death; he could not be found, because God had taken him away. For before he was taken, he was commended as one who pleased God. And without faith it is impossible to please God, because anyone who comes to him must believe that he exists and that he rewards those who earnestly seek him."** *Hebrews 11:5,6*

3. Noah's *separating* faith: this illustrates *witness* (*Hebrews 11:7*).

4. Abraham's *obedient* faith: this illustrates *trust* (*Hebrews 11:8*).

5. Sarah's *strengthening* faith: this illustrates *productiveness* (*Hebrews 11:11*).

6. Isaac's *patient* faith: this illustrates our *selfish human nature* (*Hebrews 11:20*).

7. Jacob's *suffering* faith: this illustrates *overcoming our wills* (*Hebrews 11:21*).

8. Joseph's *hopeful* faith: this illustrates *waiting on God* (*Hebrews 11:22*).

9. Moses' *enduring* faith: this illustrates *yielding ourselves to God* (*Hebrews 11:23-27*).

10. Israel's *victorious* faith: this illustrates *joy* (*Hebrews 11:29*).

11. Israel's *walking* faith: this illustrates *good actions* (*Hebrews 11:30*).

12. Rahab's *saving* faith: this illustrates *peace* (*Hebrews 11:31*).

13. God's godly followers' *living* faith: this illustrates *reward* (*Hebrews 11:32-40*).

Quote TO PONDER

"... the believer has something better: faith sweeps away the refuge of lies, and the believer turns to his God, and says, 'O God, thou shalt be my refuge.'"
George Whitefield

Forgiveness

MEANING In the Bible forgiveness means to pardon a wrong or cancel a debt. Through forgiveness God is able to deal with our sins.

Aphiemi is the word used most often for "forgiveness" in the New Testament. It means to send away, release, or dismiss.

General Bible teaching

In the Old Testament the scope of God's forgiveness is shown in the metaphors that are used to describe forgiveness:

- Our sins are put out of sight: see *Isaiah 38:17*. **"You will again have compassion on us; you will tread our sins underfoot and hurl all our iniquities into the depths of the sea."** *Micah 7:19*
- Our sins are put out of reach: see *Psalm 103:12*.
- Our sins are put out of mind: see *Jeremiah 31:34*.
- Our sins are no longer taken into account: see *Psalm 103:10*.

Jesus and forgiveness

Jesus taught that forgiveness means the removal of a burden or stain, bringing immediate relief to a sinner. In his parable of the prodigal son Jesus portrays forgiveness as the young spendthrift is received back and restored by his compassionate father. See *Luke 15:11-32*.

Quote TO PONDER

"When Christ's hands were nailed to the cross, he also nailed your sins to the cross." *Bernard of Clairvaux*

Wisdom

MEANING In the Bible wisdom refers to the ability to make right choices.

General Bible teaching

1. God's wisdom

God himself is spoken of as being "the only wise God." (*Romans 16:27*). God is the source of all true wisdom. See *Daniel 2:20-23*. **"To God belong wisdom and power; counsel and understanding are his."** *Job 12:13*

God's wisdom is seen in two main ways:

- In God's creative activity in the world (see *Psalm 136:5; Proverbs 3:19*). **"How many are your works, O Lord! In wisdom you made them all; the earth is full of your creatures."** *Proverbs 104:24*

- In God's plan of redemption (see *Romans 11:33*) which was revealed in Jesus (see *1 Corinthians 1:24*) and is spread through his church. **"His intent was that now, through the church, the manifold wisdom of God should be made known to the rulers and authorities in the heavenly realms."** *Ephesians 3:10*

2. Human wisdom

To be happy we need to find wisdom (see *Proverbs 3:13*), and wisdom is so exalted that it is often personified (see *Proverbs 9:1-6*). Wisdom is highly desirable. **"Wisdom is more precious than rubies, and nothing you desire can compare with her."** *Proverbs 8:11*

Quote TO PONDER
"Wisdom is the right use of knowledge. To know is not to be wise. Many people know a great deal, and are all the greater fools for it. There is no fool so great as the knowing fool. But to know how to use knowledge is to have wisdom." *C.H. Spurgeon*

21

"The fear of the LORD is the beginning of wisdom, and knowledge of the Holy One is understanding."
Proverbs 9:10

Obedience

MEANING To obey is to follow commands given by someone in authority. The Hebrew word for "obey," *shama'*, and the Greek word for "obey," *hypakouo*, are both very close to the word "hear" or "listen." The correct response to anyone "hearing," that is paying attention to God, is to obey him.

"If you love me, you will obey what I command. ... Whoever has my commands and obeys them, he is the one who loves me. ... If anyone loves me, he will obey my teaching."
John 14:15,21,23

General Bible teaching
The Bible teaches that obedience is the secret to blessing. **"Keep his [God's] decrees and commands, which I am giving you today, so that it may go well with you and your children after you."** *Deuteronomy 4:40*

Jesus and obedience
In the matter of obedience Jesus is our model:
- Jesus went about his Father's business. See *Luke 2:49* KJV.
- Jesus' food was to do his Father's will. See *John 4:34*.
- Jesus was obedient, even in suffering (see *Hebrews 5:8*), and even to death. **"And being found in appearance as a man, he [Jesus] humbled himself and became obedient to death – even death on a cross."** *Philippians 2:8*
- Jesus' obedience was motivated by love, as our actions should be. **"This is love for God: to obey his commands."** *1 John 5:3*

Quote TO PONDER
"We are God's glory, when we follow his ways."
Florence Nightingale

Temptation

MEANING To tempt someone is to entice him/her to sin.

General Bible teaching

How temptation comes to us
Temptation may come in a very direct way, as it did with Eve and the serpent, see *Genesis 3*.

But temptation can come through friends, even through a close friend, as it did to Jesus from Peter. See *Matthew 16:22,23*.

Temptation often comes from within ourselves. See *James 1:14,15*.

Does God tempt us?
The devil tempts us because he wants to leads us away from God. But God never tempts us, although he often tests us so that spiritually we may become stronger.
See *James 1:13; John 6:6; 2 Corinthians 13:5*.

Jesus and temptation

Jesus was tempted. See *Matthew 4:1-11*. From this we deduce that being tempted is not in itself sinful. It is only when we give way to temptation that we go wrong.

Jesus was tempted in every way. "We do not have a high priest who is unable to sympathize with our weaknesses, but we have one who has been tempted in every way, just as we are – yet was without sin." *Hebrews 4:15*. From this we deduce that godly people are not immune from temptation.

Quote **TO PONDER**
"The devil tempts that he may ruin; God tests that he may crown." *Ambrose*

"No temptation has seized you except what is common to man. And God is faithful; he will not let you be tempted beyond what you can bear. But when you are tempted, he will also provide a way out so that you can stand up under it."
1 Corinthians 10:13

Name

General Bible teaching

1. To identify
Names were given as personal labels in the Bible in the same way that we use names today. Adam gave names to the animals. See *Genesis 2:19,20.*

2. To signify
More importantly, many biblical names made statements about character. Abigail said of her husband, **"He is just like his name – his name is Fool, and folly goes with him."** *1 Samuel 25:25.* Abraham was given a new name to indicate that he would be father of a nation. See *Genesis 17:5,6.* Jacob was given the new name of Israel at a turning point in his life. See *Genesis 32:28.*

3. To typify
The word "name" was also used in a metaphorical way. So, in *Philippians 2:9,10,* Jesus' great dignity is implied by the words, **"Therefore God exalted him [Jesus] to the highest place and gave him the name that is above every name, that at the name of Jesus every knee should bow."**

4. To unify
In order to indicate that God's people have a relationship with God they are called by the name of the Lord. See *Deuteronomy 28:9,10; Numbers 6:27; Isaiah 43:7.*

Quote TO PONDER
"How sweet the Name of Jesus sounds
In a believer's ear!
It soothes his sorrows, heals his wounds,
And drives away his fear."
John Newton

"She [Mary] will give birth to a son, and you are to give him the name Jesus, because he will save his people from their sins." *Matthew 1:21*

Holy, holiness, sanctification

MEANING In the Bible, the words "holy," and "holiness" refer to:
- God's essential nature
- people, places, or things set apart or consecrated to God
- a person who lives in harmony with God's will.

The Hebrew word *qodesh* and the Greek word *hagios* refer to a person who is separate from impurity.

General Bible teaching

Because God is so utterly holy (see *Isaiah 6:3*), his followers also need to be holy (see *Leviticus 27:2*). "But just as he who called you is holy, so be holy in all you do; for it is written: 'Be holy, because I am holy' [*Leviticus 11:44,45; 19:2; 20:7*]." *1 Peter 1:15,16*

Sanctification

The word "sanctification" means "consecration" or "dedication." Hence the Sabbath Day was made "holy" (see *Genesis 2:3*), and was set apart for God.

In the New Testament the word "sanctification" is only applied to Christians. We are already sanctified. See *1 Peter 1:2*. But we are also being sanctified throughout our lives, since sanctification is a life-long process. See *2 Corinthians 3:18; 1 Thessalonians 5:23*.

Christians are sanctified:
- through God's Word. See *John 17:17*
- **"through the sanctifying work of the Spirit"** *2 Thessalonians 2:13*.

Quote TO PONDER

"The serene beauty of a holy life is the most powerful influence in the world next to the power of God." *Blaise Pascal*

"You [God] alone are holy." *Revelation 15:4*

Praise

26

"Rejoice in the Lord always, I will say it again: Rejoice!"
Philippians 4:4

MEANING In the Old Testament the words used for "praise" are *halal*, which means making a noise, and *yadah*, which refers to movements of the body and gestures linked with praise.

In the New Testament the favorite word used for "praise" is *eucharistein*, which means "to give thanks."

General Bible teaching

The whole of the Bible is full of spontaneous praise of God. God's people are meant to be characterized with a joy that stems from praising God.

All creation, including angels, expresses its joy in praise. See *Job 38:4-7; Revelation 4:6-11.*

Humankind was created to rejoice in God's creation: see *Psalm 90:14-16.* Accepting God's gifts is one way of showing that we delight ourselves in God. See *Ecclesiastes 8:15; 9:7; 11:9.*

"Finally, brothers, whatever is true, whatever is noble, whatever is right, whatever is pure, whatever is lovely, whatever is admirable – if anything is excellent or praiseworthy – think about these things." *Philippians 4:8*

The psalms and praise

There are psalms in which individuals praise God, but many psalms of praise are set in the context of a congregation. See *Psalm 22:25; 34:3; 35:18.*

Dancing was used as a way of expressing praise. See *Exodus 15:20; 2 Samuel 6:14.* This kind of praise also took place in the Temple. See *Psalm 149:3.* "Praise the Lord with tambourine and dancing." *Psalm 150:4*

Quote TO PONDER

"The chief work of men and women is the praise of God."
Augustine

Prayer

MEANING Prayer includes all the attitudes of the human spirit in its approach to God. For the Christian, prayer, in its simplest sense, is talking with God.

General Bible teaching

The Bible teaches that there are many aspects to prayer. Prayer includes:

- worship and adoration: see *Revelation 1:12-18*
- confession of sin to God: *Psalm 51*
- praising God: see *Psalm 103*
- giving thanks to God: see *Luke 17:11-19*
- asking God to grant certain things: see *2 Samuel 7:18-25; 1 Samuel 1:9-11*
- praying to God for other people: see *Genesis 18:23-33; Numbers 21:7*
- fellowship with God: see *Luke 10:39.*

Jesus and prayer

"Jesus told his disciples a parable to show them that they should always pray and not give up." *Luke 18:1.* Jesus then told his parable about the persistent widow. See *Luke 18:2-5.* See also *1 Thessalonians 5:17.*

To encourage his disciples to pray Jesus gave them a pattern prayer, which we know as the "The Lord's Prayer." See *Luke 11:1-4.*

Quote TO PONDER

"It is possible to move men and women, through God, by prayer alone." *Hudson Taylor*

"The Spirit himself intercedes for us with groans that words cannot express. ... [And] the Spirit intercedes for the saints in accordance with God's will." *Romans 8:26,27*

Peace

MEANING The Old Testament word for "peace" *shalom* means "soundness," "completeness," "wholeness" and "well-being." This "peace" may include material prosperity (see *Psalm 73:3*), physical safety (see *Psalm 4:8*), and is linked to righteousness and truth, but never wickedness (see *Psalm 85:10; 57:19-21*). **"If only you had paid attention to my commands, your peace would have been like a river, your righteousness like the waves of the sea. ... 'There is no peace,' says the Lord, 'for the wicked.'"** *Isaiah 48:18, 22*

General Bible teaching

Shalom was always conditional:
- As the gift of God. See *Numbers 6:26*.
- As one of the promises of the covenant. See *Isaiah 54:10; Ezekiel 34:25; 37:26*.
- Only comes with faith and righteousness. See *Psalm 72:3-7; 85:8-11*. **"The fruit of righteousness will be peace; the effect of righteousness will be quietness and confidence for ever."** *Isaiah 32:17*

"Peace I leave with you; my peace I give you. I do not give to you as the world gives. Do not let your hearts be troubled and do not be afraid." *John 14:27*

Jesus and peace

Jesus brought no easy peace (Greek *eirene*). The peace of the kingdom is only given to people who are worthy of receiving it. See *Matthew 10:34; Luke 19:38,42*.

For peace is not man-made, but God-given. See *Philippians 1:2*.

Peace comes through Jesus' own sacrifice. See *John 14:27; Luke 24:36; Acts 10:36; Romans 5:1; Colossians 1:20*.

Quote TO PONDER

**"Drop thy still dews of quietness,
    Till all our strivings cease;
Take from our souls the strain and
    stress,
And let our ordered lives confess
    The beauty of thy peace."**
John Greenleaf Whittier

28

Truth

"I am the way and the truth and the life. No-one comes to the Father except through me."
John 14:6

MEANING Truth meant the opposite of a lie to Homer, and the opposite of mere appearance to later writers. In this way truth stood for reality, and the nature of things.

In the Old Testament the Hebrew nouns for truth are *emeth, emunah,* and the verb is *aman,* from which we derive the word "amen." In the Old Testament truth stands for reliability and steadfastness. Hence *Deuteronomy 32:4* states: **"A faithful God who does no wrong, upright and just is he."**

In the New Testament truth (Greek *aletheia*) is the actual state of things as they really are. Humans can never discover the truth by thinking with all their might, as truth is always revealed by God's Spirit. See *John 16:13.*

General Bible teaching

In the New Testament truth refers to God revealing reality. He does this in two ways:
- through natural revelation. See *Psalm 19:1.*
- through special revelation. **"The faith and love that spring from the hope that is stored up for you in heaven and that you have already heard about in the word of truth, that gospel that has come to you."** *Colossians 1:5*

29

Jesus and truth

The truth is in Jesus. See *John 1:14.* Since Jesus spoke and acted depending completely on God, his word is true. See *John 5:30; 8:26.* He is the truth. See *John 14:6; 6:32, 33; 15:1.*

Quote TO PONDER
"A thing is not necessarily true because badly uttered, nor false because spoken magnificently."
Augustine

Salvation

MEANING Salvation means deliverance, by God, from some great distress.

In the Old Testament nearly all the 353 occurrences of Hebrew word for salvation, *yasha*, refer to a particular historical situation, such as an invasion by an enemy. In *Exodus 14:13* the Israelites are said to be delivered or "saved" out of their slavery in Egypt. But salvation also had a deeply spiritual meaning in the Old Testament: **"With joy you will draw water from the wells of salvation."** *Isaiah 12:3*

In the New Testament nearly all of the references to salvation (*soteria* in Greek) refer to God acting in Jesus to deliver his followers from Satan, sin, and death. The 24 New Testament occurrences of the Greek word *soter*, Savior, refer to God the Father (eight times), and to Jesus (16 times).

General Bible teaching
Salvation:
- originates in the grace of God: see *Titus 2:11*
- was achieved through the death of Jesus: see *Isaiah 53*
- is received by faith: see *Ephesians 2:8–10*
- is worked out in the life of the believer as he/she consecrates his/her life to God: see *Philippians 2:12*.

The tenses of salvation

1. The past tense
"For the grace of God that brings salvation *has appeared* to all men." *Titus 2:11*

"Who has *saved us* and called us to a holy life – not because of anything we have done but because of his own purpose and grace. This grace *was given* us in Christ Jesus before the beginning of time." *2 Timothy 1:9*

Note how grace is linked with salvation in these verses.

2. The present tense
"It teaches us to say 'No' to ungodliness and worldly passions, and to live self-controlled, upright and godly lives *in this present age*, ... to redeem us from all wickedness and to purify for himself a people that *are* his very own, eager to do what is good." *Titus 2:12, 14*

"We *are* God's workmanship." *Ephesians 2:10*

Note how Christians are meant to live godly lives in the world.

"This is what the Sovereign LORD, the Holy One of Israel, says: 'In repentance and rest is your salvation.'" *Isaiah 30:15*

3. The future tense

"While we wait for the blessed hope – the glorious appearing of our great God and Savior, Jesus Christ." *Titus 2:13*

"What we will be has not yet been made known. But we know that when he appears, we shall be like him, for we shall see him as he is." *1 John 3:2*

Note how salvation is linked to Jesus' second coming.

The three phases of salvation

The three tenses or phases of salvation can be thought of as:

- salvation accomplished,
- salvation experienced, and
- salvation expected.

The believer *has been saved* from the *penalty of sin*: "For it is by grace you *have been saved*, through faith – and this is not from yourselves, it is the gift of God." *Ephesians 2:8*

The believer is *being saved* from the *power of sin*: "For the message of the cross is foolishness to those who are perishing, but to us who *are being saved* it is the power of God." *1 Corinthians 1:18*

The believer *will be saved* from the *presence of sin* and from the attacks of temptation when he/she goes to be with Jesus: "... until the coming of salvation that is ready to be revealed in the last time." *1 Peter 1:5*

Grace

MEANING Grace means unmerited favor. In the Old Testament see *Jeremiah 31:2; Lamentations 3:22.*

In the Bible grace refers to God's undeserved act of love in providing us with his salvation.

- For Paul's teaching about grace, see *2 Corinthians 12:9,10; Ephesians 3:8; 4:7.*
- For Peter's teaching about grace, see *1 Peter 5:5; 2 Peter 3:18.*

G od's
R iches
A t
C hrist's
E xpense

Quote TO PONDER

"Grace is the free, undeserved goodness and favor of God to humankind."
Matthew Henry

32

Types of grace

Atoning grace	See *Hebrews 2:9*
Saving grace	See *Ephesians 2:8,9*
Access grace	See *Hebrews 4:16*
Needed grace	See *Hebrews 4:16*
Establishing grace	See *Hebrews 13:9*
Abundant grace	See *Hebrews 13:25*
Working grace	See *Acts 11:21-23*
Strengthening grace	See *2 Corinthians 12:9*
Sustaining grace	See *2 Corinthians 9:8*
Serving grace	See *1 Corinthians 15:10*
Supplying grace	See *John 1:16*

"It is by grace you have been saved."
Ephesians 2:5

Law *versus* Grace

"I do not set aside the grace of God, for if righteousness could be gained through the law, Christ died for nothing."
Galatians 2:21

Quote TO PONDER
"The Law works fear and wrath; grace works hope and mercy."
Martin Luther

Law contrasted with grace

Law	Grace
Law reveals what God demands everyone to do. *Exodus 20:1-17*	Grace reveals what God has done for everyone. *1 Corinthians 15:3,4*
Law demands perfect obedience or death.*Ezekiel 18:20; James 2:10*	Grace gives life so we may obey God. *John 10:10; 14:23*
The law commands us to love God. *Matthew 22:37*	Grace tells us that God loves us. *1 John 3:16; 4:8-10,19*
The law tells us to love our neighbor as ourself. *Matthew 22:39*	Grace fills us with God's love for our neighbor. *2 Corinthians 5:14*
The law pronounces a curse on us. *Galatians 3:10*	Grace pronounces a blessing on us. *Galatians 3:14*
The law gives sin power. *1 Corinthians 15:56*	Grace is the power of God. *Romans 1:16*
The law demands holiness. *Deuteronomy 6:24,25*	Grace produces holiness. *Romans 6:14-22*

"For the law was given through Moses; grace and truth came through Jesus Christ."
John 1:17

The Holy Spirit

MEANING The Holy Spirit is the third member of the Trinity. In the Old Testament, he is referred to as:
- the Spirit
- the Spirit of God
- the Spirit of the Lord.

In the New Testament, he is referred to as:
- the Holy Spirit (most often)
- the Spirit of Jesus
- the Spirit of Christ
- the Spirit of his [God's] Son.

The Holy Spirit and Pentecost

On the day of Pentecost after Jesus' resurrection the Spirit came to:
- work permanently in a new way. See *John 7:39*
- to be with Christians all the time. See *John 14:16*
- to be the spiritual life in the Christian church. See *1 Corinthians 12*
- to be the source and sustenance of the spiritual life in individual Christians. See *1 Corinthians 6:19.*

"But when he, the Spirit of truth, comes, he will guide you into all truth. He will not speak on his own; he will speak only what he hears, and he will tell you what is yet to come."
John 16:13

General Bible teaching

1. The Holy Spirit is personal

The Holy Spirit is always referred to as a Person, rather than being an influence or a thing. The KJV translation of *Romans 8:26* is a mistranslation: **"the Spirit *itself* maketh intercession for us ..."** This verse is correctly translated in the NIV as: **"the Spirit helps us in our weakness."**

Jesus referred to the Holy Spirit as a person in *John 16:13*, for the Holy Spirit is as much one person of the triune God as are the Father and the Son. See *Matthew 28:19; 1 Corinthians 12:4-6; 2 Corinthians 13:14.*

2. The Holy Spirit is eternal

He did not start his work at Pentecost, for he shared in the work of creation. See *Genesis 1:2; 2:7.* He inspired the prophets not to speak their own words, but the word of God. See *2 Peter 1:21.*

3. The Holy Spirit is the Counselor/Comforter

- He comes alongside us in difficult times. See *Acts 9:31.*
- He helps us when we pray. See *Romans 8:26.*
- He assures us that we are God's children. See *Romans 8:16.*

4. The Holy Spirit is Jesus' Ambassador

- The Holy Spirit has been called "the Executive of the Godhead" because he carries out God's wishes in Christians today.
- The Holy Spirit presents Jesus to the hearts/lives of Christians. See *John 14:17.*
- The Holy Spirit reminds us about Jesus. See *John 14:26; 15:26.*
- The Holy Spirit makes Jesus real to us. See *John 16:7,14.*

5. The Holy Spirit strengthens us

- The Holy Spirit enables God's servants to work for God. See *Acts 1:8; 6:3.*
- The Holy Spirit gives his spiritual gifts so that Christians can build up the whole body of the Christian church. See *1 Corinthians 12; 14.*

Quote TO PONDER
"Our nature is so vitiated, and has such a propensity to sin, that unless it is renewed by the Holy Spirit, no person can do or will what is good of himself or herself." *Basil*

Power

MEANING Power is the ability to accomplish something. One of the Greek words used for "power" in the New Testament is *dunamis*, from which we derive our word "dynamite." The Holy Spirit gave the early Christians power in their witness. See *Acts 1:8*.

General Bible teaching

1. The power of God

True power, and the ability to exercise authority, belongs to God alone. See *Psalm 62:11*.

1 Chronicles 28:11 speaks of "the greatness and the power" of the Lord. God's power is seen clearly in:

- creation. See *Psalm 148:5*.
- creation being sustained. See *Psalm 65:5-8*.
- God's mighty acts carried out for the benefit of humanity. See *Psalm 111:6*
- God's power is supremely seen in the life, and especially in the resurrection, of Jesus. See *Romans 1:4; Ephesians 1:19,20*

2. The power of Jesus

Jesus' power is often described as the authority he exercised in his ministry. Jesus showed his authority/power in:

- his teaching. **"He [Jesus] taught as one who had authority, and not as their teachers of the law."** *Matthew 7:29*

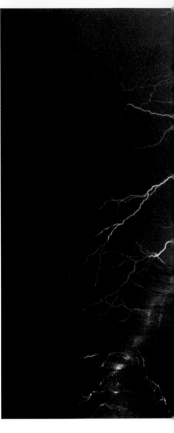

- his right to forgive sins. See *Matthew 9:6*
- in the miracles he performed. See *Luke 5:17*.

Jesus will also show his power in his second coming. See *Luke 21:27*.

All Christians have direct access to Jesus' power. See *2 Corinthians 12:9*.

> "But they are your people, your inheritance that you brought out by your great power and your outstretched arm."
> *Deuteronomy 9:29*

The Holy Spirit enabled the early Christians:

- to perform miracles: **"Men of Israel [said Peter], why does this [the healing of a crippled beggar] surprise you? Why do you stare at us as if by our own *power* or godliness we had made this man walk?"** *Acts 3:12*
- to witness powerfully about Jesus: **"With *great power* the apostles continued to testify to the resurrection of the Lord Jesus, and much grace was upon them all."** *Acts 4:33*
- to be strong spiritually: **"I pray that out of his glorious riches he may *strengthen* you with *power* through his Spirit in your inner being."** *Ephesians 3:16*

Quote TO PONDER

"If a person is filled with the Holy Spirit, his witness will not be optional or mandatory – it will be inevitable." *Richard C. Halverson*

3. The power of the Holy Spirit

In the Old Testament, God's power was seen in the coming of the Holy Spirit on specific people for specific tasks, as in the ministry of the prophet Elijah. But Christians today, living after Pentecost, are permanently empowered by the Holy Spirit. See *Acts 1:8; 2:1-3.*

Witness

MEANING The Greek word *martus* means "witness" and is the word from which we derive the word "martyr." A martyr is a witness who has been faithful to death. See *Revelation 2:10*.

General Bible teaching
Christians should be able to speak about Jesus from first-hand experience. See *Acts 1:22; 10:39*.

Christians should prepare themselves to be effective witnesses for Jesus: **"But in your hearts set apart Christ as Lord. Always be prepared to give an answer to everyone who asks you to give the reason for the hope that you have."** *1 Peter 3:15*. Paul then adds that "gentleness and respect" for the person one is witnessing to should be the hallmarks of the Christian's witness for Jesus.

Jesus and witness
Jesus' last recorded words in Matthew's Gospel concerned his instructions about witnessing and apply to his followers in every century: **"Therefore go and make disciples of all nations, baptizing them in the name of the Father and the Son and of the Holy Spirit, and teaching them to obey everything I have commanded you."** *Matthew 28:19,20*

Quote TO PONDER
"Show me that you are redeemed and then I will believe in your Redeemer." *Friedrich Nietzsche*

Joy

MEANING In the Old Testament the 27 different Hebrew words used for joy teach that it is found in God and his acts and that God's followers express their delight in God in public worship.

One of the most outstanding facets about joy taught in the New Testament is that it has been given by the Holy Spirit to Christians. See *Romans 14:7; Galatians 5:22*.

General Bible teaching

What may we rightly rejoice in?
Christians may rejoice in the natural world, remembering that it is God **"who richly provides us with everything for our enjoyment."**
2 Timothy 6:17
Joy is to be found in:
• youthfulness. See *Ecclesiastes 11:9*
• physical strength. See *Psalm 19:5*
• the harvest, and all God's provision. See *Isaiah 9:3*
• a happy marriage. See *Proverbs 5:18*
• the birth of a baby. See *John 16:21*
• human friendships. See *1 Samuel 20:41,42*.

Jesus and joy
In the Gospels joy is linked with Jesus' birth (see *Matthew 2:10*), his resurrection (see *Matthew 28:8*), suffering persecution for him (see *Luke 6:23*), answered prayer (see *John 16:24*).

Quote **TO PONDER**
"Into our lives, in many simple, familiar, homely ways, God infuses this element of joy from the surprises of life, the strain of music, the sunset glory, the unsought word of encouragement. These are the overflowing riches of his grace, these are his free gifts." *S. Longfellow*

"I have told you this so that my joy may be in you and that your joy may be complete." *John 15:11*

Love, divine love

MEANING When the New Testament writers came to write about God's love they used a Greek word, *agape*, that was hardly ever found in classical Greek. This distinguished God's love from *eros* (sexual love) and *philia* (brotherly love or friendliness.) *Agape* expresses God's love for us, which is sacrificial, redeeming, and unmerited.

General Bible teaching

1. God's nature
God's nature is love. **"Whoever does not love does not know God, because God is love."** *1 John 4:8*

2. Jesus and God's love
Jesus spoke about the love the Father had for him, **"before the creation of the world."** *John 17:24*

As Jesus started his public ministry God the Father said of him, **"This is my Son, whom I love."** *Matthew 3:17*

Throughout his earthly life Jesus experienced God's love for him. See *John 10:17*.

3. God's love and us
God demonstrated his love for all men and women in creation and especially to his chosen people. **"Because he [the Lord] loved your forefathers and chose their descendants after them, he brought you out of Egypt by his Presence and his great strength."** *Deuteronomy 4:37*

God's compassion for us is recorded in *Isaiah 54:8*: **"'With everlasting kindness I will have compassion on you,' says the Lord your Redeemer."** *Isaiah 54:8*

Quote TO PONDER
"You will find all that is lacking in your heart in the heart of Jesus, dying on the cross. Then you will be enabled to love those whom you would naturally, in your pride, hate and crush." *François Fénelon*

"As a father has compassion on his children, so the Lord has compassion on those who fear him." *Psalm 103:13*

Love, human love

General Bible teaching

1. Love God
Our most important duty on earth is to love God. **"Love the LORD your God with all your heart and with all your soul and with all your strength."** *Deuteronomy 6:5*

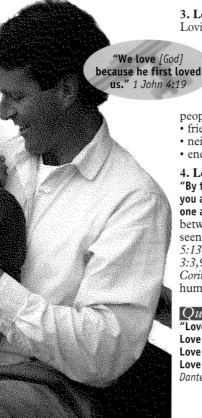

"We love *[God]* because he first loved us." *1 John 4:19*

2. Obey God
Obeying God's teaching and following his will is proof of our love for him. **"And now, O Israel, what does the LORD your God ask of you but to fear the LORD your God, to walk in all his ways, to love him, to serve the LORD your God. ..."** *Deuteronomy 10:12*

3. Love people
Loving God and hating people should be impossible. **"If anyone says, 'I love God,' yet hates his brother, he is a liar."** *1 John 4:20*
This love for other people should be shown to:
• friends. See *John 15:13*
• neighbors. See *Mark 12:31*
• enemies. See *Matthew 5:44*.

4. Love fellow-Christians
"By this all men will know that you are my disciples, if you love one another." *John 13:35* Love between Christians should be seen in service (see *Galatians 5:13*), generosity (see *1 Peter 3:3,9*), suffering (see *2 Corinthians 12:15*), and humility (see *Romans 12:10*).

Quote TO PONDER
"Love shall be our token;
Love be yours and love be mine;
Love to God and all men,
Love for plea and gift and sign."
Dante Gabriel Rossetti

Life

> "The fear of the LORD is a fountain of life, turning a man from the snares of death."
> *Proverbs 14:27*

MEANING Three of the most important meanings of the numerous ways in which the word "life" is used in the Bible are natural life, resurrection life, and spiritual life.

General Bible teaching about natural life

All life is a gift from God
God gave life in the first place. See *Genesis 2:7; Job 33:4*. Every day God sustains life (see *Daniel 5:23; Acts 17:25,28*). God sometimes prolongs life (see *Psalm 91:16*), and God brings life to a close (see *Job 1:21; Ecclesiastes 12:7*).

Human life is very special
From the beginning, see *Genesis 4:1-13*, human life is so precious that it was protected by God-given laws, see *Exodus 20:13*.

Jesus and resurrection life
Jesus told his first disciples, **"Because I live, you also will live."** *John 14:19*

Jesus overcame death so that everyone who believes in him will share in his resurrection life. **"Christ has indeed been raised from the dead, the firstfruits of those who have fallen asleep."** *1 Corinthians 15:20*

In a Christian's resurrection life we will have spiritual bodies for this entirely new kind of existence. **"So it will be with the resurrection of the dead. The body that is sown is perishable, it is raised imperishable. ... It is sown a natural body, it is raised a spiritual body."** *1 Corinthians 15:43,44*

Quote TO PONDER
"It is vanity to desire a long life and to take no heed of a good life." *Thomas à Kempis*

Eternal life

MEANING Eternal life allows Christians to share God's spiritual life, his nature, and his values.

Key New Testament passages on eternal life

- Eternal life is a gift from God and is given to all who believe in Jesus. Those who reject Jesus **"will not see life."** *John 3:15,16*
- Jesus lays down his life for us. He said, **"I give them eternal life, and they shall never perish; no one can snatch them out of my hand."** *John 10:10-28*
- Before Jesus raised Lazarus from the dead he spoke about himself being the resurrection and the life. *John 11:1-43*
- The new spiritual life of the Christian enables him/her to be righteous in God's sight. *Romans 8:1-11*

- Like everybody Christians experience physical death. But the dead in Jesus will be raised again, and will be immortal and imperishable. *1 Corinthians 15*
- Believers "live by faith in the Son of God" as Jesus' Spirit lives in them. *Galatians 2:19,20*

Quote TO PONDER

"Live near to God, so that all things will appear to you little in comparison with eternal realities." *Robert Murray McCheyne*

43

"God has given us eternal life, and this life is in his Son." *1 John 5:11*

Baptism

MEANING The word "baptize" means to dip or to submerge.

General Bible teaching

1. Baptism and the work of the Holy Spirit
In the New Testament baptism is linked closely to the Holy Spirit (see *Matthew 3:11; Acts 1:5; 11:16*). Only the Holy Spirit can bring about conviction of sin (see *John 16:7,9*), which leads to turning away from sin and to faith in Jesus.

2. Baptism and Jesus' death and resurrection
Believers are said to be buried with Jesus in baptism and raised with Jesus through faith in him. See *Colossians 2:12; Romans 6:3,4*.

3. Baptism and conversion
Baptism is an outward sign of a person's inner faith in Jesus. In the early Church a person was baptized as soon as he/she was converted. See *Matthew 28:19; Acts 2:38,41; 8:36-38; 9:18*.

4. Household baptism
Many Christians believe that, even in a Christian home, children should not be baptized until they are old enough to have made their own profession of faith in Jesus. Those who believe that babies should be baptized use two main arguments. They point to:
- the Old Testament practice of infant circumcision. See *Genesis 17:11*
- the homes where whole households were baptized in the New Testament, in which children may have been present. See *Acts 16:33; 1 Corinthians 1:16*.

5. What is the correct method of baptism?
Some Christians say that people should be fully immersed in water at baptism, showing that baptism is being buried with Jesus (see *Romans 6:4*), while others pour water over those being baptized, as a symbol of putting on Jesus (see *Galatians 3:27*).

> "We were all baptized by one Spirit into one body."
> *1 Corinthians 12:13*

Quote TO PONDER

"Those who see baptism only as confession of our faith have missed the main point. Baptism is tied to the promise of forgiveness. 'Whoever believes and is baptized will be saved' (Mark 16:16)." *John Calvin*

Worship

45

MEANING The word "worship" in the Bible is linked to service, the kind of service a slave would give to his master. It includes the ideas of reverence, wonder, and awe.

General Bible teaching

1. Old Testament
In the Old Testament worship of God was usually accompanied by great formality and ritual and very often was a congregational act.

"Then David said to the whole assembly, 'Praise the LORD your God.' So they all praised the LORD, the God of their fathers; they bowed low and fell prostrate before the LORD and the king."
1 Chronicles 29:20

2. New Testament
Worship was linked to the Lord's Day. See *Acts 20:7*. Worship often took place in people's homes. See *Colossians 4:15*.

Worship included singing God's praises, readings from God's Word, and the exercise of God's spiritual gifts. See *Ephesians 5:19; Colossians 3:16; 1 Corinthians 14:26*.

Worship often centered round a shared meal, which has been called "the love-feast," which was followed by the Lord's Supper. See *1 Corinthians 11:23-28*.

"Then the man bowed down and worshiped the Lord, saying, 'Praise be to the Lord, the God of my master Abraham, who has not abandoned his kindness and faithfulness to my master.'" *Genesis 24:26*

Jesus and worship
- Jesus regularly attended public worship in synagogues. See *Luke 4:16*.
- Jesus observed Jewish feasts. See *Luke 22:11; John 7:10*.
- Jesus warned against the dangers of hypocrisy in worship. See *Matthew 15:8*.
- Jesus taught that God should be worshiped **"in spirit and in truth"** and not just in outward forms of words. See *John 4:24*.

Quote TO PONDER
"To worship is:
to quicken the conscience by the holiness of God,
to feed the mind on the truth of God,
to purge the imagination by the beauty of God,
to open the heart to the love of God,
to devote the will to the purpose of God."
William Temple

Assurance

MEANING Assurance refers to the idea that a believer not only possesses God's salvation, but can be certain about this.

General Bible teaching

1. Historical assurance

The Christian faith is not based on a fairy tale or some myth that can be traced back to the dawn of time. Rather it is founded on the solid rock of events that took place in history. Peter underlines that he was himself an eyewitness of things that actually happened.

"We did not follow cleverly invented stories when we told you about the power and coming of our Lord Jesus Christ, but we were eye-witnesses of his majesty." *2 Peter 1:16*

Christians believe in the birth, life, death of Jesus because they really took place. And Jesus' resurrection was the crowning proof that he was who he claimed to be – the Son of God. See *Romans 1:4.*

2. Personal experience

Alongside these objective historical facts, "Anyone who believes in the Son of God has this testimony in his heart." *1 John 5:10*

God's Holy Spirit convinces believers that beyond all doubt they are God's children. "The Spirit himself testifies with our spirit that we are God's children." *Romans 8:16*

Christians are assured that they can go to God in prayer. "Let us draw near to God with a sincere heart in full assurance of faith." *Hebrews 10:22*

Quote TO PONDER

"What a wonderful thing it is to be sure of one's faith! How wonderful to be a member of the evangelical church, which preaches the free grace of God through Christ as the hope of sinners! If we were to rely on our works, what would become of us?" *G.F. Handel*

"He who has the Son has life; he who does not have the Son of God does not have life. I write these things to you who believe in the name of the Son of God so that you may know that you have eternal life." *1 John 5:12,13*

Humility

MEANING A helpful way to fully appreciate the meaning of the word "humility" is to observe a humble person. True humility is the opposite of pride. A humble person is one who has learnt to depend on God.

General Bible teaching

- A humble person is one who is dependent on God and walks in his ways. See *Micah 6:8*.
- A humble person is not caught up in his/her own importance. **"Do nothing out of selfish ambition or vain conceit, but in humility consider others better than yourselves. Each of you should look not only to your own interests, but also to the interests of others."** *Philippians 2:3,4*. See also *Romans 12:10-16*.
- Humility is no optional extra. In the New Testament humility is frequently demanded. See *Colossians 3:12; Titus 3:2; James 3:13; 4:6; 1 Peter 3:8; 5:5.*

Jesus and humility

Jesus **"made himself nothing"** when he was born as a helpless human baby, and also **"humbled himself and became obedient to death."** *Philippians 2:3,4*

QUOTE TO PONDER

"He that is down need fear no fall,
He that is low no pride."
John Bunyan

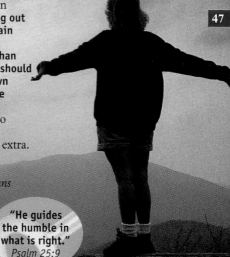

"He guides the humble in what is right."
Psalm 25:9

The cross of Jesus

MEANING The Greek word for "cross," *stauros*, was a single stake on which criminals were nailed as a form of execution. Ancient writers also used the word "cross," (in Latin *crux*) to refer to a T-shaped cross. It is this type of cross that the earliest Christians writers say Jesus was crucified on.

Whenever the New Testament writers refer to the "cross" of Jesus, or to the "blood" of Jesus they are always talking about Jesus' death by crucifixion.

The symbol of Christianity

Because of what Jesus achieved by dying on a cross, the cross has become the universal and most respected symbol of Christianity.

Taking up Jesus' cross

Jesus taught that his followers must identify with him, and even be prepared to be martyred on his account. **"Jesus said to his disciples, 'If anyone would come after me, he must deny himself and take up his cross and follow me.'"** *Matthew 16:24*

Quote TO PONDER
"By the cross we know the gravity of sin and the greatness of God's love towards us." *John Chrysostom*

Key teaching about Jesus' cross

1. It was for our salvation

"The cross of Christ" (*1 Corinthians 1:17*) refers to Jesus being crucified for humankind in order to procure their salvation.

The cross is the means of our salvation: **"And through him [Jesus] to reconcile to himself all things, whether things on earth or things in heaven, by making peace through his blood, shed on the cross."** *Colossians 1:20*

2. It was for our reconciliation to God

Paul teaches that it is through the cross of Jesus that we are reconciled to God. **"His [Christ's] purpose was to create in himself one new man [the united body of believers] out of the two [believing Jews and believing Gentiles], thus making peace, and in this one new body to reconcile both of them to God through the cross, by which he put to death their hostility."** *Ephesians 2:15,16*

3. Jesus' death on the cross was predetermined

See *Acts 2:23; 1 Peter 1:18-20; Revelation 13:8.*

> "Carrying his own cross, he [Jesus] went out to the place of the Skull (which in Aramaic is called Golgotha)."
> *John 19:17*

4. Jesus' death on the cross was voluntary

It is not true that Jesus found himself trapped in Jerusalem and so was crucified against his will. See *John 10:17,18; Galatians 2:20.*

5. Jesus' death on the cross was for us (vicarious)

"For Christ died for sins once for all, the righteous for the unrighteous, to bring you to God." *1 Peter 3:18.* See also *1 Corinthians 15:3; Romans 4:25.*

6. Jesus' death on the cross was in our place (substitutionary)

"He himself bore our sins in his body on the tree [cross], so that we might die to sins and live for righteousness; by his wounds you have been healed." *1 Peter 2:24*

Quote TO PONDER

"The cross cannot be defeated for it is defeat."
G.K. Chesterton

Atonement

MEANING Atonement means "at-one-ment." Through faith in Jesus humankind can become "at one" with God. Atonement is the act of restoring harmony between two people who have been at odds with each other.

In the Old Testament, the Hebrew word for "atone," *kapar*, means to purify or cover over. A person would go to the priest, acknowledge his guilt, and present an animal to be killed and burned as a sacrifice on the altar. Hence *Leviticus 4:26* says, **"In this way the priest will make *atonement* for the man's sin, and he will be forgiven."**

"God presented him [Jesus] as a sacrifice of atonement, through faith in his blood. He did this to demonstrate his justice, because in his forbearance he had left the sins committed beforehand unpunished." *Romans 3:25*

General Bible teaching

1. Through the atonement we are justified
Because of the atonement it is "just-as-if-I'd" never sinned. **"While we were still sinners, Christ died for us. Since we have now been justified by his blood, how much more shall we be saved from God's wrath through him!"** *Romans 5:8,9*

2. Through the atonement we are redeemed
"In him [Jesus] we have redemption through his blood, the forgiveness of sins." *Ephesians 1:7*

3. Through the atonement we come close to Jesus
"Now in Christ Jesus you who once were far away have been brought near through the blood of Christ." *Ephesians 2:13*

Scripture, Word of God, inspiration

MEANING The Greek word *gramma* means "document," and *graphe* means writings. The phrase "the Scriptures" in the New Testament, refers to the Old Testament. Peter says that Paul's writings were quickly accepted in the early church, as equal to **"the other Scriptures"** *2 Peter 3:16*.

"All scripture is given by inspiration of God [is God-breathed NIV], and is profitable for doctrine, for reproof, for correction, for instruction in righteousness." *2 Timothy 3:16,17 KJV*

General Bible teaching

The Bible describes itself in a wide variety of ways. Each description sheds light on one facet of the Word of God. The Bible likens itself to:

- **water:** "... cleansing her [the Christian church] by the washing with water through the word." *Ephesians 5:26*
- **a lamp and a light:** "Your word is a lamp to my feet and a light to my path." *Psalm 119:105*
- **fire:** many evangelists have experienced a similar conviction to the one Jeremiah had: "... his word is in my heart like a fire, a fire shut up in my bones. I am weary of holding it in, indeed I cannot." *Jeremiah 20:9*
- **a hammer:** see *Jeremiah 23:29*
- **a sword:** see *Hebrews 4:12*
- **seed:** "For you have been born again, not of perishable seed, but of imperishable, through the living and enduring word of God." *1 Peter 1:23*

Quote TO PONDER
"The holy and inspired Scriptures are sufficient of themselves for the preaching of the Truth." *Athanasius*

Heaven, hell, judgment

MEANING "Heaven," in Hebrew *shamayim*, and in Greek *ouranos*, refers to the created universe beyond planet earth, the spiritual realm and the "home" of God, and the whole material universe, in the case of "the heavens and the earth."

General Bible teaching

Sheol
The word *sheol* in Hebrew describes the place people go to when they die. **"For my soul is full of trouble and my life draws near the grave."** *Psalm 88:3*

Hades
For all the occurrences of the Greek word *Hades*, see *Matthew 11:23; 16:18; Luke 10:15; 16:23; Acts 2:27,31; 1 Corinthians 15:55; Revelation 1:18; 6:8; 20:13,14. Hades* is never used to refer to the place of final judgment, which we refer to as hell. However, the place of final judgment is mentioned in *Matthew 5:22* and *Mark 9:43*.

The "gates of *Hades*" (see *Matthew 16:18*), refers to the rallying point of Satan's forces, just as the city gate was the rallying point for armies.

Gehenna
The word *gehenna* derives its name from the deep ravine on the south side of Jerusalem, which was used as a giant rubbish pit. This was called the "Valley of Hinnon," in Hebrew *ge hinnom*. Figuratively, it was thought of as the place of final judgment.

Paradise
Paradise is the place to which God's people go immediately after death. See *Luke 23:43*.

Election, predestination

MEANING In the Bible, the word "election" refers to free, personal, and sovereign choice by God of the children of Israel. Bible translations often prefer to use the word "chosen" in place of "election" or "elected." Hence the Israelites are referred to as, **"my chosen one."** *Isaiah 42:1.*

General Bible teaching

Predestination and free will
Predestination is perfectly compatible with freedom of choice by an individual. **"The Spirit and the bride say, 'Come!' And let him who hears say, 'Come!' Whoever is thirsty, let him come; and whoever wishes, let him take the free gift of the water of life."** *Revelation 22:17.* See also *Matthew 11:28-30.*

This paradox the Christian is happy to accept as he knows that God is just. He/she knows the correct answer to the rhetorical question posed in *Genesis 18:25:* **"Will not the judge of all the earth do right?"**

Election and salvation
The doctrine of election, God's choice of us, reminds us that our salvation does not depend just on our choice of God, but rather on God's choice of us. See *John 15:16.*

Our eternal security is fully guaranteed. See *Romans 8:35-39.*

Confident of this Christians can live for God in a positive way. See *Colossians 3:12-17.*

3. Chosen for special work
God selects some people for special tasks. This was true in the case of:
• Moses. See *Psalm 106:23.*
• Jeremiah. See *Jeremiah 1:5.*
• Paul. See *Acts 9:15.*

53

Quote TO PONDER
"Those of humankind that are predestinated to life, God, before the foundation of the world was laid, according to his eternal and immutable purpose, and the secret counsel and good pleasure of his will, has chosen in Christ, for everlasting glory, out of his free grace and love alone."
Loraine Boettner

Repentance

MEANING The Old Testament uses the Hebrew word *shub*, meaning "to turn back" or "to return," for the word "repentance." For example, it means a turning from idols to God.

The equivalent word for "repentance" in the New Testament is the Greek verb *metanoein*, which occurs 30 times, and the noun *metanoia*, which is nearly as frequent. It means more than the literal meaning of *metanoia*, a mere change of mind, as it indicates a turning to God. Like faith, repentance itself is a gift of God. See *Acts 5:31; 11:18; Romans 2:4; 2 Timothy 2:25.*

Old Testament examples of repentance

1. Nehemiah's prayer
"Remember the instruction you [the LORD] gave your servant Moses, saying, 'If you are unfaithful, I will scatter you among the nations, but *if you return to me* and obey my commands, then even if your exiled people are at the farthest horizon, I will gather them from there and bring them to the place I have chosen as a dwelling for my Name.'" *Nehemiah 1:8,9*

2. Isaiah's message
"*Return* to him [the LORD Almighty] you have so greatly

revolted against, O Israelites. For in that day every one of you will reject the idols of silver and gold your sinful hands have made."
Isaiah 31:6,7

"Godly sorrow brings repentance"

Paul links godly sorrow with repentance, and repentance with salvation in *2 Corinthians 7:9,10:* "Your sorrow led you to repentance. For you became sorrowful as God intended. ... Godly sorrow leads to salvation and leaves no regret, but worldly sorrow brings death."

Messages about repentance

The importance of repentance is shown in:
- John's message of repentance. See *Matthew 3:1,2.*
- Jesus' message of repentance. See *Matthew 4:17; Luke 24:47.*
- The twelve apostles' message of repentance. See *Mark 6:12.*
- Peter's message of repentance in the first Christian sermon. See *Acts 2:38:* "Peter replied: 'Repent and be baptized, every one of you, in the name of Jesus Christ for the forgiveness of your sins.'"
- Paul's message of repentance. See *Acts 26:20.*

"But when he [John the Baptist] saw many of the Pharisees and Sadducees coming to where he was baptizing, he said to them: 'You brood of vipers! Who warned you to flee from the coming wrath? Produce fruit in keeping with repentance.'"
Matthew 3:7,8

Repentance and sin

Repentance is a God-given change of heart towards sin, righteousness, and God himself. See *Romans 2:4; 2 Timothy 2:25.*

As well as being sorrow for sin, repentance is hatred of sin: "Let those who love the LORD hate evil." *Psalm 97:10*

Results of repentance
- Joy in heaven. See *Luke 15:7,10.*
- Pardon and forgiveness: "Let the wicked forsake his way and the evil man his thoughts. Let him turn to the LORD, and he will have mercy on him, and to our God, for he will freely pardon." *Isaiah 55:7*

55

Church

56

MEANING The word used in English today for "church" comes from the Greek word *kuriakos*, meaning "the Lord's." It came to be used in a phrase like *kuriakon doma*, "the Lord's house," the building where local Christians met.

However, in the New Testament, the word for "church" is the Greek word *ekklesia*, which means "assembly." The word *ekklesia* appears 92 times in Acts and in the New Testament letters, where it describes a community of Christians who have been called and set apart by God. In the New Testament the word "church" never refers to a building or to an institution.

General Bible teaching
Numerous images are used to describe the church in the New Testament.

1. The church as the body of Christ
Christians are members of Christ's body on earth and are meant to grow towards maturity. **"And he [Christ] is the head of the body, the church."** *Colossians 1:18*. See also *1 Corinthians 12:12-31; Ephesians 1:22; 4:1-16*.

2. The church as the family of the Father
Christians have God as their Father and fellow-Christians are brothers and sisters in God's family. **"For this reason I kneel before the Father, from whom his whole family in heaven and on earth derives its name."** *Ephesians 3:14*. See also *John 13:33,34; Ephesians 5:1,2; 1 John 5:1,2*.

3. The church as the temple of the Holy Spirit
Christians are described as living stones in God's holy temple. **"As you come to him, the living Stone ... you also, like living stones, are being built into a spiritual house."** *1 Peter 2:4,5*. See also *Ephesians 2:21,22*.

Quote TO PONDER
"The church is the only institution supernaturally endowed by God. It is the one institution of which Jesus promised that the gates of hell will not prevail against it."
Chuck Colson

"In the church at Antioch there were prophets and teachers."
Acts 13:1

Fellowship

"They devoted themselves to the apostles' teaching and to the fellowship, to the breaking of bread and to prayer." *Acts 2:42*

MEANING The Greek word *koinonia* is translated in a variety of ways including "sharing," "communion," "participation," "partnership," "contribution," and "fellowship." Fellowship refers to an intimate relationship and to a close-knit community.

General Bible teaching

1. Fellowship as the union between Jesus and Christians

Paul says that we have been called into fellowship with his Son. See *1 Corinthians 1:9; 1 John 1:3,7.* **"And our fellowship is with the Father and with his Son, Jesus Christ."** *1 John 1:4.* The relationship between Christians and Jesus is so close that Paul described it in terms of a marriage. See *Ephesians 5:25-27.*

2. Fellowship between Christians

Koinonia describes the deep relationship Christians have with each other. *Acts 2:46,47* captures this bond between fellow believers: **"Every day they continued to meet together in the temple courts. They broke bread in their homes and ate together with glad and sincere hearts, praising God and enjoying the favor of all the people."**

The first Christians:
- enjoyed sharing in the Lord's Supper together. See *1 Corinthians 10:16*
- were active in Christian service. See *2 Corinthians 8:4; Philippians 1:15*
- knew that their fellowship with other Christians depended on fellowship with the Spirit. See *Philippians 1:2*
- knew that there was fellowship in suffering for the sake of Jesus. See *Philippians 3:10.*

57

Quote TO PONDER

"Some people become tired at the end of ten minutes or half an hour of prayer. What will they do when they have to spend eternity in the presence of God? We must begin the habit here and become used to being with God."
Sadhu Sundar Singh

The Lord's Supper

MEANING The Lord's Supper is a celebration of Jesus' death and was instituted by Jesus at his last meal on earth. It has been given various names: "Holy Communion," "Eucharist," which means "thanksgiving," and by Roman Catholics "The Mass," after the Latin word *missa*, which comes at the end of the service as worshipers are dismissed and sent away.

General Bible teaching

Jesus' last meal is recorded and described in *Matthew 26:17-30, Mark 14:12-25*, and *Luke 22:7-20*. John's Gospel records Jesus washing the disciples' feet during the meal, along with the conversations held during the meal. See *John 13–16*.

1. Luke's instruction

Only in Luke's Gospel are the following words found: **"Do this in remembrance of me."** From this Christians deduce that:

- Jesus commanded his followers to continue to celebrate the Lord's Supper after his death.
- the Lord's Supper should be a time when Jesus' sacrifice is remembered.

2. Paul and the Lord's Supper

Paul explains the meaning of the Lord's Supper in *1 Corinthians 11:23-26*. After quoting Jesus' own words Paul adds, **"For whenever you eat this bread and drink this cup, you proclaim the Lord's death until he comes."** *1 Corinthians 11:26*

From this it is clear that the Lord's Supper should be held periodically, but no instruction is given as to how often.

Paul warns against taking part in the Lord's Supper "in an unworthy manner." *1 Corinthians 11:27*

Paul says that before coming to the Lord's Supper a person should "examine himself." *1 Corinthians 11:28*

Quote TO PONDER

"The sacraments have been given to us in order to stimulate our faith. In fact, they are means of grace mainly because they are means of faith. And the Lord's Supper is a means of faith because it sets forth in dramatic visual symbolism the good news that Christ died for our sins in order that we might be forgiven."
John Stott

58

Gospel, preaching

MEANING To preach the gospel, in Greek *euangelizo*, is to announce good news, like announcing a military victory, or spreading the news about two people becoming engaged.

General Bible teaching

1. Preaching news from God in the Old Testament

Examples of preachers in the Old Testament are:

- Noah. In *2 Peter 2:5* Noah is referred to as **"a preacher of righteousness."**
- Jonah. God said to Jonah, **"Go to the great city of Nineveh and proclaim to it the message I give you."** *Jonah 3:2*

2. Preaching the gospel in the New Testament

The angels announced the birth of Jesus to shepherds. **"But the angel said to them, 'Do not be afraid. I bring you good news of great joy that will be for all the people.'"** *Luke 2:10*

In Acts Paul communicated the gospel in a variety of ways:

- He argued or "reasoned" with people in Thessalonica. See *Acts 17:2.*
- He "spoke" until midnight at Troas. See *Acts 20:7.*
- He "preached" at Ephesus. See *Acts 20:20.*
- He "explained" and "declared" the kingdom of God in Rome. See *Acts 28:20.*

Christian preachers should be commissioned by God. **"And how can they preach unless they are sent?"** *Romans 10:15*

59

Quote TO PONDER

"Preaching should break a hard heart, and heal a broken heart." *John Newton*

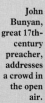

John Bunyan, great 17th-century preacher, addresses a crowd in the open air.

Righteousness

MEANING In the Bible the Hebrew word for righteousness, *tsedeq*, and the Greek word for righteousness, *dikaiosyne*, mean living in harmony with God and in line with one's obligations to him.

English translations of these Hebrew and Greek words focus on two roots: "right," "righteous," and "righteousness," and "just," "justice," and "justification." But the Hebrew and Greek words include both meanings.

General Bible teaching

"Righteousness" is used in a wide variety of ways in the Bible:

1. Divine righteousness

Throughout the Old Testament, God's justice and fairness in his dealings with his creatures, that is his righteousness, are seen.

- God's righteousness was celebrated: **"They will celebrate your abundant goodness and joyfully sing of your righteousness."** *Psalm 145:7*
- Jeremiah calls Israel's Savior "The Lord our Righteousness." **"In his days Judah will be saved and Israel will live in safety. This is the name by which he [the Lord] will be called: The LORD Our Righteousness."** *Jeremiah 23:6*
- God's righteous dealings with humankind are the model for his followers. **"He [God] has showed you, O man, what is good. And what does the LORD require of you? To act justly and to love mercy and to walk humbly with your God."** *Micah 6:8*

A summary of the Old Testament teaching about God's righteousness comes in *Psalm 11:7:* **"For the LORD is righteous, he loves justice; upright men will see his face."**

2. Our own righteousness is no good

We can never, through our own efforts, attain the kind of righteousness that is acceptable in God's sight. Judged by God's perfect standards our own ideas of righteousness are like a polluted set of clothes. **"All of us have become like one who is unclean, and all our righteous acts are like filthy rags."** *Isaiah 64:6*

Paul came to realize that if we are to be accepted by God it can never be on the grounds of our own righteousness. See *Romans 10:1-6; Philippians 3:9; Titus 3:5.*

Quote TO PONDER

"The righteousness of God is not acquired by acts frequently repeated, as Aristotle taught, but is imparted by faith." *Martin Luther*

3. Imputed righteousness

There is only one way we can stand before God. We have to be clothed in righteousness. And the only way Christians can have such righteousness is if it is given to us by God. This righteousness needs to be received by us as a wonderful gift from God.

> "Abram believed the Lord, and he credited it to him as righteousness."
> *Genesis 15:6*

- "This righteousness from God comes through faith in Jesus Christ to all who believe." *Romans 3:22*
- This righteousness has nothing to do with any good deeds we may have done: **"David ... speaks of the blessedness of the man to whom God credits righteousness apart from works."** *Romans 4:6*
- Jesus is our route to righteousness; **"It is because of him that you are in Christ Jesus, who has become for us wisdom from God – that is, our righteousness, holiness and redemption."** *1 Corinthians 1:30*
- We can only be righteous because of Jesus' righteousness: **"God made him who had no sin to be sin for us, so that in him we might become the righteousness of God."** *2 Corinthians 5:21*
- We are clothed in righteousness: The righteousness of Jesus that we wear can be likened to wearing special wedding

clothes which cover our own sins and deficiencies with Jesus' splendor. It is as if when God looks at us all he sees is Jesus' righteousness. See *Matthew 22:11,12*.

"I delight greatly in the Lord; my soul rejoices in my God. For he has clothed me with garments of salvation and arrayed me in a robe of righteousness." *Isaiah 61:10*

4. Spiritual righteousness

Christians are meant to display the fruit of the Spirit, and to be just, fair, generous, and kind in their behavior. That is another way of saying that our lives should be characterized by righteousness. **"This is my prayer ... that you may be ... filled with the fruit of righteousness that comes through Jesus Christ."** *Philippians 1:9-11*

Quote TO PONDER

"No condemnation now I dread,
Jesus, and all in him, is mine;
Alive in him, my living Head,
And clothed in righteousness divine,
Bold I approach the eternal throne,
And claim the crown, through Christ, my own."
Charles Wesley

61

Kingdom of heaven, kingdom of God

MEANING The Jews tried never to utter the name of God, so Matthew, not to offend his Jewish readers, spoke about "the kingdom of heaven." However, Mark and Luke knew that such a phrase would not be readily understood by their non-Jewish readers, and so used the phrase, "the kingdom of God." "Kingdom of heaven" and "kingdom of God" mean the same thing. The Greek word for "kingdom," *basileai*, refers to God's rule on earth.

> "From that time on Jesus began to preach, 'Repent, for the kingdom of heaven is near.'" *Matthew 4:17*

Matthew chapter 13

Many of Jesus' parables about the kingdom of heaven are recorded in *Matthew 13*. There Jesus answers the question: "What is the kingdom of heaven like?"

1. The parable of the sower
Matthew 13:2-9,18-23 explains how some people respond and other people fail to respond to the message about the kingdom. See also *Psalm 2; 18:43-50; 72:8-11; 110; Isaiah 9:7; Micah 5:4; Zechariah 45:4,5.*

2. The parable of the weeds and the parable of the net
Matthew 13:24-30,36-43,47-50 shows how in the kingdom of God this age ends with the good and evil being separated. See also *Psalm 21:8-12; 72:1-4,12-14.*

3. The parable of the hidden treasure and the parable of the pearl
Matthew 13:44,45-46 explains that the kingdom must be sought for and how it should be valued above everything else. See also P*salm 72:6,7; 132:13-18; Isaiah 11:6-9; Jeremiah 23:6; Amos 9:13; Joel 4:18.*

4. The parable of the mustard seed and the parable about yeast
Matthew 13:31-33 teaches that God's kingdom produces results which are out of all proportion to its seemingly insignificant start. See also *Psalm 45:4,5.*

Quote TO PONDER
"There can be no kingdom of God in the world without the kingdom of God in our hearts."
Albert Schweitzer

Second Coming

"This same Jesus, who has been taken from you into heaven, will come back in the same way you have seen him go into heaven." *Acts 1:11*

MEANING

1. *Parousia*: The phrase "second coming" does not appear in the Bible. It refers to the physical, personal return of Jesus to earth. In the New Testament, this event is mentioned over 300 times, most often with the Greek word *parousia*, meaning "presence" or "arrival." Some of the important New Testament passages are: *Matthew 19:28; 23:39; 24:1-51; Mark 13:24-37; Luke 12:35-48; 21:25-28; Romans 11:25-27; 1 Corinthians 11:26; 15:51-58; 1 Thessalonians 4:13-18; 2 Thessalonians 1:7-10; 2 Peter 3:10-12; Revelation 16:15; 19:11-21.*

2. *Eschatos*: The study of Jesus' return is also called "eschatology" (from the Greek word *eschatos*, meaning "last") from which the phrase "the doctrine of the last things" is derived.

Quote TO PONDER

"We must never speak to simple, excitable people about 'the Day' without emphasizing again and again the utter impossibility of prediction." *C.S. Lewis*

General Bible teaching

1. Jesus will appear for a second time
"… he [Christ] will appear a second time, not to bear sin, but to bring salvation to those who are waiting for him." *Hebrews 9:28*

2. What about Christians who have already died?
Paul assures the Thessalonians that Christians who die before Jesus' coming again will not miss out at his parousia.
"According to the Lord's own word, we tell you that we who are still alive, who are left till the coming of the Lord, will certainly not precede those who have fallen asleep."
1 Thessalonians 4:15

3. When will Jesus return?
A number of events, such as war, famine, and earthquakes, will take place before Jesus' return, and so the date of Jesus' return has often been predicted. However, the New Testament teaches that the date or time of Jesus' return is not known.
"No one knows about that day or hour, not even the angels in heaven, nor the Son, but only the Father." *Matthew 24:36*

Index

Key
Bible
People
made easy

Adam and Eve

Adam

Meaning of name: Mankind

Point of interest: The first person created by God.

Family links: Adam was Eve's husband. His children were Cain, Abel, and Seth.

New Testament link: "Therefore, just as sin entered the world through one man, and death through sin, and in this way death came to all men, because all sinned." *Romans 5:12*

Quote: "I heard you in the garden, and I was afraid because I was naked; so I hid." *Genesis 3:10*

Link to Jesus: As Adam was the head of the human race, so Jesus was the Head of the new creation: *Romans 5:12-14; 1 Corinthians 15:21,22,45; Galatians 3:22,26; Ephesians 1:22,23.*

Key verse: Speaking to the serpent, the Lord God foretells the long conflict between the children of God and the children of evil. This is the first reference in the Bible to the salvation which Jesus brought. Jesus is the One who will crush the serpent's head, that is defeat evil. "And I will put enmity between you and the woman, and between your offspring and hers; he will crush your head, and you will strike his heel." *Genesis 3:15*

More Information: *Genesis 1:26,27; 2:1–5:5*

The result of Adam's sin

The New Testament shows how Jesus deals with the results of Adam's sin.

	Adam's sin		New Testament
1.	*Genesis 3:8,9*	Separation	*Mark 15:34*
2.	*Genesis 3:16*	Pain	*Acts 2:24*
3.	*Genesis 3:17*	God's curse	*Galatians 3:13*
4.	*Genesis 3:17*	Sorrow	*Matthew 27:29*
5.	*Genesis 3:18*	Thorns	*Mark 15:17*
6.	*Genesis 3:19*	Sweat	*Luke 22:44*
7.	*Genesis 3:19*	Death	*Philippians 2:8*

Eve

Meaning of name: Life

Point of interest: Eve was the first woman God created.

Family links: Eve was Adam's wife. Her children were Cain, Abel, and Seth.

New Testament link: "But I am afraid that just as Eve was deceived by the serpent's cunning, your minds may somehow be led astray from your sincere and pure devotion to Christ." *2 Corinthians 11:3*

Quote: "The serpent deceived me and I ate." *Genesis 3:13*

Link to Jesus: To her cost, Eve discovered that Satan was a liar. The serpent said to Eve, "Did God really say, 'You must not eat from any tree in the garden'?" *Genesis 3:1*. In *John 8:44*, Jesus says of the devil, "he is a liar and the father of lies."

Key verse: "She [Eve] took some [fruit of the tree] and ate it." *Genesis 3:6*

More Information: *Genesis 2:18–3:20*

The Temptation of Adam and Eve, façade, Milan Cathedral, Italy

Eve and temptation

Just as Eve was tempted in three ways, so we are tempted today. *See Genesis 3:6.*

1. Temptation comes through our eyes: Eve saw the fruit.
2. Temptation comes through our desires: Eve desired the fruit.
3. Temptation comes as a result of our actions: Eve took the fruit.

"In Adam", but also "in Christ"

The apostle Paul speaks of Christians as being "in Adam" as well as being "in Christ." "For as in Adam all die, so in Christ all will be made alive." *1 Corinthians 15:22*

Before we become Christians, we are "in Adam" in that we are rooted in sin.

But as Christians, we are "in Christ" and related to Jesus, forgiven of our sin and renewed with his spiritual life.

Cain and Abel

Cain and Abel

Meaning of names: "Cain" means "acquire"; "Abel" means "shepherd."

Point of interest: Cain murdered Abel.

Family links: Cain and Abel were sons of Adam and Eve.

New Testament link: "By faith Abel offered God a better sacrifice than Cain did. By faith he was commended as a righteous man, when God spoke well of his offerings. And by faith he still speaks, even though he is dead." *Hebrews 11:4*

Quote: Replying to God's question, "Where is your brother Abel?" Cain said, "Am I my brother's keeper?" *Genesis 4:9*

Key verse: "Then the Lord said to Cain, 'Why are you angry? Why is your face downcast? If you do what is right, will you not be accepted? But if you do not do what is right, sin is crouching at your door; it desires to have you, but you must master it.'" *Genesis 4:7*

More Information: *Genesis 4:1,2*

The first murder

Cain was Adam and Eve's eldest son. He farmed the land. God rejected Cain's sacrifice, but accepted Abel's animal sacrifice. Cain was so jealous and angry that he killed Abel in a field.

Job

Job

Meaning of name: Persecuted

Point of interest: Job endured terrible, undeserved suffering.

Family links: Before he suffered Job had:
- 7 sons
- 3 daughters
- 7,000 sheep
- 3,000 camels
- 500 yoke of oxen
- 500 donkeys.

  After he suffered God blessed Job with:
- 7 sons
- 3 daughters
- 14,000 sheep
- 6,000 camels
- 1,000 yoke of oxen
- 1,000 donkeys.

New Testament link: "You have heard of Job's perseverence." *James 5:11*

Quote: "I know that my Redeemer lives." *Job 19:25*

Link to Jesus: Job endured suffering, in which he was patient, and from which he was delivered.

Key verse: Job said: "But he [God] knows the way that I take; when he has tested me, I shall come forth as gold." *Job 23:10*

More Information: The book of *Job*

Job as an example of righteousness

The prophet Ezekiel mentions Job, along with Noah and Daniel, as an example of righteousness in *Ezekiel 14:14*.

"I despise myself"

The opening verse of the book of Job characterizes Job as someone who was "blameless and upright, who feared God and shunned evil." But at the end of the book Job says of himself: "I despise myself and repent in dust and ashes." *Job 42:6*

The more we grow in the grace of God, the more we realize that we are only sinners saved by God's grace.

Enoch and Methuselah

Enoch

Meaning of name: Teacher

Point of interest: Enoch was one of only two people (the other being Elijah in 2 Kings 2:11) whom the Bible says were "translated" to heaven, into the presence of God, without dying.

Family links: Enoch's father was Jared. Enoch was the father of Methuselah.

New Testament link: "By faith Enoch was taken from this life, so that he did not experience death; he could not be found, because God had taken him away. For before he was taken, he was commended as one who pleased God." *Hebrews 11:5*

Key verse: "Enoch walked with God; then he was no more, because God took him away." *Genesis 5:24*

More Information: *Genesis 5:18-24*

Methuselah

Meaning of name: Man of the javelin

Point of interest: Methuselah was the oldest person to have lived. He died when he was 969 .

Family links: His father was Enoch, and he was the father of Lamech, and grandfather of Noah.

New Testament link: In Luke's genealogy of Jesus, Methuselah is mentioned: " ... the son of Methuselah, the son of Enoch ..." *Luke 3:37*

Key verse: In Genesis 5:25,26 Methuselah is mentioned, and is the eighth patriarch listed in this chapter.

More Information: *Genesis 5:21-27; Luke 3:37*

Walking with God

"Walking with God" is a picture of having close fellowship with God.

> "Noah was a righteous man, … and he walked with God." *Genesis 6:9*

> "And what does the Lord require of you? To act justly and to love mercy and to walk humbly with your God." *Micah 6:8*

> "True instruction was found in his mouth and nothing false was found on his lips. He walked with me in peace and uprightness, and turned many from sin." *Malachi 2:6*

Noah

Noah

Meaning of name: Rest

Point of interest: Noah was a "preacher of righteousness." See *2 Peter 2:5*

Family links: Noah had three sons: Shem, Japheth, and Ham.

New Testament link: "By faith Noah, when warned about things not yet seen, in holy fear built an ark to save his family. By his faith he condemned the world and became heir of the righteousness that comes by faith." *Hebrews 11:7*

Words spoken about: "Noah was a righteous man, blameless among the people of his time, and he walked with God." *Genesis 6:9*

Link to Jesus: Noah prepared the way of salvation: *Genesis 6:14; Hebrews 11:7*

Noah finished God's work: *Genesis 6:22; John 19:30*

Key verse: "Noah did everything just as God commanded him." *Genesis 7:22*

More Information: *Genesis 5–9; Luke 3:36; 1 Peter 3:20; 2 Peter 2:5*

The sign of the rainbow

After the flood God made a promise to Noah for all time: he would never again send a flood to destroy all living things. God gave the rainbow as a sign of that promise. See *Genesis 9:11-17*.

Rainbows are very significant in the Bible. They announce God's judgments in a vivid, pictorial way:

- "Like the appearance of a rainbow in the clouds on a rainy day, so was the radiance around him." *Ezekiel 1:28*.
- "Then I saw another mighty angel coming down from heaven. He was robed in a cloud, with a rainbow above his head …" *Revelation 10:1*.

Abraham

Abraham

Meaning of name: Father of multitudes. Abraham was also called "Abram"

Point of interest: Abraham was the founder of the Jewish nation.

Family links: Abraham's father was Terah, his nephew was Lot, his wife was Sarah (Sarai), and his son was Isaac.

New Testament link: Jesus claimed to have existed before Abraham's time. "'I tell you the truth,' Jesus answered, 'before Abraham was born, I am!'" *John 8:58*

Quote: "God himself will provide the lamb for the burnt offering, my son." *Genesis 22:8*

Link to Jesus:
- Abraham expressed his concerns freely, and with great faith, in his prayer life. "Abraham said, 'O Sovereign Lord, what can you give me since I remain childless? ... You have given me no children.'" *Genesis 15:2,3*
- In all the critical moments of his life Abraham prayed to God. See *Genesis 18:16-33; 20:7.*

Key verse: "Abram believed the Lord, and he credited it to him as righteousness." *Genesis 15:6*

More Information: *Genesis 11:1–25:11; Matthew 1:1,2; Acts 7:2,3; Hebrews 11:8-19*

By faith

The book of Hebrews gives a summary of Abraham's wonderful life of faith.

"By faith Abraham, when called to go to a place he would later receive as his inheritance, obeyed and went, even though he did not know where he was going.

"By faith he made his home in the promised land like a stranger in a foreign country; he lived in tents, as did Isaac and Jacob, who were heirs with him of the same promise. For he was looking forward to the city with foundations, whose architect and builder is God.

"By faith Abraham, even though he was past age – and Sarah herself was barren – was enabled to become a father because he considered him faithful who had made the promise. And so from this one man, and he as good as dead, came descendants as numerous as the stars in the sky and as countless as the sand on the seashore.

"All these people were still living by faith when they died. They did not receive the things promised; they only saw them and welcomed them from a distance. And they admitted that they were aliens and strangers on earth.

"People who say such things

show that they are looking for a country of their own. If they had been thinking of the country they had left, they would have had opportunity to return.

"Instead, they were longing for a better country – a heavenly one. Therefore God is not ashamed to be called their God, for he has prepared a city for them.

"By faith Abraham, when God tested him, offered Isaac as a sacrifice. He who had received the promises was about to sacrifice his one and only son, even though God had said to him, 'It is through Isaac that your offspring will be reckoned.' Abraham reasoned that God could raise the dead, and figuratively speaking, he did receive Isaac back from death."

Hebrews 11:8-19

Summary of life

Abraham lived around 2000 BC. He grew up in the prosperous town of Ur in Mesopotamia.

- God called Abraham to leave Ur and to set off into the unknown. He then lived in Haran, before he traveled to Canaan.
- Abraham believed God's promise that a great nation would descend from him, even though Sarah was past the age of child-bearing.
- After his son Isaac was born, Abraham showed his faith and obedience to God by being prepared to sacrifice Isaac.

Melchizedek

Melchizedek

Meaning of name: King of righteousness

Point of interest: Melchizedek was a mysterious king of Salem (Jerusalem) to whom Abraham paid a tithe.

Family links: Melchizedek was said to be, "Without father or mother, without genealogy, without beginning of days or end of life . . ." *Hebrews 7:3*

New Testament link: According to *Hebrews 7:3*, Melchizedek, "like the Son of God he remains a priest forever."

Quote: Melchizedek blessed Abram, saying, "Blessed be Abram by God Most High, Creator of heaven and earth. And blessed be God Most High, who delivered your enemies into your hand." *Genesis 14:19,20*

Link to Jesus: Melchizedek, the priest-king, *Genesis 14:18-20*, is a type of the priesthood of Jesus, *Hebrews 6:20; 7:1-17,24,25*.

Key verse: "Jesus . . . has become a high priest forever, in the order of Melchizedek." *Hebrews 6:20*

More Information: *Genesis 14:18-20; Psalm 110:4; Hebrews 5:6; 7:3*

King and priest

Melchizedek was king of Salem (Jerusalem). He was also priest of the most high God, and he blessed Abraham.

Melchizedek is a prophetic symbol of Jesus who was both King and Priest.

Isaac

Isaac

Meaning of name: Laughing
Point of interest: Being the second of the patriarchs of the Israelites.
Family links: Isaac's very elderly parents were Sarah and Abraham. Isaac's bride, Rebekah, was found by Abraham's faithful servant. Isaac and Rebekah had twins, Jacob and Esau.
New Testament link: Isaac is referred to as a son of promise in *Romans 4:16-21; 9:7-9*.
Words spoken to: At Beersheba, the Lord said to Isaac, "I am the God of your father Abraham. Do not be afraid, for I am with you; I will bless you and will increase the number of your descendants for the sake of my servant Abraham." *Genesis 26:24*
Key verse: "Was not our ancestor Abraham considered righteous for what he did when he offered his son Isaac on the altar?" *James 2:21*
More Information: *Genesis 21:1–28:9; 35:27-29; Matthew 1:2*

13

The ram

God ordered Abraham to sacrifice his son Isaac. As he raised his knife to kill his tied up son, the angel of the LORD called out, "Abraham, Abraham."

Abraham replied, "Here I am."

"'Do not lay a hand on the boy,' he said. 'Do not do anything to him. Now I know that you fear God, because you have not withheld from me your son, your only son.'" *Genesis 22:12*

Then Abraham saw a ram caught in a thicket, which he sacrificed in place of Isaac. The idea of Jesus as our substitute is detailed in *Hebrews 10:5-10*.

An unexpected blessing

In Isaac's old age, when he was nearly blind, he was tricked into blessing Jacob with the blessing that was rightly Esau's. But the New Testament even looks at this through the eyes of faith.

"Isaac blessed Jacob and Esau in regard to their future." *Hebrews 11:20*

Joseph and his brothers

Joseph

Meaning of name: Increaser

Point of interest: His coat of "many colors." This was a richly ornamented coat that had long sleeves. It was given to the heir in a family. So it was hardly surprising that Joseph's brothers were mad with jealousy when Jacob gave Joseph, the youngest but one in the family, this coat.

Family links: Joseph was Rachel's first son, but Jacob's eleventh son. Joseph had one brother and ten half-brothers.
Joseph and Asenath, daughter of Potiphera, priest of On, had two sons, Ephraim and Manasseh.

New Testament link: "By faith Joseph, when his end was near, spoke about the exodus of the Israelites from Egypt and gave instructions about his bones." *Hebrews 11:22*

Quote: "I am your brother Joseph, the one you sold into Egypt! *Genesis 45:4*

Link to Jesus: Joseph is seen to be a type of Jesus in many ways:
- Joseph was stripped of his coat/robe. Compare *Genesis 37:23* with *John 19:23, 24.*

- Joseph was sold for the price of a slave. Compare *Genesis 37:28* with *Matthew 26:15.*
- Joseph was taken into Egypt. Compare *Genesis 37:24* with *Matthew 2:14, 15.*
- Joseph was falsely accused. Compare *Genesis 39:16-18* with *Matthew 26:59, 60.*
- Joseph was placed with two prisoners, one of whom was delivered and one of whom was lost. Compare *Genesis 40: 2,3,21,23* with *Luke 23:32,33,39-43.*
- Joseph started his ministry, aged 30. Compare *Genesis 41:46* with *Luke 3:23.*
- Joseph became a blessing to Gentile nations. Compare *Genesis 45:46-57* with *John 1:12.*

Key verse: "You intended to harm me, but God intended it for good to accomplish what is now being done, the saving of many lives." *Genesis 50:20*

More Information: *Genesis 30:20-24; 37–50*

Joseph's eventful life

After his two significant dreams Joseph was sold by his brothers as a slave and ended up in Egypt. There Joseph became the steward in the home of a leading soldier, Potiphar.

- Joseph was falsely accused of having sex with Potiphar's wife and so was thrown into prison.
- Joseph was released from prison, interpreted the king of Egypt's dreams, and on the strength of that was made the equivalent of vice-president of Egypt.

Through Joseph, Jacob's family was saved from the terrible seven-year-long famine. Joseph's family had to settle in Egypt where Joseph looked after them.

Learning from Joseph's life
- Joseph's refusal to be seduced by Potiphar's wife is admirable. Joseph reasoned, "No one is greater in this house than I am. My master has withheld nothing from me except you, because you are his wife. How then could I do such a wicked thing and sin against God?" *Genesis 39:9*
- Later when Potiphar's wife approached Joseph again, Joseph took evasive action and ran out of the house. See *Genesis 39:11,12.*

Crops being assessed for taxing. Egyptian tomb painting from around 1400 BC.

Moses

Meaning of name: Drawer out

Point of interest: Moses led the Israelites out of their slavery in Egypt, after the ten terrible plagues, into the desert, where God gave him the Ten Commandments.

Family links: Moses had one sister, Miriam, and one brother Aaron. Moses was brought up in the king of Egypt's palace because an Egyptian princess found the baby Moses, hidden in a basket among the reeds of the River Nile.

After Moses had killed a cruel Egyptian taskmaster, he was forced to flee from Egypt. He found refuge in the desert with Jethro, whose daughter, Zipporah, Moses married. They had two sons, Gershom, *Exodus 2:22; 18:3,* and Eliezer, *Exodus 18:4.* Moses named his children after events he experienced in his life. "Gershom" sounds like the Hebrew for "an alien here." Moses said, "I have become an alien in a foreign land."

"Eliezer" means "my God is helper." Moses said, "My father's God was my helper; he saved me from the sword of Pharaoh."

New Testament link: "Moses was faithful in all God's house." *Hebrews 3:2*

Quote: "You will see the deliverance the Lord will bring you today." *Exodus 14:13*

Link to Jesus: Jesus himself used the example of the bronze snake Moses put on a pole in the desert, *Numbers 21:6-9,* which saved anyone who looked to it in faith from dying of a snake bite. Jesus used it as a picture of his own resurrection.

"Just as Moses lifted up the snake in the desert, so the Son of Man must be lifted up, that everyone who believes in him may have eternal life." *John 3:14,15*

Key verse: "There the angel of the Lord appeared to him in flames of fire from within a bush. Moses saw that though the bush was on fire it did not burn up." *Exodus 3:2*

More Information: The complete books of *Exodus, Leviticus, Numbers,* and *Deuteronomy,* and *Luke 9:28-36; Hebrews 11:23-29*

16

By faith Moses ...

The writer of the letter to the Hebrews does not think of the events in Moses' life as mere secular history. He saw them as instances of how Moses lived his courageous life of faith.

"By faith Moses' parents hid him for three months after he was born, because they saw he was no ordinary child, and they were not afraid of the king's edict.

By faith Moses, when he had grown up, refused to be known as the son of Pharaoh's daughter. He chose to be mistreated along with the people of God rather than to enjoy the pleasures of sin for a short time. He regarded disgrace for the sake of Christ as of greater value than the treasures of Egypt, because he was looking ahead to his reward. By faith he left Egypt, not fearing the king's anger; he persevered because he saw him who is invisible. By faith he kept the Passover and the sprinkling of blood, so that the destroyer of the firstborn would not touch the firstborn of Israel.

By faith the people passed through the Red Sea as on dry land; but when the Egyptians tried to do so, they were drowned." *Hebrews 11:23-29*

The tabernacle

In the desert God gave Moses very detailed instructions about how the Israelites were to worship him. The portable tent, known as the tabernacle, was erected for the sole purpose of worshiping God.

"Then have them make a sanctuary for me, and I will dwell among them. Make this tabernacle and all its furnishings exactly like the pattern I will show you." *Exodus 25:8,9*

The writer to the Hebrews explains that the tabernacle has a most important spiritual meaning, which has been surpassed and fulfilled in Jesus.

"For Christ did not enter a man-made sanctuary that was only a copy of the true one; he entered heaven itself, now to appear for us in God's presence." *Hebrews 9:24*

Joshua

Joshua

Meaning of name: God is salvation

Point of interest: Joshua led the people of Israel into the Promised Land.

Family links: Joshua was the son of Nun.

New Testament link: "By faith the walls of Jericho fell, after the people had marched around them for seven days." *Hebrews 11:30*

Words spoken to: "Be strong and courageous. Do not be terrified; do not be discouraged, for the Lord your God will be with you wherever you go." *Joshua 1:9*

Key verse: "But as for me and my household, we will serve the Lord." *Joshua 24:15*

More Information: *Exodus 17:9-13; 24:13; Numbers 13–14;* the whole book of *Joshua*

Characteristics of Joshua

- Joshua was both a military and a spiritual leader.
- In the wilderness Joshua was Moses' right hand man.
- With Caleb, Joshua spied out the land of Canaan and encouraged the Israelites to attack it. He said that with God's help they could conquer the land.
- After Moses' death Joshua became the leader of the Israelites and led them into the Promised Land.

Rahab

"Rahab" means "broad." Rahab had been a prostitute, *Joshua 2:1.* But she later served God very faithfully and hid two of Joshua's spies. As a result of this when Jericho was captured by Joshua, "Rahab, her father and mother and all who belonged to her" were spared. See *Joshua 6:23.*

The letter to the Hebrews commends Rahab for acting out of faith in God:

"By faith the prostitute Rahab, because she welcomed the spies, was not killed with those who were disobedient." *Hebrews 11:31*

Ruth

Ruth

Meaning of name: Companion

Point of interest: Ruth was faithful to her mother-in-law, Naomi, and returning with her to Bethlehem, where Ruth met a relative of Naomi's, Boaz, and married him.

Family links: Ruth's son, Obed, was the father of Jesse, whose son was King David.

New Testament link: Matthew includes Ruth's name in his genealogy of Jesus, in *Matthew 1:5*.

Quote: "Don't urge me to leave you or to turn back from you. Where you go I will go, and where you stay I will stay. Your people will be my people and your God my God." *Ruth 1:16*

Key verse: "The woman said to Naomi: 'Praise be to the Lord who this day has not left you without a kinsman-redeemer.'" *Ruth 4:14*

More Information: The whole of the book of *Ruth; Matthew 1:5*.

Naomi
Naomi had:
• lost her husband, *Ruth 1:3*
• lost her sons, *Ruth 1:5*
• lost her joy, *Ruth 1:20*

But, through the faithfulness of Ruth and the generosity of Boaz, Naomi's joy was restored after she returned to Bethlehem.

"Then Naomi took the child; laid him in her lap and cared for him. The women living there said, 'Naomi has a son.'"*Ruth 4:16*

Gideon

Gideon

Meaning of name: Great warrior

Point of interest: Gideon, Israel's fifth judge and ruler, defeated the Midianites and the Amalekites — semi-nomadic peoples — and so gave the Israelites 30 years of peace.

Family links: Gideon's father was Joash. Gideon's two named sons were Jether and Abimelech. Gideon "had seventy sons of his own, for he had many wives." *Judges 8:30*

New Testament link: Gideon is only mentioned once in the New Testament. The book of Hebrews says that Gideon lived a life of faith in God. "And what more shall I say? I do not have time to tell about Gideon, Barak, Samson, Jephthah, David, Samuel and the prophets, who through faith conquered kingdoms, administered justice, and gained what was promised; who shut the mouths of lions, quenched the fury of the flames, and escaped the edge of the sword; whose weakness was turned to strength; and who became powerful in battle and routed foreign armies." *Hebrews 11:32-34*

Quote: "When I and all who are with me blow our trumpets, then from all around the camp blow yours and shout, 'For the Lord and for Gideon.'" *Judges 7:18*

Link to Jesus: Gideon was the fifth judge of the Israelites. He brought Israel back into fellowship with God by smashing his father's statue of Baal. Jesus, our advocate, brings us back into fellowship with God, as we confess our sins and ask for his forgiveness. See *1 John 1:7, 9; 2:1*.

Key verse: "The Lord said to Gideon, 'With the three hundred men that lapped I will save you and give the Midianites into your hands.'" *Judges 7:7*

More Information: *Judges 6–8*

Samson

Samson

Meaning of name: Distinguished

Point of interest: His physical strength.

Family links: Samson's father was Manoah. Samson's mother, who is not named, had been sterile and so was childless. But an angel appeared to her and told her that she would conceive and give birth to a son. Samson's parents were told that their child would be especially dedicated to God as a Nazirite who would save the Israelites from the Philistines. See *Judges 13:1-24*.
Samson married a Philistine woman from Timnah, whom the Philistines killed. Samson later fell in love with another Philistine, Delilah. Samson died childless.

New Testament link: Apart from a fleeting mention in *Hebrews 11:32*, Samson is not mentioned in the New Testament.

Quote: "'No razor has ever been used on my head,' he said, 'because I have been a Nazirite set apart to God since birth. If my head were shaved, my strength would leave me, and I would become as weak as any other man.'" *Judges 16:17*

Key verse: As a blinded prisoner, Samson's last prayer, just before he pulled down the Philistine temple on the Philistines and on himself was: "'O Sovereign Lord, remember me. O God, please strengthen me just once more, and let me with one blow get revenge on the Philistines for my two eyes.'" *Judges 16:28*

More Information: *Judges 13–16*

Samson's riddle

Samson gave the Philistines this riddle to solve. If they could not solve it they had to give him 30 linen garments and thirty sets of clothes.

> "Out of the eater, something to eat;
> out of the strong, something sweet."
> *Judges 14:14*

The answer to the riddle and what happened when the Philistines gave Samson the right answer is in *Judges 14:12-20*.

Samson destroys the Philistine temple: Gustav Doré.

Samuel

Samuel

Meaning of name: Asked of God

Point of interest: Samuel was the last great warrior-judge of Israel, and one of their first prophets.

Family links: Samuel's parents were Hannah and Elkanah. He was born in answer to Hannah's prayers. Like his mentor Eli, Samuel was unable to influence his sons to lead a godly life. See *1 Samuel 8:3*.

New Testament link: Acts 3:24 views Samuel as the first of the prophets. Samuel was the last of the judges: "After this, God gave them judges until the time of Samuel the prophet." *Acts 13:20*

Quote: "As for me, far be it from me that I should sin against the Lord by failing to pray for you." *1 Samuel 12:23*

Key verse: Samuel's final act was to anoint David, privately, to be the next king of Israel. "So Samuel took the horn of oil and anointed him [David] in the presence of his brothers, and from that day on the Spirit of the Lord came upon David in power." *1 Samuel 16:13*

More Information: *1 Samuel 1–4; 7–16*

Samuel's understanding compared with teaching in the New Testament

- Samuel told Saul that the Lord had looked for a man after God's own heart (David), and had appointed him leader of his people. Compare *1 Samuel 13:14* with *Acts 13:21, 22*.

- Samuel knew that to obey is better than sacrifice. Compare *1 Samuel 15:22* with *Mark 12:23*.

- Samuel knew that the Lord does not look on the outward appearance of a person. Compare *1 Samuel 16:7* with *2 Corinthians 10:7*.

Saul

Saul

Meaning of name: Asked

Point of interest: Saul was the first king of Israel.

Family links: Saul was son of Kish. His wives were Ahinoam and Rizpah. His children were Jonathan, Malki-Shua, Abinadab, Esh-baal (Ish-Bosheth), Armoni, Mephibosheth, Merab, Michal.

New Testament link: King Saul is not mentioned in the New Testament.

Quote: "As they danced, they sang: 'Saul has slain his thousands, and David his tens of thousands.' Saul was very angry; this refrain galled him. 'They have credited David with tens of thousands,' he thought, 'but me with only thousands. What more can he get but the kingdom?' And from that time on Saul kept a jealous eye on David." *1 Samuel 18:7-9*

Key verse: At the end of his life Saul consulted the witch of Endor. "So Saul disguised himself, putting on other clothes, and at night he and two men went to the woman. 'Consult a spirit for me,' he said, 'and bring up for me the one I name.'" *1 Samuel 28:8*

More Information: *1 Samuel 8–31; 2 Samuel 1*

The decline and fall of Saul

There are more things in Saul's life to avoid than to follow. Self-will and stubbornness were two characteristics that marred Saul's life. See *1 Samuel 15:19-23*. Saul's sin is:

- forbidden by God: see *2 Chronicles 30:8; Psalm 95:8*
- unbelief: see *2 Kings 7:14*
- pride: see *Nehemiah 9:16,29*
- refusing to listen to God: see *Proverbs 1:24*
- an evil heart: see *Jeremiah 7:24*
- rebelling against God: see *Psalm 78:8*
- resisting God's Spirit: see *Acts 7:51*.

David

David

Meaning of name: Beloved

Point of interest: David was Israel's second and greatest king, who loved the Lord with all his heart.

Family links: David was the great-grandson of Ruth and Boaz, and son of Jesse, from the tribe of Judah. He was the youngest of eight brothers. Eight of David's wives are named: Michal, Ahinoam of Jezreel (their child Amnon), Abigail, widow of Nabal (Kileab or Daniel), Maacah (Absalom), Haggith (Adonijah), Abital (Shephatiah), Eglah (Ithream), Bathsheba (Shimea, Shobab, Nathan, Solomon). Ten other children whom David had by other wives are named: see *1 Chronicles 3:6-9; 14:3,4*, not to mention other sons from David's concubines: *1 Chronicles 3:9*.

New Testament link: David is listed as an ancestor of Jesus in the two family trees of Jesus in the New Testament. "David was the father of Solomon" *Matthew 1:6*; "… the son of David …" *Luke 3:31*

Quote: After David's adultery with Bathsheba, he confessed his sin to God by saying, "Against you, you only, have I sinned and done what is evil in your sight." *Psalm 51:4*

Link to Jesus: In the Bible no one else is called David. This underlines the unique place David has as the ancestor, forerunner and foreshadower of the Lord Jesus Christ, who is great David's greater son. Jesus is repeatedly called "Son of David."

Paul says that Jesus "was a descendant of David." *Romans 1:3* Jesus himself is recorded by John as saying "'I am the Root and the Offspring of David.'" *Revelation 22:16*

Key verse: 73 of the psalms are said to be "David's" psalms. Jesus in Luke 20:42 spoke of David being the author of Psalm 110, from which he quotes to make clear how he was the Messiah. "The Lord says to my Lord: 'Sit at my right hand until I make your enemies a footstool for your feet.'" *Psalm 110:1*

More Information: The whole of *1 Samuel* and *2 Samuel; 1 Chronicles 11–29*

Goliath

"an exile" or "soothsayer"

Goliath, the Philistine champion, was over 9 feet tall. He was protected in heavy armor, and just the tip of his spear weighed 15 pounds.

- When the Israelites saw Goliath, they said that he was too big to defeat.
- When David saw Goliath, he said that he was too big to miss!

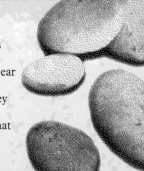

Bathsheba

"the seventh daughter"

The Bible holds up David as a spiritual giant. But it does not gloss over his faults and very serious sins. His most infamous failing came as a result of seeing Bathsheba taking her bath. Not only did he commit adultery with her, but he instigated the death of her husband, Uriah. Psalm 51 is David's great lament in which he pours out his heart to God, asking for his forgiveness.

The point about David's sins is that even though he committed them, he repented, so God was able to continue to use him in very special ways.

Absalom

"father of peace"

David greatly loved his son Absalom, but Absalom tried to steal the heart of the Israelites so he could gain his father's throne. He met his death in a most unusual way.

"Now Absalom happened to meet David's men. He was riding his mule, and as the mule went under the thick branches of a large oak, Absalom's head got caught in the tree. He was left hanging in mid-air, while the mule he was riding kept on going." *2 Samuel 18:9*

Joab and his men then killed Absalom.

Solomon

"Peace"

Solomon was the son of David and Bathsheba. Solomon succeeded David on Israel's throne. He build a magnificent temple in Jerusalem to honor the Lord.

Solomon used 30,000 men of Israel to transport cedar and pine logs from Lebanon.

"Solomon had seventy thousand carriers and eighty thousand stone-cutters in the hills, as well as thirty-three hundred foremen who supervised the project and directed the workmen." *1 Kings 5:15*

Elijah

Elijah

Meaning of name: The Lord is my God
Point of interest: His confrontation with the prophets of Baal on Mount Carmel.
Family links: Nothing is known about Elijah's family.
New Testament link: *Malachi 4:5,6* says that Elijah's ministry will be revived before the coming of the great and dreadful day of the Lord. Jesus said that this all applied to John the Baptist. See *Matthew 11:14; 17:11,12* Elijah appeared in person when Jesus was transfigured. See *Mark 9:4*.

Quote: "'How long will you waver between two opinions? If the Lord is God, follow him; but if Baal is God, follow him.'" *1 Kings 18:21*
Key verse: Elijah was the greatest ecstatic prophet in the Old Testament and his Spirit-led actions often left people confused. "'But now you tell me to go to my master and say, "Elijah is here." I don't know where the Spirit of the Lord may carry you when I leave you. If I go and tell Ahab and he doesn't find you, he will kill me.'" *1 Kings 18:11,12*
More Information: *1 Kings 17–19; 2 Kings 1–2; Luke 4:25, 26; Romans 11:2-4; James 5:17,18*

The most prominent prophet

Elijah was the most prominent prophet of his time, 875–850 BC. He lived at a critical time in the history of Israel. The evil king, Ahab, married Jezebel who was the daughter of Ethbaal, king of Sidon. Jezebel persuaded Ahab to adopt the worship of Baal.

Elijah spent his energy in confronting Queen Jezebel and King Ahab as they attempted to draw the Israelites away from the worship of the one true God.

Prophets of Israel

Before Elijah and Elisha there were three prophets who prophesied to the northern kingdom of Israel: Ahijah, Iddo, and Jehu.

After Elijah and Elisha there were two prophets who prophesied to the kingdom of Israel: Amos and Hosea.

View from the top of Mount Carmel.

Elisha

Elisha

Meaning of name: God is Savior

Point of interest: Elisha was Elijah's disciple. He carryied on the prophetic work after watching Elijah being "translated" as he was caught up in a chariot of fire. Elisha performed 14 miracles, the most notable one being the curing of General Naaman of his leprosy.

Family links: Elisha's father was Shaphat.

New Testament link: *Luke 4:27* is the only New Testament reference to Elisha.

Quote: "Let me inherit a double portion of your spirit." *2 Kings 2:9*

Key verse: "The company of the prophets from Jericho, who were watching, said, 'The spirit of Elijah is resting on Elisha.'" *2 Kings 2:15*

More Information: *1 Kings 19:16,19-21; 2 Kings 2–9; 13:14-20*

Kings of Israel

After the Israelites split into two kingdoms, the northern kingdom of Israel was ruled by seventeen kings before it was captured by Assyria in 722 BC.

The kings of Israel were: Jeroboam I, Nadab, Baasha, Elah, Zimri, Omri, Ahab, Ahaziah, Jehoram, Jehu, Jehoahaz, Jehoash, Jeroboam II, Zechariah, Shallum, Manahem, Pekahiah, Pekah, and Hoshea.

Elijah and Elisha were prophets in the reigns of Ahab, Ahaziah, and Jehoram.

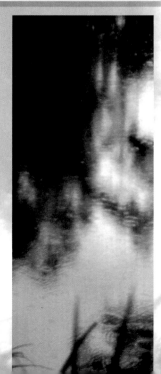

Isaiah

Isaiah

Meaning of name: Salvation of God

Point of interest: His call to be a prophet, recorded in *Isaiah 6:1-13*, when he saw an awe-inspiring vision of God.

Family links: Isaiah was the son of Amoz. He lived in Jerusalem. We are not told the name of Isaiah's wife. She is just called "the prophetess" in *Isaiah 8:3*.

Isaiah gave his children significant names. His first son was called Shear-Jashub meaning "a remnant will return." Isaiah's second son was called, Maher-Shalal-Hash-Baz, meaning, "quick to the plunder." "And the Lord said to me, 'Name him Maher-Shalal-Hash-Baz. Before the boy knows how to say "My father" or "My mother," the wealth of Damascus and the plunder of Samaria will be carried off by the king of Assyria'" *Isaiah 8:3,4*. This meant that the enemies of King Ahaz would be plundered.

New Testament link: *Isaiah 7:14* is quoted in *Matthew 1:23* as a prophecy about the virgin birth of Jesus.

Quote: "My eyes have seen the King, the Lord Almighty." *Isaiah 6:5*

Link to Jesus: Jesus fulfilled *Isaiah 42:1-4*. See *Matthew 12:18-21*.

Key verses: *Isaiah 52:13–53:12* is the most detailed Old Testament prophecy about the death of Jesus, the messiah and suffering servant.

More Information: The whole of the book of *Isaiah,* especially *Isaiah 1:1; 7:3; 8:1-4*

Isaiah and the kings of Judah

According to the opening verse of the book of Isaiah, the prophet gave his prophecies during the reigns of Uzziah, Jotham, Ahaz, and Hezekiah.

There were nine kings of Judah before this: Rehoboam, Abijam, Asa, Jehoshaphat, Jehoram, Ahaziah, Athaliah, Joash, and Amaziah.

After Isaiah's ministry there were seven further kings of Judah, before Jerusalem fell to the Babylonians in 586 BC: Manasseh, Amon, Josiah, Jehoahaz, Jehoiakim, Jehoiachin, and Zedekiah.

Jonah

Jonah

Meaning of name: Dove

Point of interest: Jonah was swallowed by a great fish. Jonah was the first Hebrew prophet to be sent into a Gentile (non-Jewish) country. He prophesied during the reign of King Jeroboam II of Israel.

Family links: Jonah's father was Amittai: *Jonah 1:1.* Jonah came from Gath Hepher, *2 Kings 14:25*, a Zebulunite town near to Nazareth.

New Testament link: Jesus mentioned Jonah. "A wicked and adulterous generation asks for a miraculous sign! But none will be given it except the sign of the prophet Jonah. For as Jonah was in the belly of a huge fish, so the Son of Man will be three days and three nights in the heart of the earth." *Matthew 12:39,40*

Quote: In chapter 2 of Jonah's prophecy, the prophet records his prayer from the belly of the huge fish: "In my distress I called to the Lord, and he answered me. From the depths of the grave I called for help, and you listened to my cry." *Jonah 2:2*

Link to Jesus: Jesus likened Jonah's experience in the belly of the fish to his own resurrection. Jesus told some of the Pharisees and teachers of the law that the sign of the prophet Jonah was the only miraculous sign they needed to see.

Key verse: From the seaport of Joppa Nineveh was 500 miles northeast across desert. Going to Tarshish meant traveling 2,000 miles west. "But Jonah ran away from the Lord and headed for Tarshish." *Jonah 1:3*

More Information: *2 Kings 14:25;* the whole of the book of *Jonah*; *Matthew 12:29-31; 16:4, 17*

Jeremiah

Jeremiah

Meaning of name: God is high

Point of interest: Jeremiah was the great prophet of Judah who prophesied, from about 625–585 BC, during the grim reigns of the last five kings of Judah: Josiah, Jehoahaz, Jehoiakim, Jehoiachin, and Zedekiah.

Family links: "The words of Jeremiah son of Hilkiah, one of the priests at Anathoth in the territory of Benjamin." *Jeremiah 1:1*

New Testament link: One of the most renowned prophecies made by Jeremiah concerns his description of a new covenant.

"'The time is coming,' declares the Lord,
'when I will make a new covenant with the house of Israel
and with the house of Judah.
It will not be like the covenant
I made with their forefathers
when I took them by the hand
to lead them out of Egypt,
because they broke my covenant,
though I was a husband to them,'
declares the Lord.
'This is the covenant that I will make
with the house of Israel
after that time,' declares the Lord.
'I will put my law in their minds
and write it on their hearts.
I will be their God,
and they will be my people.'"
Jeremiah 31:31-33
Compare this with *Hebrews 8:8-10; 10:16, 17.*

Quote: "Can the Ethiopian change his skin or the leopard its spots?" *Jeremiah 13:23*

Link to Jesus: Jeremiah speaks of "The Lord our Righteousness." *Jeremiah 23:6.* Paul explains how Jesus is our righteousness in *Romans 3:21, 22.*

Key verse: Jeremiah constantly called the Israelites to obey God. "Obey me, and I will be your God and you will be my people." *Jeremiah 7:23*

More Information: The whole of the book of *Jeremiah.*

Jeremiah: the prophet no one listened to

Jeremiah was given a thankless task by God. For 40 years Jeremiah warned the people who lived in Jerusalem that unless they turned back to God they would be captured and taken away by the Babylonians. Most of the time his preaching fell on deaf ears.

- Jeremiah was rejected: *Jeremiah 11:18-21.*
- Even Jeremiah's friends were fickle: *Jeremiah 12:2-6.*
- Jeremiah was plagued by false prophets. He confronted them face to face: *Jeremiah 14:13-16; 28:10-17.*
- Jeremiah was often threatened with violence and endured persecution: *Jeremiah 15:10-18.*

Jeremiah's prophecy comes true

Jeremiah not only warned the people that Jerusalem would be captured, he also predicted that the Israelites would return to Jerusalem 70 years later.

1. Jerusalem was captured

"Nebuzaradan commander of the imperial guard, who served the king of Babylon, came to Jerusalem. He set fire to the temple of the Lord, the royal palace and all the houses of Jerusalem. Every important building he burned down." *Jeremiah 52:12,13*

- Jeremiah predicted this in *Jeremiah 25:8-11.*
- The book of *Lamentations*, also written by Jeremiah, is a description of Jerusalem after it had been ransacked.

2. Israelites return to Jerusalem

70 years later Cyrus, king of Persia, allowed Israelites to return to Jerusalem. See *2 Chronicles 36:15-23.*

Deportation of Assyrian captives

- Jeremiah was put in the stocks: *Jeremiah 20:1,2.*
- On a number of occasions Jeremiah barely escaped with his life: *Jeremiah 26:8, 36:26.*
- Accused of treason, Jeremiah was imprisoned: *Jeremiah 32:2,3; 37:11-15.*
- Jeremiah had some of his prophecies burned by King Jehoiakim: *Jeremiah 36:22-25.*
- Jeremiah was lowered by ropes into a cistern and left to die: *Jeremiah 38:6.* If it had not been for the courage of Ebed-Melech, who alerted King Zedekiah to the evil behind this action, Jeremiah would have died. As it was, Ebed-Melech rescued him.
- Jeremiah was bound in chains: *Jeremiah 40:1.*

Esther

Esther

Point of interest: Esther saved the Jews from being massacred.

Family links: Esther was an orphan. She was brought up by her uncle, Mordecai.

New Testament link: Esther is not mentioned in the New Testament.

Quote: "Esther said, 'The adversary and enemy is this vile Haman.'" *Esther 7:6*

Link to Jesus: Mordecai has been seen as a type of Jesus for the following reasons:

- Mordecai adopted Esther: *Esther 2:7* Although we were orphans, and in the world without hope, Jesus received us into God's family: *John 1:12; Ephesians 2:8, 9, 12, 13.*
- As Mordecai was despised, *Esther 3:5,* so was Jesus, *Isaiah 53:3; John 15:25.*
- As Mordecai was tested, *Esther 4:1,* so was Jesus, *Matthew 4:1-11; Luke 22:42.*
- As Mordecai finally received a place of honor, *Esther 6:1-3; 8:7,8,* so did Jesus in his resurrection, *Ephesians 1:20-23; Hebrews 1:3.*

Key verse: "'For if you remain silent at this time, relief and deliverance for the Jews will arise from another place, but you and your father's family will perish. And who knows but that you have come to royal position for such a time as this.'" *Esther 4:14*

More Information: The whole book of Esther.

The beauty queen
When King Xerxes looked for a new wife a competition took place to find him "beautiful young virgins," *Esther 2:2.* Esther, "who was lovely in form and features," *Esther 2:7,* won the beauty competition and became the new queen.

Brave Esther
When Mordecai told Esther that the king's minister, Haman, plotted to kill all the Jews, Esther pleaded with Xerxes for the Jews, even though she risked her own life in doing this.

Daniel

Daniel

Meaning of name: "God is my judge"

Point of interest: Daniel was thrown into a lions' den, and spending a whole night with them, without being harmed.

Family links: Daniel came from an aristocratic Jerusalem family, but apart from that we know nothing about his family. When Jerusalem was captured by Nebuchadnezzar, Daniel, as a teenager, was exiled to Babylon, where he rose to prominence because of his ability to interpret dreams. Following the custom of the time he was given a Babylonian name, Belteshazzar, *Daniel 1:7.*

New Testament link: The allusion in *Hebrews 11:33* to lions, "who shut the mouths of lions," seems a clear reference to Daniel's experience recorded in *Daniel 6.*

Quote: "O king, live forever! My God sent his angel, and he shut the mouths of the lions. They have not hurt me, because I was found innocent in his sight." *Daniel 6:22*

Link to Jesus: Jesus is seen by Daniel:
• as the Ancient of Days, *Daniel 7:9*
• a son of man, *Daniel 7:13*
• the Prince of princes, *Daniel 8:25*
• the most holy, *Daniel 9:24,*
• the Anointed One, *Daniel 9:25.*

Key verse: "'In my visions ... one like a son of man ... was given authority, glory, and sovereign power; all peoples, nations and men of every language worshiped him. His dominion is an everlasting dominion that will not pass away, and his kingdom is one that will never be destroyed.'" *Daniel 7:13, 14*

More Information: The whole book of *Daniel; Matthew 24:15*

Ezekiel and the prophets of Judah

Not well received

Many of Ezekiel's prophecies were badly received.

> "And you, son of man, they will tie with ropes; you will be bound so that you cannot go out among the people."
> *Ezekiel 3:25*

Not followed

Even when the Jews did listen to Ezekiel they did not do what he told them to.

> "Indeed, to them you are nothing more than one who sings love songs with a beautiful voice and plays an instrument well, for they hear your words but do not put them into practice." *Ezekiel 33:32*

Ezekiel and salvation

Ezekiel gives many pictures and visions depicting what happens when God saves us. In chapter 16 Ezekiel says that:

- God makes us alive: *verse 6*
- God cleanses and washes us: *verse 9*
- God clothes us: *verses 8,11*
- God claims us for himself: *verse 8*
- God crowns us: *verse 12*.

Ezekiel

Meaning of name: God strengthens

Point of interest: Ezekiel comforted the Jews who were in exile in Babylon. Ezekiel had been exiled from Jerusalem and lived in Babylon with a community of Jews at Talabib on the River Chebar, *Ezekiel 1:1*. There he told the Jews that God would restore Jerusalem to them and they would be able to rebuild God's temple.

Family links: Ezekiel was the son of Buzi the priest. Ezekiel's wife died the day Nebuchadnezzar besieged Jerusalem, *Ezekiel 24:1,2, 15-17*. No mention is made of any children.

New Testament link: Ezekiel predicts a caring shepherd, calling him "my servant David," "'I will place over them one shepherd, my servant David, and he will tend them; he will tend them and be their shepherd.'" *Ezekiel 34: 23*. A favorite description of Jesus is recorded in John's Gospel, "'I am the good shepherd. The good shepherd lays down his life for the sheep.'" *John 10:11*

Quote: "You will know that I am the Lord." *Ezekiel 6:7*. This phrase comes more than 60 times in the book named after Ezekiel.

Link to Jesus:
- *Ezekiel 17: 22-24*, depicts the Messiah as a tender twig that becomes a stately cedar on a high mountain. Jesus is also called the Branch in *Isaiah 11:1; Jeremiah 24:5; 33:15;* and *Zechariah 3:8; 6:12*.
- The Messiah is the King who has the right to rule, *Ezekiel 21:26,27*, and he is the true Shepherd who will deliver and feed his flock, *Ezekiel 34:11-31*.

Key verse: "The hand of the Lord was upon me, and he brought me out by the Spirit of the Lord and set me in the middle of a valley; it was full of bones." *Ezekiel 37:1*

More Information: The whole book of *Ezekiel*

The prophets of Judah

Five prophets, who do not have books in the Bible named after them, nevertheless prophesied to the people of Judah:

- Shemaiah
- Hanani
- Huldah.
- Azariah
- Jahaziel

Seven prophets, who do have books in the Bible recording their prophecies, spoke to the people of Judah:

- Joel
- Micah
- Habakkuk
- Ezekiel.
- Isaiah
- Zephaniah
- Jeremiah

Ezra

Ezra

Meaning of name: The Lord helps

Point of interest: Ezra led a second group of Israelite exiles from Babylon back to Jerusalem. In this way Ezra shows how God fulfilled his promise to return his people to Jerusalem after their 70 years of exile.

New Testament link: Ezra shows how God kept his promise to keep David's descendants alive. Zerubbabel, a leader of a group who returned from exile *(Ezra 3–5)* is part of the messianic line as he was the grandson of Jeconiah. See *1 Chronicles 3:17-19* and *Matthew 1:12,13.*

Quote: "'O my God, I am too ashamed and disgraced to lift up my face to you, my God, because our sins are higher than our heads and our guilt has reached to the heavens." *Ezra 9:7*

Link to Jesus: The book of Ezra as a whole typifies Jesus' work of forgiveness and restoration.

Key verse: "For Ezra had devoted himself to the study and observance of the Law of the Lord, and to teaching its decrees and laws in Israel." *Ezra 7:10*

More Information: The whole book of Ezra; *Nehemiah 8:1-9; 12:36*

Godly Ezra

Ezra was a godly man with:
• a strong trust in the Lord:
  Ezra 9:6-15
• moral integrity:
  Ezra 10:9-17
• an outrage about people sinning against God:
  Ezra 9:3,4.

Nehemiah

Nehemiah and prayer
- Nehemiah began his work in prayer: *Nehemiah 1:4.*
- Nehemiah continued his work in prayer: *Nehemiah 4:9.*
- Nehemiah did not stop praying when he had finished his work: *Nehemiah 13:31.*

Joseph

Joseph

Meaning of name: May (God) add
Family links: Joseph, a carpenter, was a descendant of king David: see *Matthew 1:20*. His wife was Mary.
Link with Jesus:
- Joseph acted as a father towards Jesus.
- Joseph took Jesus to Jerusalem for the purification, *Luke 2:2*.
- Joseph took the toddler Jesus and Mary to Egypt, to escape King Herod's murderous intentions.
- Joseph took Jesus and Mary from Egypt to Nazareth and settled there, *Matthew 2:19-23*.
- Joseph took Jesus to Jerusalem for the Passover, *Luke 2:41*.

- It seems probable that at least by the time Jesus was twelve years old he knew that Joseph was not his father. "'Why were you searching for me?' he [Jesus] asked. 'Didn't you know I had to be in my Father's house?'" *Luke 2:49*

Key verse: "'Joseph son of David, do not be afraid to take Mary home as your wife, because what is conceived in her is from the Holy Spirit.' *Matthew 1:20*

More Information: *Matthew 1:20-25; 2:13-23; Luke 1:27–2:52*

Joseph obeys

Little is known about Jesus' foster father Joseph. But his utter obedience to God is clear from the way he obeyed what God told him to do in his dreams.
- "The Lord appeared to him [Joseph] in a dream and said, 'Joseph … take Mary home as your wife.'" *Matthew 1:20*
- "An angel of the Lord appeared to Joseph in a dream. 'Get up,' he said, 'take the child and his mother and escape to Egypt.' … So he got up, took the child and his mother during the night and left for Egypt." *Matthew 2:13,14*.

- "An angel of the Lord appeared in a dream to Joseph in Egypt and said, 'Get up, take the child and his mother and go to the land of Israel.'" *Matthew 2:19,20*

What happened to Joseph?

The last time we hear about Joseph being alive was when Jesus visited the temple as a twelve-year-old. Joseph is not mentioned during Jesus' ministry.

Mary

Mary

Meaning of name: "Mary" is a form of "Miriam" meaning "strong"

Point of interest: Mary was the mother of Jesus.

Family links: Mary was living in Nazareth, a town in Galilee, engaged to Joseph, when an angel told Mary that, although she was still a virgin, she would be the mother of Jesus. Mary visited her relative Elizabeth who later gave birth to John the Baptist.

Old Testament link: Mary knew that the birth of Jesus was in fulfillment of the prophecy of *Isaiah 7:14*, which stated that a virgin would give birth to a son. See *Matthew 1:22,23*.

Quote: "'I am the Lord's servant,' Mary answered. 'May it be to me as you have said.'" *Luke 1:38*

Link with Jesus: Mary was not only the mother of Jesus, but was also present at different points in Jesus' ministry, such as the turning of water into wine at Cana, *John 2:1-22*. Mary also watched Jesus being crucified, and was with Jesus' apostles after Jesus' resurrection. "They all joined together constantly in prayer, along with the women and Mary the mother of Jesus, and with his brothers." *Acts 1:14*

Key verse: "His mother [Mary] said to the servants, 'Do whatever he [Jesus] tells you.'" *Luke 2:5*

More Information: *Matthew 1–2; Mark 3:31-35; Luke 1–2; 11:27,28; John 2:1-22; 19:25-27; Acts 1:14*

Mary's faith

Mary expressed her faith when on her visit to Elizabeth, she said a song of praise, which we now call the Magnificat.

"My soul glorifies the Lord
    and my spirit rejoices in God
    my savior,
for he has been mindful
    of the humble state of his
    servant."
Luke 1:46-48

The life of Jesus

Jesus

Meaning of name: The Lord is salvation

Point of interest: Jesus is the Savior of the world.

Family links: Jesus' conception was miraculous. Mary was still a virgin when Jesus was conceived. The angel told the virgin Mary, "You will be with child and give birth to a son, and you are to give him the name Jesus." *Luke 1:31*

Matthew traces Jesus' family tree through Joseph back to Abraham. "A record of the genealogy of Jesus Christ the son of David, the son of Abraham." *Matthew 1:1*

Luke traces Jesus' family tree back to Adam: *Luke 3:23-38.*

Old Testament link: "'Do not think that I have come to abolish the Law or the Prophets; I have not come to abolish them but to fulfill them.'" *Matthew 5:17*

Quote: Jesus' crucifixion was planned by God and did not take Jesus by surprise. In the same way Jesus' resurrection should not have taken the disciples by surprise. "And he [Jesus] said, 'The Son of Man must suffer many things and be rejected by the elders, chief priests and teachers of the law, and he must be killed and on the third day be raised to life.'" *Luke 9:21, 22*

Key verse: Jesus tells us who God is like. "In the past God spoke to our forefathers through the prophets at many times and in various ways, but in these last days he has spoken to us by his Son, whom he appointed heir of all things, and through whom he made the universe. The Son is the radiance of God's glory and the exact representation of his being, sustaining all things by his powerful word." *Hebrews 1:1-3*

More Information: The whole of *Matthew, Mark, Luke,* and *John*

Events in Jesus' life

Jesus' childhood

Event	Place	Date	Reference in the Gospels
Birth of Jesus	Bethlehem	c. 6/5 BC	*Matthew 1:18-25; Luke 2:1-7*
Visit by shepherds	Bethlehem		*Luke 2:8-20*
Presentation in the temple	Jerusalem		*Luke 2:21-40*
Visit by the Magi	Bethlehem		*Matthew 2:1-12*
Escape to Egypt	Nile Delta		*Matthew 2:13-18*
Return to Nazareth	Lower Galilee		*Matthew 2:19-23*
Visit to temple	Jerusalem	c. AD 7/8	*Luke 2:41-52*

None of the four Gospels give any details about Jesus' life from the time that he went to the temple, aged twelve years old, to when Jesus arrived at the River Jordan and was baptized by John the Baptist.

All we have is the following two-verse summary by Luke.

> "Then he [Jesus] went down to Nazareth with them [Mary and Joseph] and was obedient to them. But his mother treasured all these things in her heart. And Jesus grew in wisdom and stature, and in favor with God and men." *Luke 2:51,52*

You would have thought that the one place where Jesus would be welcome was the place where he grew up. Yes and no. Yes, "All spoke well of him." *Luke 4:22*

No, "They got up, drove him [Jesus] out of the town, and took him to the brow of the hill ... in order to throw him down the cliff. But he walked right through the crowd and went on his way." *Luke 4:29,30*

First year of Jesus' public ministry

Event	Place	Date	Reference in the Gospels
Jesus is baptized	River Jordan	c. AD 26	*Matthew 3:13-17*
Jesus is tempted by Satan	Desert		*Matthew 4:1-11*
Jesus' first miracle	Cana		*John 2:1-11*
Jesus and Nicodemus	Jerusalem		*John 3:1-21*
Jesus and the Samaritan woman	Samaria	c. AD 27	*John 4:5-42*
Jesus heals the nobleman's son	Cana		*John 4:46-54*
People try to kill Jesus	Nazareth		*Luke 4:16-31*

Events in Jesus' life

Jesus' year of popularity

Event	Place	Date	Reference in the Gospels
Four fishermen follow Jesus	Capernaum	AD 28	*Matthew 3:13-17*
Jesus preaches in Galilee			*Matthew 4:23-25*
Jesus chooses his twelve disciples			*Mark 3:13-19*
Jesus preaches the Sermon on the Mount			*Matthew 5:1–7:29*

The most famous part of the Sermon on the Mount is the Beatitudes:

"Blessed are the poor in spirit, for theirs is the kingdom of heaven.
Blessed are those who mourn, for they will be comforted.
Blessed are the meek, for they will inherit the earth.
Blessed are those who hunger and thirst for righteousness, for they will be filled.
Blessed are the merciful, for they will be shown mercy.
Blessed are the pure in heart, for they will see God.
Blessed are the peacemakers, for they will be called sons of God.
Blessed are those who are persecuted because of righteousness, for theirs is the kingdom of heaven.
Blessed are you when people insult you, persecute you and falsely say all kinds of evil against you because of me. Rejoice and be glad, because great is your reward in heaven, for in the same way they persecuted the prophets who were before you."
Matthew 5:1-12

Jesus' year of opposition

Event	Place	Date	Reference in the Gospels
John the Baptist beheaded	Machaerus	AD 29	*Matthew 14:1-12*
Peter says Jesus is the Son of God	Caesarea Philippi		*Matthew 16:21-26*
Jesus is transfigured			*Matthew 17:1-13*
Jesus brings Lazarus back to life	Bethany		*John 11:1-44*
Jesus sets off for Jerusalem		AD 30	*Luke 17:11*

Jesus' last week

Event	Place	Day	Reference in the Gospels
Palm Sunday	Jerusalem	Sunday	*Matthew 21:1-11*
Jesus curses the fig-tree		Monday	*Matthew 21:18,19*
Jesus cleanses the temple		Monday	*Matthew 21:18,19*
Jesus' authority challenged		Tuesday	*Matthew 21:23-27*
Jesus teaches in the temple		Tuesday	*Matthew 21:28–23:39*
Jesus is anointed	Bethany	Tuesday	*Matthew 26:6-13*
Jesus is plotted against	Jerusalem	Wednesday	*Matthew 26:17-29*
The Last Supper		Thursday	*Matthew 26:17-29*
Jesus teaches his disciples		Thursday	*John 14:1–16:33*
Jesus in the Garden of Gethsemane		Thursday	*Matthew 26:36-46*
Jesus' arrest and trials		Thurs/Fri	*Matthew 26:47–27:26*
Jesus is crucified		Friday	*Matthew 27:27-56*
Jesus is buried	Joseph's tomb	Friday	*Matthew 27:57-66*

In his life

"In his life Christ is an example,
showing us how to live;
In his death he is a sacrifice,
satisfying for our sins;
In his resurrection, a conqueror;
In his ascension, a king;
In his intercession, a high
priest." *Martin Luther*

Jesus' resurrection

Event	Place	Day	Reference in the Gospels
The empty tomb	Jerusalem	Sunday	*Matthew 28:1-10*
Mary Magdalene sees the risen Jesus	Jerusalem	Sunday	*Mark 16:9-11*
Jesus appears to the two going to Emmaus		Sunday	*Mark 16:12,13*
Jesus appears to ten disciples	Jerusalem	Sunday	*John 20:19-25*
Jesus appears to eleven disciples	Jerusalem	1wk later	*John 20:26-31*
Jesus talks to some of his disciples	Sea of Galilee	1 wk later	*John 21:1-25*
Jesus ascends to his Father in heaven	Mount of Olives	40 days later	*Luke 24:44-53*

Elizabeth and Zechariah

Elizabeth

Meaning of name: God is my oath

Point of interest: Elizabeth was the mother of John the Baptist. This was a miraculous conception as Elizabeth was barren and "well on in years." See *Luke 1:7.*

Family links: Wife of Zechariah, who was also descended from the high priest Aaron.

Quote: When Mary visited Elizabeth, Elizabeth greeted Mary with the words: "Blessed are you among women, and blessed is the child you shall bear!" *Luke 1:42*

Link with Jesus: Elizabeth's son baptized Jesus.

Key verse: "When Elizabeth heard Mary's greeting, the baby leaped in her womb, and Elizabeth was filled with the Holy Spirit." *Luke 1:41*

More Information: *Luke 1*

Zechariah

Meaning of name: The Lord remembers

Point of interest: Zechariah was the father of John the Baptist.

Family links: Zechariah was a godly priest who belonged to the priestly division of Abijah.

Old Testament link: David had separated the priests into different divisions "for their appointed order of ministering." *1 Chronicles 24:3* "The eighth [lot fell] to Abijah." *1 Chronicles 24:10*

Quote: When an angel told Zechariah that his wife Elizabeth would have a son, Zechariah was incredulous. So Zechariah was unable to speak until his baby was born and named John.

Link with Jesus: Zechariah's son baptized Jesus.

Key verse: "Then they made signs to his father, to find out what he would like to name the child. He asked for a writing tablet, and to everyone's astonishment he wrote, 'His name is John.'" *Luke 1:63*

More Information: *Luke 1*

Simeon and Anna

Two people in the temple
When Joseph and Mary took the baby Jesus to the temple in Jerusalem, just five miles from Bethlehem, in order to present him to the Lord, they met two godly people.

Simeon

Meaning of name: He hears
Point of interest: Simeon was given special insight by God's Spirit to recognize Jesus as the Christ.
Quote: The words Simeon said of Jesus are sometimes called the *Nunc Dimittis*, after the first words of the Latin Vulgate translation: "[You] now dismiss."

Link with Jesus: Simeon took him [Jesus] in his arms and praised God, saying: "Sovereign Lord, as you have promised, you now dismiss your servant in peace." *Luke 2:29*
More Information: *Luke 2:25-35*

Anna

Meaning of name: Grace
Point of interest: Anna greeted the baby Jesus in the temple, whom she recognized as the Messiah.
Family links: Daughter of Phanuel, of the tribe of Asher.
Old Testament link: Anna was a prophetess, *Luke 2:36*. Prophetesses in the Old Testament include Miriam, *Exodus 15:20;* Deborah, *Judges 4:4*, and Huldah, *2 Kings 22:14*.
Link with Jesus: "Coming up to them [Joseph, Mary, and the baby Jesus] at

that very moment, she gave thanks to God and spoke about the child to all who were looking forward to the redemption of Jerusalem." *Luke 2:38*
Key verse: Anna was very old, either 84 years old, or she had been a widow for 84 years, which would make her over 100 years old. "She never left the temple but worshiped night and day, fasting and praying." *Luke 2:37*
More Information: *Luke 2:36-38*

Augustus, Tiberius, and Herod

Augustus

Meaning of name: "August"
Point of interest: When he became the first Roman Emperor he took the name Octavian, ruling from 31 BC to AD 14. The census which brought Joseph and Mary to Bethlehem for Jesus' birth was ordered by Augustus.
Family links: He was the nephew and successor of Julius Caesar.
More Information: See *Luke 2:1*

Tiberius

Meaning of name: "Son of Tiber"
Point of interest: Also known as Claudius Caesar Augustus. He was Roman Emperor from AD 14 to AD 37, that is during most of Jesus' lifetime.
Key verse: "In the fifteenth year of the reign of Tiberius Caesar … " *Luke 3:1*

Herod

Meaning of name: [Herod, known as Herod the Great] Heroic
Point of interest: Herod ordered the massacre of all the male babies under the age of two in Bethlehem.
Family links: By murdering his rivals Herod became king of Judea in 37 BC, and ruled until 4 BC. Herod murdered many of his sons, fearing their plots against him.
Quote: To the Magi, Herod said, "Go and make a careful search for the child. As soon as you find him, report to me, so that I too may go and worship him." *Matthew 2:8*
Link with Jesus: Joseph took Mary and Jesus to Egypt after he had been warned in a dream that Herod was "going to search for the child to kill him." *Matthew 2:13*
Key verse: "After Jesus was born in Bethlehem in Judea, during the time of King Herod … " *Matthew 2:1*. As Herod died in 4 BC, we know that Jesus must have been born before 4 BC, rather than in 0 AD.
More Information: *Matthew 2; Luke 1:5*

John the Baptist

John

Meaning of name: The Lord is gracious

Point of interest: John baptized Jesus.

Family links: John's Father, Zechariah, was a priest. As John's mother, Elizabeth, was related to Mary the mother of Jesus, John was related to Jesus.

Old Testament link: John looked like an Old Testament prophet, with his camels' hair clothes and leather belt. He lived in the desert eating wild honey and locusts.

Luke said that John fulfilled Isaiah's prophecy:

"A voice of one calling in the desert, 'Prepare the way for the Lord, make straight paths for him ...
And all mankind will see God's salvation.'" *Luke 3:4-6*

Quote: John was outspoken in his condemnation of the Pharisees and Sadducees. "He said to them: 'You brood of vipers! Who warned you to flee from the coming wrath? Produce fruit in keeping with repentance. And do not think you can say to yourselves, "We have Abraham as our father."'" *Matthew 3:7-9*

Link with Jesus: Speaking about John the Baptist, Jesus said, "'I tell you the truth: Among those born of women there has not risen anyone greater than John the Baptist ... '" *Matthew 11:11*

Key verse: John the Baptist told Herod the tetrach off for marrying his brother Philip's wife while Philip was still alive. This led to John being beheaded. "'It is not lawful for you to have her.'" *Matthew 14:4*

More Information: *Matthew 3; 11:1-19; 14:1-12; Mark 1:1-8; Luke 1; John 1:1-34*

Peter

Peter

Meaning of name: Rock

Point of interest: Peter said that Jesus was the Christ. "'Who do you say I am?' Simon Peter answered, 'You are the Christ, the Son of the living God.'" *Matthew 16:16*

Family links: Andrew was Peter's brother.

Old Testament link: On the Day of Pentecost, when Peter preached the first Christian sermon, he included the following quotation from *Joel 2:28*: "'In the last days, God says, I will pour out my Spirit on all people.'" *Acts 2:17*

Quote: Peter denied knowing Jesus three times. "Then he [Peter] began to call down curses on himself and he swore to them, 'I don't know the man!'" *Matthew 26:74*

Link with Jesus: In the list of Jesus' twelve apostles Peter always comes at the top of the list as he was their outspoken leader.

Key verse: Although Peter had been tempestuous as a young follower of Jesus, in his old age he encouraged others with these words: "Humble yourselves, therefore, under God's mighty hand, that he may lift you up in due course." *1 Peter 5:6*

More Information: *Acts 1–12;* the whole of *1 Peter* and *2 Peter*. Peter is often mentioned in the four Gospels.

48

Peter and the New Testament

Traditionally it is thought that much of Mark's Gospel was derived from Peter and may have been a summary of his preaching.

The two letters *1 Peter* and *2 Peter* were written by Peter.

Peter's death

According to tradition Peter was crucified upside-down in Rome in the AD 60s, during the reign of Nero.

Andrew

Andrew

Meaning of name: Manly

Point of interest: Andrew introduced Peter to Jesus.

Family links: Andrew, with his brother Peter, and with James and John, ran a small fishing partnership on Lake Galilee.

Quote: Andrew brought a boy, who had his own packed lunch, to Jesus, which Jesus miraculously used to feed more than 5,000 people. "Andrew, Simon Peter's brother, spoke up, 'Here is a boy with five small barley loaves and two small fish, but how far will they go among so many?'" *John 6:8, 9*

Link with Jesus: Andrew became one of Jesus' first disciples.

Key verse: "Andrew, Simon Peter's brother, was one of the two who heard what John had said and who had followed Jesus. The first thing Andrew did was to find his brother Simon and tell him, 'We have found the Messiah' (that is, the Christ). And he brought him to Jesus." *John 1:40-42*

More Information: *Matthew 4:18-20; Mark 1:16-18; John 1:35-42; 6:8,9*

49

Loaves and fish: mosaic at Tabgha, on the shores of Lake Galilee.

James

James

Meaning of name: "James" is a form of "Jacob" which means "supplanter"

Point of interest: James was one of Jesus' disciples.

Family links: James' brother was John, another of Jesus' disciples. The two brothers, with their father, Zebedee, ran a small family business as fishermen. James and John were given the nicknames of "Sons of Thunder," presumably because they had stormy natures. "Jesus … appointed twelve … apostles … James son of Zebedee and his brother John (to them he gave the name Boanerges, which means Sons of Thunder)." *Mark 3:13,14,17*

Old Testament link: When Jesus was setting out for Jerusalem he sent messengers ahead of him to a Samaritan village to get things ready for him. However, this village did not welcome Jesus. The Sons of Thunder then asked Jesus, "'Lord, do you want us to call fire down from heaven to destroy them?'" *Luke 9:54*. This is an allusion to the prophet Elijah. "Elijah answered the captain, 'If I am a man of God, may fire come down from heaven and consume you and your fifty men!' Then the fire fell from heaven and consumed the captain and his men." *2 Kings 1:9*

Link with Jesus: James was called by Jesus to be one of his special followers. "When he [Jesus] had gone a little farther, he saw James son of Zebedee and his brother John in a boat, preparing their nets. Without delay he called them, and they left their father Zebedee in the boat with the hired men and followed him." *Mark 1:9-20*

Key verse: With Peter and his brother John, James became one of Jesus' inner circle of three friends and experienced special moments with Jesus, such as the transfiguration of Jesus. "After six days Jesus took with him Peter, James and John the brother of James, and led them up a high mountain by themselves." *Matthew 17:1*

More Information: *Matthew 4:21,22; 10:2; 17:1-13; 26:37; Mark 5:37; 10:35-45; Luke 9:51-56; Acts 12:2*

James' death

James was beheaded by Herod Agrippa I about ten years after Jesus' death. See *Acts 12:2*.

John

John

Meaning of name: The Lord is gracious

Point of interest: John was "the disciple whom Jesus loved." In John's Gospel, the author, John, never mentions himself by name, but instead uses the expression, "the disciple whom Jesus loved." See *John 13:23; 19:26; 21:7*.

Family links: John's brother was James, also one of Jesus' disciples, and their father was Zebedee.

Old Testament link: John, the writer of the fourth Gospel, was a Jew and clearly very familiar with the Old Testament. He begins his Gospel with the words, "In the beginning was the Word, and the Word was with God, and the Word was God," an echo of *Genesis 1:1:* "In the beginning God created the heavens and the earth."

Quote: "Lord, who is going to betray you?" *John 21:20*

Link with Jesus: Jesus must have completely trusted John as he entrusted his mother into his care. "Near the cross of Jesus stood his mother ... When Jesus saw his mother there, and the disciple whom he loved standing nearby, he said to his mother, 'Dear woman, here is your son,' and to the disciple, 'Here is your mother.' From that time on, this disciple took her into his home." *John 19:25-27*

Key verse: John not only wrote the fourth Gospel, but also three New Testament letters, 1, 2, and 3 John, as well as the book of Revelation. John states why he wrote his Gospel: "Jesus did many other miraculous signs in the presence of his disciples, which are not recorded in this book. But these are written that you may believe that Jesus is the Christ, the Son of God, and that by believing you may have life in his name." *John 20:30,31*

More Information: *Matthew 4:21,22; 20:20-23; John 13:23-25; 19:25-27; Acts 1:13; 3–4; Galatians 2:9; 1, 2, and 3 John, Revelation 1:1*

The other apostles and Matthias

Bartholomew

Meaning of name: Son of Talmai
Link with Jesus: We know nothing about Bartholomew who is only mentioned in the New Testament in the list of all Jesus' apostles. See *Matthew 10:3*

James

Meaning of name: "James" is a form of "Jacob" which means "supplanter"
Family links: Two of Jesus' twelve apostles were called James. This James, who was not the brother of John, is identified as the son of Alphaeus, but nothing more is known about him. See *Matthew 10:3; Acts 1:13*

Judas

Meaning of name: Praise
This Judas is to be identified as the same person who is called Thaddaeus. To distinguish him from the Judas who betrayed Jesus, this Judas is called, "Judas, not Iscariot."See *Luke 6:16; Acts 1:13*

Judas Iscariot

Meaning of name: Judas means "praise" Iscariot means "a man of Keriot," a town twelve miles from Hebron
Family links: Judas was the son of a man called Simon.
Link with Jesus: Judas, the treasurer for the twelve apostles, betrayed Jesus for 30 silver pieces. When John asked Jesus at the Last Supper which of the twelve apostles would betray him, Jesus replied: "It is the one to whom I will give this piece of bread when I have dipped it in the dish." *John 13:26.* Jesus then gave this piece of bread to Judas. "As soon as Judas took the bread, Satan entered into him." *John 13:27.* John adds, "As soon as Judas had taken the bread, he went out. And it was night." *John 13:30*
Judas betrayed Jesus with a kiss, a mark of friendship, in the Garden of Gethsemane so Jesus could be identified in the dark and arrested. Later, when Judas realized the wrong he had done, in a fit of remorse, he returned the 30 silver pieces to the priests and then committed suicide by hanging himself. See *Matthew 26:1–27:10; Acts 1:15-26*

Matthew

Meaning of name: Gift of the Lord

Link with Jesus: Matthew, who was also known as Levi, was a tax-collector when Jesus called him to follow him. Matthew then held a party in his home which Jesus went to. "While Jesus was having dinner at Levi's house, many tax collectors and 'sinners' were eating with him and his disciples, for there were many who followed him. When the teachers of the law who were Pharisees saw him eating with 'sinners' and tax collectors, they asked his disciples: 'Why does he eat with tax collectors and sinners?'" *Mark 2:15, 16*

This indicates that tax collectors were greatly despised. Also, to the ordinary Jew, they were regarded as traitors, working for their occupying power, the Romans. Jesus gave this reply to the question the Pharisees asked: "'It is not the healthy who need a doctor, but the sick. I have not come to call the righteous, but sinners.'" *Mark 2:17*

Nathanael

Meaning of name: God has given

Link with Jesus: He is mentioned only in John's Gospel and is most likely to be identified as the Bartholomew who is mentioned in the other Gospels. Nathanael first heard about Jesus from Philip. "When Jesus saw Nathanael approaching, he said of him, 'Here is a true Israelite, in whom there is nothing false.'" *John 1:47*

Philip

Meaning of name: Lover of horses

Link with Jesus: Like Andrew and Peter, Philip was a fisherman from Bethsaida. He brought Bartholomew (Nathanael) to Jesus. In answer to Philip's question about the Father, Jesus said, "'Anyone who has seen me has seen the Father.'" *John 14:9*

Simon

Meaning of name: Hearing

Link with Jesus: This Simon, who was a different person from Simon Peter, was known as Simon the Zealot, because he was most probably a member of a revolutionary group who wanted to drive the Romans from Israel. See *Matthew 10:4*

Thomas

Meaning of name: Twin. Thomas' Greek name was Didymus

Link with Jesus: Thomas is forever labeled as "doubting" Thomas because he did not initially believe that Jesus rose from the dead. But when he did see the risen Lord Jesus he said to him, "'My Lord and my God!'" *John 20:28*

Matthias

Meaning of name: God's gift

Link with Jesus: Matthias replaced Judas as an apostle. See *Acts 1:23,26*

Nicodemus

Nicodemus

Meaning of name: Conqueror of the people

Point of interest: Nicodemus met Jesus under the cover of night.

Who was Nicodemus?
- A pharisee
- A member of the Jewish ruling council
- Jesus called Nicodemus, "Israel's teacher."

Words spoken to: "I tell you the truth, no one can see the kingdom of God unless he is born again." *John 3:3*

Link with Jesus: Nicodemus is mentioned three times in the New Testament. Each time the focus of attention is on Jesus.

Key verse: "Nicodemus ... came to Jesus at night." *John 3:1,2*

More Information: *John 3:1-21; 7:45-52; 19:39*

Nicodemus meets Jesus

Jesus' conversation with Nicodemus and his following words include the most famous words from the Bible:

> "Just as Moses lifted up the snake in the desert, so the Son of Man must be lifted up, that everyone who believes in him may have eternal life."
> *John 3:15*

> "For God so loved the world that he gave his one and only Son, that whoever believes in him may have eternal life."
> *John 3:16*

Nicodemus stands up for Jesus

Jesus was not exactly the most popular man in town with the Jewish hierarchy. The chief priests and Pharisees were furious with the temple guards for not arresting Jesus and scornfully asked the guards, "Has any of the rulers or the Pharisees believed in him?" *John 7:48*

Nicodemus bravely leapt to Jesus' defense, and asked, "Does our law condemn a man without first hearing him to find out what he is doing?" *John 7:51*

Nicodemus helps to bury Jesus

The last cameo John's Gospel gives us of Nicodemus is when Nicodemus brought 75 pounds of "a mixture of myrrh and aloes" to help Joseph of Arimathea bury Jesus.
John 19:39

Caiaphas

Caiaphas

Meaning of name: Depression

Point of interest: Caiaphas masterminded Jesus' arrest and condemnation.

Family links: Caiaphas was son-in-law of Annas who had been high priest from AD 6 to 13.

Old Testament link: The work of the Old Testament high priesthood is found in *Deuteronomy 33:8-10*. Caiaphas was an important member of the Jewish priesthood and was high priest in Jerusalem from AD 18 to 36.

Quote: Caiaphas advised the Jewish authorities that one man, Jesus, should die for all the people. "Then ... Caiaphas, who was high priest that year, spoke up, ... 'You do not realize that it is better for you that one man die for the people than that the whole nation perish.' He did not say this on his own, but as high priest that year he prophesied that Jesus would die for the Jewish nation, and not only for that nation but also for the scattered children of God, to bring them together and make them one." *John 11:51, 52*

Link with Jesus: Caiaphas presided over the illegal trial of Jesus when he was hauled up in front of the Sanhedrin. Caiaphas pronounced that Jesus was guilty of blasphemy.

Key verse: "Again the high priest asked him [Jesus], 'Are you the Christ, the Son of the Blessed One?' 'I am,' said Jesus." *Mark 14:61, 62*

More Information: *Matthew 26:3-5, 57-68; Mark 14:53-55; Luke 3:2; John 11:49-51; 18:12-14, 19-24; Acts 5:27*

Caiaphas and the first Christians

Caiaphas persecuted the early Christians:

"Having brought the apostles, they made them appear before the Sanhedrin to be questioned by the high priest. 'We gave you strict orders not to teach in this name,' he said. 'Yet you have filled Jerusalem with your teaching and are determined to make us guilty of this man's blood.' Peter and the other apostles replied: 'We must obey God rather than men!'"
Acts 5:27-29

Pilate

Pilate

Meaning of name: Javelin carrier

Point of interest: Pilate handed Jesus over to the Jews so that he would be crucified.

Pilate's position: Pilate was commander-in-chief of the Roman soldiers in Judea. Although the Jews hated the Romans they had to bring Jesus before Pilate as he could order the death sentence, which the Jews were not allowed to do.

Quote: Pilate had the following notice, written in Aramaic, Latin and Greek, put on Jesus' cross: "JESUS OF NAZARETH, THE KING OF THE JEWS." The chief priests protested to Pilate, "'Do not write "The King of the Jews," but that this man claimed to be king of the Jews.'" *John 19: 21*

To this, Pilate made his famous reply: "'What I have written, I have written.'" *John 19:22*

Link with Jesus: Pilate found Jesus "not guilty" of the false charges the Jews accused him of. "Once more Pilate came out and said to the Jews, 'Look, I am bringing him out to you to let you know that I find no basis for a charge against him.'" *John 19:4*

Key verse: "Finally Pilate handed him [Jesus] over to them to be crucified." *John 19:16*

More Information: *Matthew 27:11-26; Mark 15:1-15; Luke 22:66–23:25; John 18:28–19:22*

Pilate's wife

"While Pilate was sitting on the judge's seat, his wife sent him this message: 'Don't have anything to do with that innocent man, for I have suffered a great deal today in a dream because of him.'" *Matthew 27:19*

Stephen

Stephen

Meaning of name: Crown

Point of interest: Stephen was the first Christian martyr.

Family links: We know nothing about Stephen's family, but he was chosen to be one of the first seven deacons to be appointed who had to be full of the Spirit and wisdom. Stephen is described as being "a man full of faith and of the Holy Spirit." *Acts 6:5*

Old Testament link: When Stephen was brought before the Sanhedrin on trumped up charges of blasphemy against Moses and against God, he gave a lengthy defense in which he outlined the Old Testament account of the history of the Jews from the time of Abraham to Jesus' crucifixion.

Quote: "'Look,' he [Stephen] said, 'I see heaven open and the Son of Man standing at the right hand of God.'" *Acts 7:56*

Link with Jesus: As Stephen was being stoned to death he prayed a prayer which echoed some words spoken by Jesus as he was being crucified: "Stephen prayed, 'Lord Jesus, receive my spirit.' Then he fell on his knees and cried out, 'Lord, do not hold this sin against them.' When he had said this, he fell asleep." *Acts 7:59, 60*

Key verse: "All who were sitting in the Sanhedrin looked intently at Stephen, and they saw that his face was like the face of an angel." *Acts 6:15*

More Information: *Acts 6:1–8:2*

Stephen and Paul

It is left to our imaginations to work out how influential Stephen's martyrdom was. However, it clearly had a great effect on one man: "the witnesses laid their clothes at the feet of a young man named Saul … And Saul was there, giving approval to his death." *Acts 7:58; 8:1*

The stoning of Stephen, by Rembrant (1625) Musée des Beaux-Arts, Lyons

Cornelius

Cornelius

Meaning of name: Of a horn

Point of interest: Cornelius was one of the famous conversion stories in the Acts of the Apostles.

Family links: We know nothing of Cornelius' family, but we do know some facts about him:

- He was a Roman centurion in the Italian Regiment, living in Caesarea.
- He was respected by the Jews at Caesarea.
- He was well known for being generous to the poor.
- He and all his family prayed to God regularly.

Quote: "Cornelius answered: 'Four days ago I was in my house praying at this hour, at three in the afternoon. Suddenly a man in shining clothes stood before me and said, "Cornelius, God has heard your prayer and remembered your gifts to the poor."'" *Acts 10:30, 31*

Link with Jesus: Peter went to Cornelius' home and preached the gospel to him and his family, saying, "You know the message God sent to the people of Israel, telling the good news of peace through Jesus Christ, who is Lord of all.'" *Acts 10:36* Whenever Peter preached he preached about Jesus.

Key verse: Cornelius, even though he was a high-ranking Roman soldier, showed his humility when Peter came into his home. "As Peter entered the house, Cornelius met him and fell at his feet in reverence." *Acts 10:25*

More Information: *Acts 10*

59

Jews and Christians
Many practicing Jews who became followers of Jesus found it hard to believe that Jesus' message applied to non-Jews as well.

"The circumcised believers who had come with Peter were astonished that the gift of the Holy Spirit had been poured out even on the Gentiles. For they heard them speaking in tongues and praising God." *Acts 10:45,46*

Entering the Roman amphitheatre, Caesarea.

Paul

Paul

Meaning of name: Before his conversion, Paul was called Saul; "Saul" means "asked" "Paul" means "small"

Point of interest: His conversion on the road to Damascus. "As he [Saul] neared Damascus on his journey [to persecute Christians], suddenly a light from heaven flashed around him. He fell to the ground and heard a voice say to him, 'Saul, Saul, why do you persecute me?'" *Acts 9:4.* Later Saul changed his name to Paul.

Family links: Paul was from the tribe of Benjamin and a zealous member of the Pharisee party, *Romans 11:1; Philippians 3:5; Acts 23:6.* While we know nothing about his family, we know that he was brought up in Tarsus and was a Roman citizen, *Acts 16:37; 21:39; 22:25-27.*

Old Testament link: Paul had been brought up as a devout Jew:
- " ... circumcised on the eighth day,
- of the people of Israel,
- of the tribe of Benjamin,
- a Hebrew of Hebrews;
- in regard to the law, a Pharisee." *Philippians 3:5*

- Paul had been a pupil of the most respected rabbi of the day, Gamaliel, *Acts 22:3.*

Quote: Paul had an unquenchable desire to preach about Jesus: "'Woe to me if I do not preach the gospel!'" *1 Corinthians 9:16*

Link with Jesus: There is no record that Paul met Jesus while Jesus was alive. However, Paul's conversion experience was so vivid that he never forgot it as being the time when he first encountered Jesus.
"'Who are you. Lord?' Saul asked.
"'I am Jesus, whom you are persecuting,' he replied. 'Now get up and go into the city, and you will be told what you must do.'" *Acts 9:5,6*

Key verse: Paul knew that he had been forgiven for all his sins, but he never forgot that he had once persecuted Christians. "'For I am the least of the apostles and do not even deserve to be called an apostle, because I persecuted the church of God.'" *1 Corinthians 15:9*

More Information: *Acts 7, 9–28;* Paul's thirteen New Testament letters

Paul and the gospel of faith

After his conversion Paul spent the rest of his life preaching about and writing about Jesus. To the Christians at Rome Paul explained what it meant to live by faith:

"For in the gospel a righteousness from God is revealed, a righteousness that is by faith from first to last, just as it is written: 'The righteous will live by faith.'" *Romans 1:17*

Paul's physical appearance

We are told nothing about the physical appearance of Jesus or any of his apostles. It is almost the same with Paul. All we know from the New Testament are in a few verses which suggest that Paul's personal appearance was not very impressive. See *1 Corinthians 2:3-4; 2 Corinthians 10:10.*

The earliest apocryphal description of Paul says that he was, "A man small in size, bald-headed, bandy-legged, well built, with eyebrows meeting, a nose somewhat hooked, full of grace – for sometimes he seemed like a man, and sometimes he had the countenance of an angel." *Acts of Paul and Thecla* (apocryphal)

Paul's letters

After Luke, we have more writings of Paul in the New Testament than of anybody else. Thirteen letters are traditionally ascribed to Paul.

- Romans
- 1 and 2 Corinthians
- Galatians
- Ephesians
- Philippians
- Colossians
- 1 and 2 Thessalonians
- 1 and 2 Timothy
- Titus
- Philemon

Paul the pioneer missionary

Paul's missionary strategy was to take a partner or team and preach the gospel in the main cities of the known world.

> "Paul stakes all his life upon the truth of what he says about the death and resurrection of Jesus." *J. Gresham Machen*

Roman coinage.

The Acropolis, Athens.

Timothy and Titus

Timothy

Meaning of name: Honoring God

Point of interest: Timothy was the apostle Paul's friend and helper.

Family links: Although Timothy's father was a Greek, Timothy was born into a strong Christian home. His mother, Eunice, was a Jew and a believer, and even his grandmother, Lois, had sincere faith in God.

Link with Jesus: In Paul's two letters to Timothy, *1 and 2 Timothy*, Paul gives Timothy advice about being a Christian leader and pastor. Timothy owed his own Christian conversion to Paul. "You then, my son, be strong in the grace that is in Christ Jesus." *2 Timothy 2:2*

Key verse: Timothy was probably shy and retiring by nature. "Don't let anyone look down on you because you are young, but set an example for the believers in speech, in life, in love, in faith and purity." *1 Timothy 4:12*

More Information: *Acts 16–17; 1 and 2 Timothy*

62

Titus

Meaning of name: Honored

Point of interest: Titus was the pastor of the Christian Church on the island of Crete.

Family links: We know nothing about Titus' family. He was one of Paul's greatly trusted friends. To some Christians who insisted that all Christians should adopt Jewish customs, Paul used Titus as an example to show how unnecessary this was. "Yet not even Titus, who was with me, was compelled to be circumcised, even though he was a Greek." *Galatians 2:3*

Words spoken about: Paul is on record as saying what a comfort Titus was to him: "But God, who comforts the downcast, comforted us by the coming of Titus." *2 Corinthians 7:6*

Link with Jesus: Paul wrote to Titus about Jesus being our Savior. See *Titus 3:6.*

Key verse: "You must teach what is in accord with sound doctrine." *Titus 2:1*

More Information: *1 Corinthians 16; 2 Corinthians 7–8; Galatians 2; the whole of Titus*

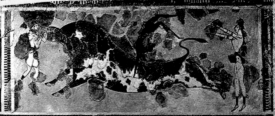

Boys and girls bull-jumping, fresco from Palace of Knossos, Crete. Minoan civilization

Luke

Luke

Meaning of name: Light giving

Point of interest: Luke wrote the Gospel which bears his name and the Acts.

Old Testament link: Although Luke is usually thought of as being a Gentile (non-Jew) it is clear from his Gospel that he realized the great links between Jesus and the Old Testament.

In *Luke 4*, for example, Luke makes four important quotations from the Old Testament. He teaches that the whole of Jesus' ministry was foretold by Isaiah, as he records Jesus reading from *Isaiah 61:1-2*, after which Jesus said, "'Today this scripture is fulfilled in your hearing.'" *Luke 4:21*

Quote: Luke explains why he wrote his Gospel in its opening verses: "Therefore, since I myself have carefully investigated everything from the beginning, it seemed good also to me to write an orderly account for you, most excellent Theophilus, so that you may know the certainty of the things you have been taught." *Luke 1:3, 4*

Link with Jesus: Luke records 17 of Jesus' parables which are not found in the other three Gospels. The most famous two of these are the Good Samaritan and the Prodigal Son. See *Luke 10:30-37; 15:11-32*.

Key verse: Luke summed up Jesus' mission in the following words of Jesus: "For the Son of Man came to seek and to save what was lost." *Luke 19:10*

More Information: *Colossians 4:2 Timothy 4;* the books of *Luke* and *Acts*

63

Luke the faithful doctor

As Paul's traveling companion, Luke was greatly appreciated. In *Colossians 4:14* Paul calls Luke, "Our dear friend Luke, the doctor." That Paul prized Luke's faithful friendship is seen in some of the last words Paul wrote: "Only Luke is with me." *2 Timothy 4:11*

Index of Bible people

Bible
Research
made
easy

Once you have read the other four titles in this handbook, *Bible Research made easy* gives you the opportunity to dig deeper into the treasures of the Bible and to explore in more depth some of the gems that await your discovery.

Bible Research made easy gives you enough ideas about different ways in which to study the Bible to last you a lifetime. It introduces you to the different Bible research methods, such as:

• Using different Bible versions
• Using chain references
• Using cross references
• Using an expository dictionary of the Bible
• Using Bible theology books
• Using the Internet for Bible study

Bible Research made easy will help you to have the same approach to Bible Study as Martin Luther used:

> "I study my Bible as I gather apples. First, I shake the whole tree that the ripest might fall. Then I shake each limb, and when I have shaken each limb, I shake each branch and every twig. Then I look under every leaf."
>
> *Martin Luther*

Contents

Introduction to Bible research

Research is ...

- If you copy what one other person has written it is called plagiarism;
- If you copy what two or more people have written it is called research!

Contemporary biblical research

A great deal of biblical research today focuses on finding something that is new, innovative or original.

This book does not approach Bible research in that way at all.

It's purpose is to show you how to use Bible reference books and to help you come to a clearer understanding of a given Bible text.

Bible reference tools

To receive benefit from this book no other book is necessary – only a Study Bible (see pages 6-7). However, 13 other books which aid detailed Bible Study will be mentioned.

It is not necessary to have these reference books to study this book. In fact, if you do not own any of them, it may be best for you to finish reading this book before deciding which ones to buy. At that point you will be in a better position to choose the books that are most appropriate for you.

5

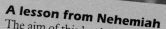

A lesson from Nehemiah

The aim of this book is summed up by the following words:

"The Levites ... instructed the people in the Law while the people were standing there. They read from the Book of the Law of God, making it clear and giving the meaning so that the people could understand what was being read. ... Then all the people went away ... to celebrate with great joy, because they now understood the words that had been known to them."
Nehemiah 8:7-8, 12

Start simple

What you need to make use of this book
- You will need a good Study Bible.
- If you don't know what a Study Bible is, a Christian bookstore will be able to show you a variety of them and demonstrate their unique features.
- With each of the major translations of the Bible, one or more Study Bibles are usually published.
- These Study Bibles are also often available in libraries.

(Unless otherwise stated, the Bible studies in this book are based on the *New International Version* of the Bible.)

Many of the topics in this book are treated on two levels.

simple start

The first level introduces the topic and suggests preliminary ways of studying the text. This will aid in understanding its meaning and allow God to speak directly to you. You will find this first level under the heading: **A simple start.**

SOLID BIBLE STUDY

The second level gives a more in-depth approach to a passage or subject. These second level studies come under the heading: **Solid Bible study.** They will suggest different avenues of Bible study which may take many months rather than a few minutes.

Pick and choose
Don't feel that you have to do *every* Bible study in this book.

Pick the studies that appeal to you and are most appropriate for your needs.

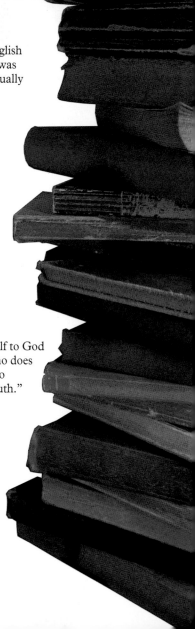

William Tyndale

When William Tyndale, the English Reformer and Bible translator, was imprisoned before he was eventually burnt at the stake, he made the following request.

"A warmer cap, a candle, a piece of cloth to patch my leggings. ... But above all, I beseech and entreat your clemency to be urgent with the Procurer that he may kindly permit me to have my Hebrew Bible, Hebrew Grammar and Hebrew Dictionary, that I may spend time with them in study."

Do you love God with your mind?

"Do your best to present yourself to God as one approved, a workman who does not need to be ashamed and who correctly handles the word of truth."
2 Timothy 2:15

Choosing a Bible version

The best selection ever
Never before has there been such a good selection of trustworthy translations of the Bible to choose from.

King James Version: KJV
The *King James Version*, also known as the *Authorized Version*, is the oldest continuously published English translation of the Bible.

It was first published in 1611, at the suggestion of King James I of England, 1566-1625. It is loved for the beauty of its traditional English. But over the centuries the meaning of some English words has changed. Therefore this version does not always communicate understandably to readers today.

New International Version: NIV
The *New International Version* is a translation of the Bible produced by over 100 scholars working from the best available Hebrew, Aramaic and Greek texts. The goals of the translators were to produce an accurate translation that would have clarity and literary quality. The *NIV* had its beginning in 1965. The *NIV* New Testament was published in 1973, and the Old Testament was finished in 1978.

It is conservative in its theological position and accurate in its translation.

New Living Translation: NLT
The New Living Translation is a completely revised edition of *The Living Bible*. It has been recommended by Billy Graham for its "greater readability and accuracy."

The Message
Designed for reading rather than for study, *The Message* is a unique, idiomatic, contemporary rendering of the Bible text in modern language by Eugene Peterson. It is helpful for devotional reading and for clarifying difficult passages.

The Living Bible: TLB
Published in 1971, Kenneth Taylor's single-author paraphrase is praised for its ability to communicate directly with the reader and for its theologically conservative stance. However, scholars have pointed out that some of the translator's own assumptions are evident and that some parts are very loosely translated. *The Living Bible* is often given to people who are unfamiliar with the Bible to help them more easily understand it.

New American Standard Bible: NASB

55 conservative scholars, using the insights of modern scholarship, produced this translation in 1971 to replace the *American Standard Version* of 1901. While preserving the literal accuracy of the 1901 *ASV*, the *NASB* has sought to render grammar and terminology in contemporary English. Special attention has been given to the rendering of verb tenses to give the English reader a rendering as close as possible to the sense of the original Greek and Hebrew texts.

The *New American Standard Bible* 1995 edition is an updated version of this word-for-word translation.

New King James Version: NKJV

The New King James Version was produced by 130 evangelical scholars in 1982. It is an updated version of the *King James Version*.

The New Revised Standard Version: NRSV

The *NRSV* is based on the *Revised Standard Version*, published in 1952, which, in turn, aimed to replace the *American Standard Version*, of 1901. The *RSV* used modern scholarship but included an occasional liberal bias. The language of the *NRSV* is modern, yet dignified, reflecting the long tradition of translation with which it is associated, that started with the 1611 *King James Version* of the Bible

Contemporary English Version: CEV

The *CEV*, which was released in 1994, was written for people who want an accurate contemporary English rendering of the Bible that remains thoroughly readable. It endeavors to put the precise meaning of the original languages into words that clearly communicate. The *CEV* was translated directly from the Greek text published by the United Bible Societies (third edition, corrected, 1983).

Questions to ask

When you choose to read or buy a Bible version, either for yourself, or for somebody else, ask:

- Is it a paraphrase or a translation?
- Is it to be used to gain a speedy acquaintance with the general meaning of the text, or is it for detailed study?
- Is it for children or for adults?
- Is there a school grade readability level associated with this version?

Comparison of eight Bible versions

The Contemporary Parallel New Testament

This is a parallel Bible, which contains in its 1,840 pages, the full text of the New Testament in the classic King James Version and in seven of the modern English translations:

- New King James Version
- New Living Translation
- The Message
- Contemporary English Version
- New Century Version
- New International Version
- New American Standard Bible

2 Corinthians 7:10

As you read this verse in different Bible versions, note the differences and what they teach about the word "repentance." Can you understand the origin of repentance?

King James Version: "For godly sorrow worketh repentance to salvation not to be repented of: but the sorrow of the world worketh death."

New King James Version: "For godly sorrow produces repentance (leading) to salvation, not to be regretted, but the sorrow of the world produces death."

New Living Translation: "For God can use sorrow in our lives to help us turn away from sin and seek salvation. We should never regret this kind of sorrow. But sorrow without repentance is the kind that results in death."

The Message: "Distress that drives us to God does that. It turns us around. It gets us back in the way of salvation. We never regret that kind of pain. But those who let distress drive them away from God are full of regrets, end up on a deathbed of regrets."

Contemporary English Version: "When God makes you feel sorry enough to turn to him and be save, you don't have anything to feel bad about. But when the world makes you feel sorry, it can cause your death."

New Century Version: "The kind of sorrow God wants makes people change their hearts and lives. This leads to salvation, and you cannot be sorry for that. But

Bible sales in the USA

New Living Translation 4%
Living Bible 1.5%
New Revised Standard Version 1.5%
Other 2%
New International Version 48%

the kind of sorrow the world has brings death."

New International Version:
"Godly sorrow brings repentance that leads to salvation and leaves no regret, but worldly sorrow brings death."

New American Standard Bible:
"For the sorrow that is according to the will of God produces a repentance without regret, leading to salvation, (or, leading to a salvation without regret) but the sorrow of the world produces death."

Making up your own eight versions

Of course, you don't have to stick to the eight versions in *The Contemporary Parallel New Testament*. You can choose other versions for additional comparisons.

Comparing only four translations would greatly increase your appreciation of the text of the New Testament. In order to supersede the effectiveness of this way of studying you would need to have a good knowledge of the original languages.

In the J.B. Phillips paraphrase one of the most memorable translations is of the first part of Romans 12:2: "Don't let the world around you squeeze you into its own mold." Compare this with the translations found in the *Contemporary Parallel New Testament* below:

King James Version: "And do not be conformed to this world."

New King James Version:
"And do not be conformed to this world."

New Living Translation: "Don't copy the behavior and customs of this world."

The Message: "Don't become so well-adjusted to your culture that you fit into it without even thinking."

Contemporary English Version: "Don't be like the people of this world."

New Century Version: "Do not change yourselves to be like the people of this world."

New International Version:
"Do not conform any longer to the pattern of this world."

New American Standard Version: "And do not be conformed to this world."

SOLID
BIBLE STUDY

Investigate the ways different Bible versions translate key New Testament passages, such as John 1:1-18; Philippians 2:1-11; Colossians 2:1-10.

Features of a Study Bible –
Character studies

People

Many Study Bibles provide a listing of the names of people mentioned in the Bible. (The studies on pages 12-15 are correct for *The New International Version* and may differ slightly in other translations.)

SOLID
BIBLE STUDY

Make a study of all the references in the New Testament about the twelve apostles and so build up your own character sketch of each of them.

Identifying the important people

Some lists identify the important people by giving a one, or two, line summary of their lives. For example, under the letter B, from among the many of names

Balaam	**Balak**	**Barnabas***
Prophet who attempted to curse Israel (Nu 22-24; Dt 23:4-5; 2 Pe 2:15; Jude 11). Killed in Israel's vengeance on Midianites (Nu 31:8; Jos 13:22).	Moabite king who hired Balaam to curse Israel (Nu 22-24; Jos 24:9).	Disciple, originally Joseph (Ac 4:36), prophet (Ac 13:1), apostles (Ac 9:27), Antioch (Ac 11:22-29; Gal 2:1-13), on the first missionary journey (Ac 13-14). Together at Jerusalem Council, they separated over John Mark (Ac 15). Later co-workers (1 Co 9:6; Col 4:10).

the following might be singled out. Key Bible verses are
supplied.

People marked with an asterisk (*) indicate that every
appearance of that person in the Bible is listed.

13

Bartholomew*
Apostle (Mt 10:3;
Mk 3:18; Lk 6:14;
Ac 1:13). Possibly also
known as Nathanael
(Jn 1:45-49; 21:2).

Baruch
Jeremiah's secretary
(Jer 32:12-16; 36;
43:1-6; 45:1-2).

Benjamin
Twelfth son of Jacob
by Rachel
(Ge 35:16-24;
46:19-21; 1 Ch 2;2).
Jacob refused to send
him to Egypt, but
relented (Ge 42-45).
Tribe of blessed
(Ge 49:27; Dt 33:12),
numbered (Nu 1:37;
26:41), allotted land
(Jos 18:11-28; Eze
48:23), failed to fully
possess (Jdg 1:21),
nearly obliterated
(Jdg 20-21), sided
with Ish-Bosheth
(2 Sa 2), but turned to
David (1 Ch 12:2, 29).
12,000 from (Rev 7:8).

Features of a Study Bible –
Chronological timelines

Timelines
Study Bibles often furnish useful information about Bible events and Bible people in the form of a chronological timeline.

These timelines offer a bird's eye view of historical events. They can also show how events recorded in the Bible relate to events which were going on in the world.

So, at the time of Jesus' birth, a New Testament timeline points out that the rulers in Palestine were under the control of the Roman Emperors.

Chronology of the Bible
Most Study Bibles provide charts giving an overview of the whole Bible. These charts attempt to date the events recorded in the Bible and position them in relation to when each Bible book was written.

You need to realize, though, that there is uncertainty about some of the dates. For example, no one is certain exactly when the book of Job was written. Some think it may have been the first Bible book written while others date it up to two thousand years later.

Certain dates continue to be hotly debated.

John the Baptist
starts his ministry
AD 26

Jesus
starts his
ministry
AD 26

John the
Baptist
imprisoned
AD 27

Jesus
baptized
AD 26

John the
Baptist
beheaded
AD 28

Jesus crucified AD 30

Jesus
ascends
AD 30

Roman Procurator
Pontius Pilate
AD 26-36

Herod the Great
37-4 BC

20 BC

Jesus born
6/5 BC

10 BC

Roman Emperor
Augustus
27 BC – AD 14

0

**Jesus in
the temple**
AD 6/7

**Roman
procurators
rule Palestine
from**
AD 6/7

AD 10

The chronology (below) of the life of Jesus should be viewed with this in mind. Many scholars believe that the dating used to determine Christ's birth was erroneous. Hence, Jesus may have been born earlier than originally calculated, placing his birth at 5 or 6 BC. Once that is understood, it then means that Jesus' boyhood visit to the temple is placed twelve years later, at AD 6 or 7. When one date is fixed it determines many of the other dates, and, of course, if the original date is wrong, the other days will not be accurate.

AD 20

15

SOLID
BIBLE STUDY

Read Matthew 21:1 –27:66; Mark 11:1 –15:47; Luke 19:28–23:56; John 12:12 –19:42, and construct your own chronology of the last week of Jesus' life. What have you learned from this?

30

Using study notes from a Study Bible

What are study notes?

Most Study Bibles include interpretative notes which are inserted throughout the Bible. These notes provide a commentary about the Bible text. They normally appear at the bottom of the page and look like extended footnotes.

The following commentary notes are taken from the *NIV Study Bible*.

1. Study notes explain concepts and important words

The study note on Matthew 3:2, "Repent, for the kingdom of God is near," reads:

3:2 **Repent**. Make a radical change in one's life as a whole. **the kingdom of heaven**. A phrase found only in Matthew, where it occurs 33 times. ... The kingdom of heaven is the rule of God and is both a present reality and a future hope. The idea of God's kingdom is central to Jesus' teaching and is mentioned 50 times in Matthew alone.

2. Study notes interpret verses which appear to contain difficulties

Did Jesus teach that we should hate our families?

The study note on Luke 14:26, "If anyone comes to me and does not hate his father and mother, his wife and children, his brothers and sisters - yes, even his own life - he cannot be my disciple" reads:

14:26 **hate his father**. A vivid hyperbole, meaning that someone must love Jesus even more than his immediate family (see Mal 1:2-3 for another use of the figure). See Mt 10:37.

3. Study notes link Bible events and Bible people

Moses is seen as a mediator.

The study note on Exodus 32:30, "Moses said to the people,

'You have committed a great sin. But now I will go up to the Lord; perhaps I can make atonement for your sin.'" reads:

32:30 **make atonement for your sin**. By making urgent intercession before God, as the mediator God had appointed between himself and Israel. No sacrifice that Israel or Moses might bring could atone for this sin. But Moses so identified himself with Israel that he made his own death the condition of God's destruction of the nations (see v. 32). Jesus Christ, the great Mediator, offered himself on the cross to make atonement for his people.

4. Study notes provide background information to shed light on a particular practice

Was there a moral question about eating meat sacrificed to animals?

The study note on 1 Corinthians 8:1, "Now about food sacrificed to idols" reads:

8:1 **Now about food**. Another matter the Corinthians had written about. **sacrificed to idols**. Offered on pagan altars. Meat left over from a sacrifice might be eaten by the priests, eaten by the offerer and his friends at a feast in the temple or sold in the public meat market. Some Christians felt that if they ate such meat, they participated in pagan worship and thus compromised their testimony for Christ. Other Christians did not feel this way.

5. Study notes show how one passage illuminates another passage

The study notes on Psalm 26:8, "I love the house where you live, O Lord, the place where your glory dwells," reads:

26:8 **where your glory dwells**. The presence of God's glory signaled the presence of God himself: (see Exodus 24:16; 33:22.) His glory dwelling in the tabernacle (see Ex 40:35), and later this temple (see 1 Ki 8:11), assured Israel of the Lord's holy, yet gracious, presence among them. John 1:14 announces that same presence in the Word become flesh who "made his dwelling among us".

SOLID BIBLE STUDY

Read through an unfamiliar book of the Bible and read through the accompanying commentary notes from a Study Bible.

Using a Bible cross reference

Raised numbers or letters

Study Bibles have tiny raised numbers or letters accompanying some of the words in most of the Bible verses.

These letters/numbers are similar to footnotes in a book. They lead you to a matching letter/number which is either at the foot of the page or in a column in the center of the page.

Following the letter/number is a cross-reference to another verse on a similar topic in the Bible.

You need eagle eyes to see the cross references

Look up Genesis 1:1. Following the word "beginning" is a tiny raised letter ᵃ.

In the margin, or at the foot of the page you will find the figure **1**. This indicates which verse numbers the cross references link to. As you look at the first verse of Genesis chapter one, you will see **1**ᵃ Ps 102:25.

The compilers of these cross references thought that it would be a good idea for us to look up Psalm 102, verse 25 in connection with the word "beginning" in Genesis 1:1

"In the beginning you laid the foundations of the earth, and the heavens are the work of your hands." *Psalm 102:25.*

Using cross-references

Use your Bible to look up the cross-references listed below for the first verse of the Bible.

When you come across the abbreviation "ver" in the cross references it means you are to look up a verse from the chapter that you are studying. So the first one you will find reads "ver 21" – you then look up and read Genesis 1, verse 21.

At the front of your Study Bible you will find a list of abbreviations used for books of the Bible.

Ps denotes Psalms, **Isa** denotes Isaiah, etc.

Genesis 1:1

Bible text	Cross references
In the beginning^a	1 ^a Ps 102:25; Pr 8:23; Isa 40:21; 41:4, 26; Jn 1:1-2
God created^b	^b ver 21, 27; Ge 2:3
the heavens^c	^c ver 6; Ne 9:6; Job 9:8; 37:18; Ps 96:5; 104:2; 115:15; 121:2; 136:5; Isa 40:22; 42:5; 51:13; Jer 10:12; 51:15
and the earth.^d	^d Ge 14:19; 2 Ki 19:15; Ne 9:6; Job 38:4; Ps 90:2; 136:6; 146:6; Is 37:16; 40:28; 42:5; 44:24; 45:12, 18; Jer 27:5; 32:17; Ac 14:15; 17:24; Eph 3:9; Col 1:16; Heb 3:4; 11:3; Rev 4:11; 10:6

As you search these verses you may find yourself following your own train of thought. Add your own references in the margin.

SOLID BIBLE STUDY

Look up all the cross references in the letter of Jude.

Make a note of the way your study will hopefully change your behavior or affect your attitude to a problem.

Using a Bible chain reference

The purpose of chain references

The chain reference system helps you learn from the links between occurrences of particular words in the Bible. The word may show you how it is used in a particular Bible book. The word may show you how different writers used the same word at different times.

How the chains work

In a chain reference Bible the text of certain words are highlighted in **bold**.

These words are found in the margin of the Bible and are in alphabetical order.

Following the bold word, Bible references are given to other places in the Bible where the word occurs.

In the following example from 2 Corinthians in *The Thompson Chain-reference Study Bible, NIV* there are a number of features to note about the notes in the margin.

- **Pilot number**: The "Pilot Number" in the numerical system–at the left of the topics on the margin–leads directly to the same topic in the Comprehensive Helps section where all references are found.
- **Forward reference in chain**: The reference at the right of the topic is the "Forward Reference" which leads to the end of the "chain." One obtains each reference in its Scriptural setting by following a "chain."

The symbol † indicates the end of a "chain". Parallel passages are marked (p.p.) in the margin.

SOLID BIBLE STUDY

Follow through the use of the word "turn" in Mark's and Luke's gospels in a Bible chain reference Bible. Note how the word is used in different ways.

Sometimes it refers directly to repentance, sometimes it illustrates what repentance is and sometimes it uses the word "turn" in other ways.

Using a Bible concordance

Using a Bible concordance

A concordance is an index of all the major or key words in the Bible along with their immediate contexts. With a concordance you find the specific word you are looking for. The various places where that word occurs are listed in order from Genesis to Revelation. Each entry provides the context by inserting a portion of the verse along with the key word. This aids in finding the particular verse you are seeking.

Most Study Bibles include a short concordance.

Choosing a Bible concordance

There are three excellent concordances for the *King James Version/AV*: *Cruden's*, *Young's* and *Strong's*. *Young's* and *Strong's* are massive and exhaustive and ideal for very detailed Bible study.

Many modern translations of the Bible have their own concordances. It's possible that you may be able to match up your favorite Bible version with a companion Bible concordance.

Why bother with Crudens' concordance?

If you were brought up on the *KJV/Authorized Version* of the Bible you may find that many of its words and phrases are permanently lodged in your mind.

For example, you may find that you want to locate the story of the man from whom Jesus expelled many demons. All you can remember is that his name was "Legion." If you are presently now using *The Good News Bible* you won't find a reference to this story from the word "Legion."

A concordance such as *Cruden's* will guide you to Mark 5:9. Then in your *Good News Bible* you will see that the word "Mob" is used for "Legion."

Look up the word "gentle" in a concordance.

You will see that the word "gentleness" follows "gentle", so it is worthwhile looking up the instances of "gentleness" as well.

This will give you a partial picture of the Bible's teaching on the subject of being gentle. There are numerous examples of gentleness in the Bible where the actual word "gentle" is not used. However, by doing this Bible study you will have a good idea about the Bible's basic teaching on this topic.

As you look up each verse ask yourself what it teaches about gentleness.

Gentle and gentleness

Old Testament instances of "gentle"
Dt 28:54; 28:56
2 Sa 18:5
1 Ki 19:12
Job 41:3
Pr 15:1; 25:15
Jer 11:19
Zec 9:9

New Testament instances of "gentle"
Mt 11:29; 21:5
Ac 27:13
1 Co 4:21
Eph 4:2
1 Th 2:7
1 Ti 3:3
1 Pe 3:4

New Testament instances of "gentleness"

2 Co 10:1	By the meekness and gentleness of Christ,
Gal 5:23	faithfulness, gentleness and self-control.
Php 4:5	Let your gentleness be evident to all.
Col 3:12	kindness, humility, gentleness and patience.
1 Ti 6:11	faith, love, endurance and gentleness.
1 Pe 3:15	But do this with gentleness and respect,

SOLID
BIBLE STUDY

Use a Bible concordance to develop your own Bible study of the nine characteristics which make up the fruit of the Spirit.

"But the fruit of the Spirit is love, joy, peace, patience, kindness, goodness, faithfulness, gentleness and self-control." Galatians 5:22-23

Leave the research and study of "love" until the end as it will be a very long study.

Using Strong's concordance

Strong's Exhaustive Concordance
- *Strong's Exhaustive Concordance* is well named.
- It is a treasure store for any "strong" Bible student.
- It is based on the *KJV* or *Authorized Version* of the Bible.
- It lists every occurrence of every word in the Bible.

Under the word "repent"
If you look up the word "repent" you will find 45 verses in which "repent" occurs. The panel below gives five examples of

the word "repent" from these 45 verses. The numbers following the book/chapter/verse notation are explained on pages 26 and 27.

Examples of verses with "repent" in it

the people **r** when they see war	Ex 13:17	5162
r of this evil against thy people	Ex 32:12	5162
began to preach, and to say, **R**	Mt 4:17	3340
but, except ye **r**, ye shall all	Lk 13:3	3340
be zealous therefore, and **r**	Rev 3:19	3340

Other forms of the word "repent"

Strong's Exhaustive Concordance also provides all forms in which the word "repent" occurs in the Bible. The following entries reveal six additional variations for the word "repent."

Forms of "repent"	Number of occurrences
Repentance	26
Repented	32
Repentest	1
Repenteth	5
Repenting	1
Repentings	1

The panel below gives an example from each of the above six listings.

Repentance	the righteous, but sinners to **r**	Mt 9:13	3341
Repented	for they **r** at the preaching of	Lk 11:32	3340
Repentest	kindness, and **r** thee of the evil	Jonah 4:2	5162
Repenteth	in heaven over one sinner that **r**	Lk 15:7	3340
Repenting	I am weary with **r**	Jer 15:6	5162
Repentings	my **r** are kindled together	Hos 11:8	5150

Using Strong's numbering system
Researching Greek and Hebrew words

**Every occurrence of every word —
plus Greek and Hebrew words**

In addition to listing every occurrence of every word
in the Bible, *Strong's Exhaustive Concordance* points
you to the Greek and Hebrew words behind the
English translation.

Strong's numbering system

The verses on pages 24-25 of the book are taken from
Strong's Exhaustive Concordance where numbers appear
after many of the words.

These numbers are the key that will lead you to the
original Greek and Hebrew words. As previously noted
each entry in *Strong's Exhaustive Concordance* consists
of three parts. From left to right they are:

• The specific reference word along with the
  surrounding scripture text.
• The book, chapter and verse where the
  specific word is found.
• And the precise number to the Hebrew
  and Greek dictionaries in the back of the
  concordance.

The Old Testament number for repent

The number 5162, for "repent" as it occurs in the Old Testament, leads you to Strong's *Dictionary of the words in the Hebrew Bible*. Under the number 5162 you will find the following entry.

5162 נָחַם **nâcham**, naw-kham'; a prim. root; prop. to sigh, i.e. *breathe* strongly; by impl. *to be sorry*, i.e. (in a favorable sense) to *pity*, *console* or (reflex.) *Rue*; or (unfavorably) to 1§ (oneself):—comfort (self), ease [one's self], repent (-er, -ing, self).

The New Testament number for repent

The number 3340, for "repent" as it occurs in the New Testament, leads you to *Strong's Dictionary of the Greek Testament*. Under the number 3340 you will find the following entry.

3340 μετανοεω **mĕtanŏĕō**, met-an-ŏ-eh'-o; from *3326* and *3539*; to *think differently* or *afterwards*, i.e. *reconsider* (mor. *feel compunction*):—repent.

You can see that the numbers in italics refer to words as they occur in the New Testament.

SOLID
BIBLE STUDY

Look up the remaining Hebrew and Greek numbers for repentance by searching in the Hebrew and Greek dictionaries.
These remaining numbers will take you to other derivative words.
- The Old Testament numbers are: **7725; 5164; 5150**.
- The New Testament numbers are: **3341; 278**.

New Testament Greek
for beginners

New Testament Greek

The Greek in which the New Testament is written is not the same as classical Greek or the Greek spoken in Greece today.

New Testament Greek is known as *koinē*, or common Greek, a simple form of classical Greek. In the apostle Paul's day *koinē* Greek was spoken by all the countries surrounding the Mediterranean Sea.

From Alpha to Omega

From the above alphabet it is easy to see that the first and last letters of the Greek alphabet are A and Ω.

Jesus is given the title of being the "Alpha" and the "Omega" in the book of Revelation. Revelation 1:8; 21:6 and 22:13. "I am the Alpha and the Omega." In each case the text reads, "αλφα ... ω," with the first letter of the Greek alphabet, A, written out in full: *alpha*; and the last letter of the Greek alphabet, Ω, written out as a lower case single letter: ω.

A characteristic of God, the originator of all things, is applied to Jesus.

Transliterations

In many Bible commentaries Greek words are used. So a commentary on Romans 1:16 may point out that the Greek word for "power" is δυναμις. "I am not ashamed of the gospel, because it is the *power* of God for the salvation of everyone who believes: for the Jew, then for the Gentile,"

Often, letters from the English alphabet are used, for the benefit of non-Greek readers. So the word is printed *dunamis*.

Such transliterations often shed light on the text. In this case *dunamis* is the word from which our word dynamite is derived. So Paul is writing that the gospel has dynamite like power.

The Greek Alphabet

Even if you never study Greek you can derive a number of benefits in your Bible research if you know a little about Greek.

Greek capital letter	Greek small letter	English name of letter	English equivalent
A	α	Alpha	a
B	β	Bēta	b
Γ	γ	Gamma	g
Δ	δ	Delta	d
E	ε	Epsilon	e
Z	ζ	Zēta	z
H	η	Ēta	ē
Θ	θ	Thēta	th
I	ι	Iōta	i
K	κ	Kappa	k
Λ	λ	Lambda	i
M	μ	Mu	m
N	ν	Nu	n
Ξ	ξ	Xi	x
O	ο	Omīcron	o
Π	π	Pi	p
P	ρ	Rhō	r
Σ	σ, ς	Sigma	s
T	τ	Tau	t
Y	υ	Upsilon	u
Φ	φ	Phi	ph
X	χ	Chi	ch
Ψ	ψ	Psi	so
Ω	ω	Ō	ō

A little more Greek

Four loves: love, love, love and love

When the writers of the New Testament wanted to convey what they meant by God's love for us, as displayed in Jesus, they had a problem. They had three Greek words for "love" but none of them expressed what they were trying to communicate. So the writers of the New Testament used a little-used term in classical Greek, *agape*. This word is transformed in the New Testament into the most powerful word imaginable for love.

1. Eros (ερος)

The New Testament writers never use this Greek word. In classical Greek it stood for sexual love, but in the world of the Greeks and Romans it had become so badly debased that it stood for lust. So the New Testament avoids it altogether. The word "erotic" is derived from *eros*.

2. Storgē (στοργη)

This Greek word stood for the natural affection between a child and a mother. But this was not the kind of love the writers of the New Testament meant by God's great love for us and so they did not use this word either.

3. Philia (φιλια)

Philia stands for affection between friends. *Philia*, and compound words constructed from its root, like *philadelphia*, are used in the New Testament and describe warm caring relationships between people.

4. Agapē (αγαπη)

Agape is a word which hardly occurs in classical Greek, but it is the one which the writers of the New Testament used of God's special self-giving love as it was displayed in Jesus. *Agapē*-love, Godlike love, is distinguished from the other three loves.

Examples of the use of *agapē*
- John 13:35
- John 14:15
- 2 Corinthians 5:14
- 1 Thessalonians 1:3
- 1 Thessalonians 3:6
- 1 John 5:3
- 2 John 1, 3, 5, 6
- 3 John 1, 6
- Revelation 2:4

Examples of the use of *philia*
- Romans 12:10
- 1 Thessalonians 4:9
- 2 Peter 1:7

The secret sign of the fish

- In the early days of Christianity the first Christians were often persecuted. As a result they used a number of secret signs with hidden meanings.
- In the catacombs underneath the city of Rome, the Christians held secret services of worship and buried their dead friends. They sometimes scratched the sign of the fish on the walls of these underground passages.

- You may have seen the sign of the fish yourself. Some people wear a small fish badge or broach. Others have the sign of the fish on the bumpers of their cars.
- So why the fish? The Greek word for fish is ichthus. Ichthus in the Greek alphabet (ιχθυς) can become the acronym below.

ι	= Iesous	= Jesus
χ	= Chrisitos	= Christ
θ	= Theou	= God's
υ	= Huios	= Son
ς	= Soter	= Savior

The first Christians used the symbol of the fish to identify themselves as followers of Jesus Christ, God's Son and Savior.

Using a Greek-English Interlinear New Testament

Finding the exact meaning

English translations sometimes struggle to convey the exact meaning of a Greek word. As an example, it is not always easy to tell which meaning of the word "love" is being referred to in some Bible versions. The *King James Version* uses both the words "charity" and "love" to refer to *agape*. The *New International Version* uses "love" for *agape* and "brotherly love" for *philia*. The *New American Standard Bible* uses "love" in 1 Thessalonians 4:9, in which *philia* is used, and "love" in 1 Thessalonians 3:6, where *agape* is used.

How it works

A Greek-English interlinear New Testament has every Greek word of the New Testament on one line with the English word written underneath. The following verse from 1 Corinthians shows how it works.

---

1 Corinthians 13:1

Below the interlinear extract are various English translations for comparison.

Εαν	ταις	γλωσςαις	των	ανθώπων	λαλω	και	των	αννγελων
If	in the	tongues	–	of men	I speak	and	–	of angels

αγαπην	δε	μη	εχω...
but love		I have not	

- **KJV** Though I speak with the tongues of men and of angels, and have not charity,
- **NRSV** If I speak in the tongues of mortals and of angels, but do not have love,
- **NIV** If I speak in the tongues of men and of angels, but have not love,
- **RSV** If I speak in the tongues of men and of angels, but have not love,

Comparing the KJV with the Greek

Note the use of the word "love" (loving) in the following verse from 1 Corinthians. The verb form of αγαπη (*agape*) is used and occurs as αγαπωσιν (*agaposin*).

---

1 Corinthians 2:9

αλλα καθωσ	γεγραπται		α
but as	it is has been written:		Things which

οφθαλμοσ ουκ ειδεν και ουσ ουκ ηκουσεν
eye saw not and ear heard not

και επι καρδιαν ανθρωπου ουκ ανεβη,
and on heart of man came not up,

οσα	ητοιμασεν ο θεοσ	τοισ	αγαπωσιν
how many	prepared – God	for the [ones]	loving

αυτον.
him.

• *KJV* "But as it is written, Eye hath not seen, nor ear heard, neither have entered into the heart of man, the things which God hath prepared for them that love him."

SOLID BIBLE STUDY

- Read 1 Corinthians 13 in an interlinear New Testament, and note the Greek word for love, agape (or one of its forms such as agapain [αγαπην]).
- Read other famous Bible verses which contain the word love in this way. Observe which Greek word is used for love.
- Read John 3:16, John 15:13, Romans 8:39, 1 Thessalonians 3:6, 1 Thessalonians 4:9, 1 John 4:7-8

Using an expository dictionary of Bible words

Vine's Expository Dictionary of New Testament Words

Using an expository Bible dictionary, such as Vine's *Expository Dictionary of New Testament Words*, gives you both a definition and a summary of the Bible's teaching on hundreds of the most important Bible words. Look at the following entry on "reconcile". Note that *Vine's Dictionary* provides other derivates under the heading of Reconcile, Reconciliation.

BIBLE STUDY

Look up other important linked words to reconcile in an expository word dictionary of the Bible. Try the following words: "reconciliation, peace, unity."

RECONCILE, RECONCILIATION
A. Verbs.

1. *katallassō* (καταλλάσσω, 2644) properly denotes "to change, exchange" (especially of money); hence, of persons, "to change from enmity to friendship, to reconcile." With regard to the relationship between God and man, the use of this and connected words shows that primarily "reconciliation" is what God accomplishes, exercising His grace towards sinful man on the ground of the death of Christ in propitiatory sacrifice under the judgment due to sin, 2 Cor. 5:19, where both the verb and the noun are used. By reason of this men in their sinful condition and alienation from God are invited to be "reconciled" to Him; that is to say, to change their attitude, and accept the provision God had made, whereby their sins can be remitted and they themselves be justified in His sight in Christ.

Rom. 5:10 expresses this in another way: "For if, while we were enemies, we were reconciled to God through the death of His Son...;" that we were "enemies" not only expresses man's hostile attitude to God but signifies that until this change of attitude takes place men are under condemnation, exposed to God's wrath. The death of His Son is the means of the removal of this, and thus we "receive the reconciliation," Rom. 5:11, RV. This stresses the attitude of God's favor toward us ...

2. *apokatallassō* (ἀποκαταλ-λάσσω, 604) "to reconcile completely", "to change from one condition to another," so as to [re]move [all en]mity [a]nd leave no impediment to unity and peace, used in Eph. 2:16, of the "reconciliation" of believing Jew [and] Gentile "in one body unto [God] through the Cross;" in Col.1:21 not the union of Jew and Gentile [is] in view, but the change wrought in the individual believer from alienation and enmity, on account of evil works, to "reconciliation with God; in Col. 1:20 the word [is] used of the Divine purpose [to] "reconcile" through Christ "[all] things unto Himself ... whether things upon the earth, or things [in] the heavens," the basis of [the] change being the peace effe[cted] "through the blood of His Cross[."]

3. *diallassō* (διαλλάσσω, 1259) "to effect an alteration, [to] exchange," and hence, "to [recon]cile," in cases of mutual hostili[ty] yielding to mutual concession, [is] used in the Passive Voice in Mat[t.] 5:24, which illustrates the point. There is no such idea as "makin[g] it up" where God and man a[re] concerned.

B. Noun.

katallagē (καταλλαγή, 264[3]) akin to A, No 1, primarily "[an] exchange," denotes "reconcilia-tion," a change on the part of on[e] party, induced by an action on th[e] part of another; in the NT, [of] "reconciliation" of men to God [by] His grace and love in Christ. [The] word is used in Rom. 5:11; 11:1[5]. The word also occurs in 2 Cor. 5:18,19, where "the ministry of reconciliation" and "the word o[f] reconciliation" are not the min-istry of teaching the doctrine of expiation, but that of beseeching men to be "reconcile[d]" to God on the ground o[f what God] has wrought in [Christ. Note 1,]

Using a Bible dictionary

A Bible dictionary

A Bible dictionary provides definitive and descriptive information on Bible words. It may even include devotional material about Bible topics which is not always found in expository dictionaries of Bible words.

The following extract below is from *Easton's Bible Dictionary*.

REPENTANCE

There are three Greek words used in the New Testament to denote repentance.

1. The verb metamelomai is used of a change of mind, such as to produce regret or even remorse on account of sin, but not necessarily a change of heart. This word is used with reference to the repentance of Judas (Matt. 27:3).

2. Metanoeo, meaning to change one's mind and purpose, as the result of after knowledge. This verb, with (3.) the cognate noun metanoia, is used of true repentance, a change of mind and purpose and life, to which remission of sin is promised.

Evangelical repentance

Evangelical repentance consists of:
1. a true sense of one's own guilt and sinfulness;
2. an apprehension of God's mercy in Christ;
3. an actual hatred of sin (Ps. 119:128; Job 42:5, 6; 2 Cor. 7:10) and turning from it to God; and
4. a persistent endeavour after a holy life in a walking with God in the way of his commandments.

The true penitent

The true penitent is conscious:
 • of guilt (Ps. 51:4, 9),
 • of pollution (Ps. 51:5, 7, 10),
 • and of helplessness (Ps. 51:11; 109:21, 22).

Thus he apprehends himself to be just what God has always seen him to be and declares him to be. But repentance comprehends not only such a sense of sin, but also an apprehension of mercy, without which there can be no true repentance.

37

Using a topical Bible

What are topical keywords?

Nave's Topical Bible is a comprehensive digest of over 20,000 topics and sub-topics with more than 1,000,000 Scripture references. It groups verses by "ideas" or "topics", thus offering a better overview of relevant Scriptures than a concordance. It provides a cross-reference system and includes the full text of the verse cited in most instances.

Nave's Topical Bible

By using *Nave's Topical Bible* many fruitful avenues for extended Bible Study are opened up, as is seen from the following entry on "repentance".

Repentance

Instances of: Joseph's brethren, of their maltreatment of Joseph, Gen. 42:21; 50:17,18. Pharaoh, of his hardness of heart, Ex. 9:27; 10:16,17. Balaam, of his spiritual blindness, Num. 22:34, with vs. 24-35. Israelites, of worshiping the golden calf, Ex 33:3,4; of their murmuring on account of lack of bread and water, when the plague of fiery serpents came upon them, Num. 21:4-7; when rebuked by an angel for not expelling the Canaanites, Judg. 2:1-5; of their idolatry, when afflicted by the Philistines, Judg. 10:6-16; 1 Sam. 7:3-6; in asking for a king, 1 Sam. 12:16-20; in the time of Asa, under the preaching of Azariah, 2 Chr. 15:1-19; under the preaching of Obed, 2 Chr. 28:9-11; under the influence of Hezekiah, 2 Chr. 30:11. Achan, of his theft, Josh. 7:20. Saul, at the reproof of Samuel for not destroying the Amaletkites, 1 Sam. 15:24, with vs. 6-31. David, at the rebuke of Nathan, the prophet, of his sins of adultery and murder, 2 Sam. 12:11,13, with vs. 7 PSALMS, PENE

Exemplified: Num. 21:7. Therefor the people came to Moses, and sai. We have sinned, for we have spoken against the Lord, and against thee: pray unto the Lord, that he take aw. the serpents form us. And Moses prayed for the people.

2 Sam. 24:10. David's heart smo him after that he had numbered th people. And David said unto the Lord, I have sinned greatly in that I have done: and now, I beseech thee, O Lord, take away the iniquity of thy servant; for I have done very fooli. ly. 17. And David spake unto u. Lord when he saw the angel that smote the people, and said, Lo, I have sinned, and I have done wickedly: but these sheep, what have they done? let thine hand, I pray thee, b. against me, and against my father . house. 1 Chr. 21:17.

2 Chr. 29:6. Our fathers have trespassed, and done that which was evil in the eyes of the L⊂ have forsaken hi. away thei.

39

Using a one volume Bible commentary

One volume commentaries

The best type of commentary to use or buy initially is a one volume commentary. Although they are often large in size they do offer you comments on some of the most significant and difficult passages in the Bible. Plus, they provide an introduction, background information and commentary notes on each book of the Bible. An excellent, devotional, one-volume classic commentary is by Matthew Henry. A simpler one-volume commentary is the *Concise Bible Commentary* by James Gray.

Psalm 51

Psalm 51 records David's heartfelt repentance. The following extract is taken from the commentary on Psalm 51 by John W. Baigent, found in *The International Bible Commentary*, (General Editor, F.F. Bruce) which is based on the NIV.

A PRAYER FOR FORGIVENESS

This individual lament is most suitably called a "Penitential Psalm". The heading links it with the experience of David recorded in 2 Samuel 11-12, and it obviously fits that situation, ... being an expansion of David's confession of 2 Samuel 12:13.

The psalm opens (vv. 1,2) with the urgent plea for forgiveness, based upon the psalmist's knowledge of the merciful character of God (cf. Exod. 34:6f.). The genuineness of his confession is demonstrated by his profound understanding of the true nature of sin in its outward, inward and Godward aspects (vv. 3-5). Verses 6-12 express his deep desire for inward cleansing and spiritual renewal; whilst vv. 13-17 declare his determination to show his gratitude not only in humble thanksgiving, but also in a public testimony to the saving acts of God (cf Psalms 9:1f.; 22; 25; 40:9f.). The conclusion (vv. 18,19) asks that God will enable Jerusalem to be rebuilt so that the ...ic observances, impossible to ...out during the exile, may be ...ned, to the pleasure of God.

... **y on** or "be gracious ...ually expresses

inferior, carrying with it the idea of unmerited favor. **your great compassion**: lit. "The multitude of thy mercies"; "mercies" here represents a word which in the singular usually means "womb" (cf. Isa. 49:15) or "Bowels" (cf. Phil. 2:1, AV), thus it signifies deeply-felt compassion. **blot out**: as from a book (cf. Exod. 32:32; Neh. 13:14). **wash**: the verb is used of washing clothes by treading them (cf. Exod. 19:10, 14; 2 Sam. 19:24; Jer. 2:22). **3. I know**: or "I acknowledge" RV (cf. Isa. 49:12). **4**. Sin, even when directed against one's fellow man, is in the last analysis rebellion against God: "sin is ultimately a religious concept rather than an ethical one" (Weiser). Cf. 2 Sam. 12:13; Gen. 39:9; Prov. 14:13; 17:5. **so that**: his confession of culpability reveals the justice of God's punishment (cf. Jos. 7:19). **justified**: lit. "Clear". **5**. There is no suggestion here that the processes of birth or conception are sinful in themselves, nor that the birth of the psalmist was illegitimate. "The Psalmist confesses his total involvement in human sinfulness, from the very beginning of his existence" (A.A. Anderson). This is not offered as an excuse, but rather as an additional evidence ...f his utt...fulness (cf. ...8:3).

41

Using a commentary on a specific book of the Bible

Building up a library
It's possible to build one's own personal library with a variety of excellent Bible commentaries. Many helpful sets of Bible commentaries on each book of the Bible exist.

A book devoted to a single book of the Bible gives a much more detailed commentary than a one-volume commentary. The following extract is taken from *The Message of Acts*, by John Stott. It is commentary on part of the first recorded Christian sermon after the death of Jesus, in which Peter stresses the importance of repentance.

Acts 2:38-39

[38]Peter replied, "Repent and be baptized, every one of you, in the name of Jesus Christ for the forgiveness of your sins. And you will receive the gift of the Holy Spirit. [39]The promise is for you and your children and for all who are far off — for all whom the Lord our God will call."

Cut to the heart, that is, convicted of sin and conscience-stricken, Peter's hearers asked anxiously what they should do (37). Peter replied that they must *repent*, completely changing their mind about Jesus and their attitude to him, and *be baptized* in his name, submitting to the humiliation of baptism, which Jews regarded as necessary for Gentile converts only, and submitting to it in the name of the very person they had obviously rejected. This would be a clear, public token of their repentance — and of their faith in him. Though Peter does not specifically call on the crowd to believe, they evidently did so, since they are termed "believers" in verse 44, and in any case repentance and faith involve each other, the turn from sin being impossible without the turn to God, and vice versa (cf. 3:19). And both are signified by baptism in Christ's name, which means "by his authority, acknowledging his claims, subscribing to his doctrines, engaging in his service, and relying on his merits" (I. Alexander).

Then they would receive two free gifts of God — the forgiveness of their sins (even of the sin of rejecting God's Christ) and the gift of the Holy Spirit (to regenerate, indwell, unite and transform them). For they must not imagine that the Pentecostal gift was for the apostles alone, or for the 120 disciples who had waited ten days for the Spirit to come, for any élitist group, or even for that nation or that generation alone. God had placed no such limitations on his offer and gift. On the contrary (39), *the promise* — or "gift" or "baptism" — of the Spirit (1:4; 2:33) was for them also (who were listening to Peter), and for all who were far off (certainly the Jews of the dispersion and perhaps also prophetically the distant Gentile world, as in Is. 49:1, 12; 57:19; cf. Eph. 2:13, 17), indeed *for all* (without exception) *whom the Lord our God will call*. Everyone God calls to himself through Christ receives both gifts. The gifts of God are coextensive with the call of God.

Using a Bible handbook

Bible handbooks and Bible encyclopedia

It is often difficult to draw distinctions between books which are published under the names of Bible handbooks and encyclopedia. They often cover the same ground and the good ones are invaluable as reference tools for Bible study. A Bible handbook provides additional, interesting information often not found in other research tools.

The following two extracts are taken from *The New Unger's Bible Handbook* (revised by Gary N. Larson) and shed light on the subject of repentance with special reference to the Old Testament sacrificial system and to redemption in the New Testament.

A theological explanation of the Old Testament sacrificial system

The sacrificial system When Moses led Israel out of Egypt, the sacrificial system was given fresh meaning in the light of experienced redemption, organized, codified and written down by inspiration in the sacrificial codes of Exodus and Leviticus.

Meaning of sacrifices for the Old Testament worshiper The fundamental idea to the Hebrew worshiper of the sacrifices was that they were a *means of approach to God*. This is evident from the underlying connotation of the broadest Hebrew term for "sacrifice" (*qorban* from the root *qrb*, "to draw near or approach"). Sinful, guilty man needed some way to draw near to the infinitely holy God with assurance of acceptance. This was divin...

The application of the Old Testament sacrifices

The typological meaning of the sacrifices For the New Testament believer the Old Testament sacrificial system is particularly instructive through its illustrations of New Testament redemption. Many of the Levitical prescriptions are typical, i.e., they were symbolically *predictive*, expressing a need that they could not satisfy, but which the coming promised Redeemer would fulfill (Eph 5:2; 1 Cor 10:11, Heb 9:14). Others serve as principles that can be applied to the New Testament dispensation, while yet others illustrate facets of God's interaction with man that are timeless in their application. This is the normal application of the Old Testament sacrifices for the New Testament believer, although not their basic or practi... meaning for the Old...

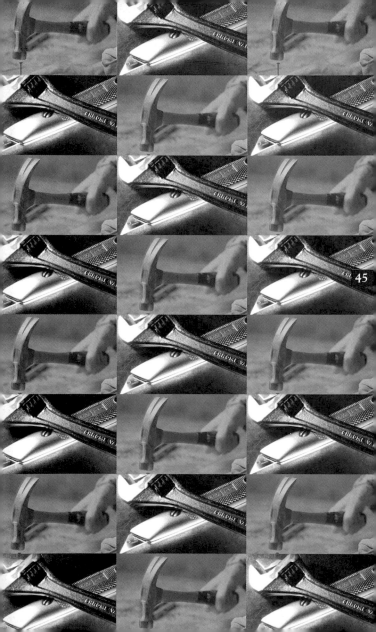

Using a Bible atlas

Key maps

Bible atlases are probably one of the most underused and undervalued of all the Bible reference tools. In order to appreciate the insight that you can gain from using maps, examine these map topics in a good Study Bible:

- The physical map of Palestine
- The ancient world at the time of the patriarchs
- The Exodus
- The empire of David and Solomon
- The kingdoms of Israel and Judah
- Palestine in New Testament times

- Jesus' Galilean ministry
- Jesus' later ministry
- Jerusalem at the time of Jesus
- Journeys of the apostles
- Paul's first journey
- Paul's second journey
- Paul's third journey
- Paul's journey to Rome

SOLID
BIBLE STUDY

1. Follow Paul's third missionary journey, Acts 18:23–21:16 and his journey to Rome, Acts 21:26–28:29, in the Acts of the Apostles with the help of good maps.
2. Locate on a map the destination of Paul's letters and see how many of them you can tie in to his pioneer missionary tours recorded in the Acts of the Apostles. For example Acts 16:1 recounts where Paul met Timothy, who became his protégé, and to whom he wrote 1 and 2 Timothy.

Reading the Acts of the Apostles with maps

The dramatic spread of the Christian gospel after Jesus' ascension is described in the Acts of the Apostles. It is impossible to fully appreciate what is recorded in the Acts of the Apostles without referring to maps.

"But you will receive power when the Holy Spirit comes on you, and you will be my witnesses in Jerusalem, and in all Judea and Samaria, and to the ends of the earth." *Acts 1:8*

Paul's second missionary journey
Acts 15:36–18:22

"Paul said to Barnabas, 'Let us go back and visit the brothers in all the towns where we preached the word of the Lord and see how they are doing.'" *Acts 1:36*

Bible reference	Map location
16:1-4	Derbe, Lystra, Iconium, Antioch
16:8	Troas
16:11	Samothrace and Neapolis
16:12-40	Philippi
17:1-10	Thessalonica
17:10-14	Berea
17:15-34	Athens
18:1-18	Corinth
18:18	Cenchrea
18:19-21	Ephesus
18:22	Caesarea, Antioch

Paul's first missionary journey
Acts 13:2–14:8

Turn to a map of Paul's first missionary journey and look up the following places as you read Acts 13:2–14:8 and see what happened in each place.

Bible reference	Map location
13:3	Seleucia
13:4	Salamis
13:4	Cyprus
13:6	Paphos
13:13	Perga
13:14-50	Pisidian Antioch
13:51–14:5	Iconium
14:6-19	Lystra
14:20-21	Derbe "They preached the good news in that city [Derbe] and won a large number of disciples." *Acts 14:21*
14:21	Lystra, Iconium and Antioch (revisited)
14:24	Pamphylia
14:25	Perga
14:25	Attalia
14:26	Antioch

47

Using a Bible theology book

The value of a Bible theology book

Good Bible theology books normally give the following information on Bible topics:

- A comparison between Old Testament teaching and New Testament teaching
- The meaning of the Hebrew or Greek word
- Links with other important Bible topics
- An aspect about the topic which must not be missed
- Mistakes about the topic that have been made
- Confusions to avoid

The following extract, written by R. Kearsley, is taken from *The New Dictionary of Theology* (edited by S.B. Ferguson and D.F. Wright).

REPENTANCE.

The OT often speaks of repentance to describe Israel's turning back to their God (e.g. 2 Ch. 7:17), in response to a promise of restored fortunes for the nation. In the NT, however, the preaching of repentance is greatly heightened and given specific content for the individual. This feature starts with the preaching of John the Baptist (Mt. 3:5-12; Li. 3:7-14). The Gk. words used throughout the NT are mainly forms related to the verb *metanoein*, "to change one's mind". This small phrase, however, describes a radical change in the individual's *disposition*, for the change of mind concerns his judgment upon himself and his sin together with an evaluation of God's demands upon him. The transformation implied, therefore, is not a matter merely of mental judgment, but of new religious and moral attitudes (a turning to *God*, 1 Thes. 1:9) and a new behavior (Acts 26:20), as John's preaching spelt out.

A continuous process

The importance of repentance is seen from the early preaching of the apostles and from its place as the first principle of the Christian message (Heb 6:1). Although there is in conversion a decisive change of mind, the renewing of the mind towards God is a *continuous* process (Rom 12:2; Eph. 4:23) just as faith is to be increased. Turning, and renewal of faith in the Christian's life, are the active side of the process called sanctification, of which regeneration and preservation are the passive aspects.

Martin Luther

Due to the increased emphasis on penitence (sorrow for sin) associated with repentance, the idea of confession and penance came to overshadow the sense of "changing one's mind", and it was Martin Luther who rediscovered the NT Gk. word, *metanoein*. With this he replaced the prevailing Latin Vulgate rendering of "do penance", and allied repentance closely to faith.

A moral act

It cannot be stressed too much that repentance is a moral act involving the turning of the whole person in spirit, mind and will to consent, and subjection, to the will of God. It is in a very real sense a moral miracle, a gift of grace. Terms often confused with repentance, such as p... remorse or penance, do n... tice to the impact of... call repentance

Using Bible computer software

Computer software

Computer software offers many benefits for Bible study. More and more Bible research tools are becoming available for computer. Most are obtaianble in CD-ROM format. Often times a CD-ROM is less expensive than the book. The one described on these two pages relates to the *New Living Translation*, the successor of the *Living Bible*.

If you are connected to the Internet, many resources are available for your use and are free of charge. See the pull-out chart in the back for a wonderful Bible research resource.

Quickverse Life Application Bible

Topic index	The Bible text

1. Touch points

This allows you to see short summaries of dozens of topics. Under "repentance" you will find:

- Why is repentance necessary?
- What is repentance?
- Is repentance a one-time event, or do we need to repent each time we sin?

Each question is answered with relevant Bible verses and a short explanation.

2. Bible topics

This is a fuller article about the Bible's teaching on repentance. It has hundreds of verses to look up, as well as numerous headings, such as:

- Repentance attributed to God
- Exhortation to repentance
- Examples of repentance
- Bible passages which exemplify repentance

In the Bible text there is often a symbol to press which gives you the Greek text for a particular word or phrase.

At Mark 1:4, for example reads in the *NLT*, "preaching that people should be baptized to show that they had turned from their sins and turned to God to be forgiven."

On pressing the symbol after the word "forgiven" the following message appears on your screen: "Mark 1:4 Greek: [this is an invitation for the viewer to look up this verse in a Greek New Testament to see the significance of some Greek word used.] 'preaching a baptism of repentance for the forgiveness of sins.'"

Insights

The Bible text has another symbol in it which takes you to insights on particular verses.

For example, the insight symbol at Matthew 4:17 takes you to an explanation about repentance. This says that repentance is turning away from self-centeredness and turning our live over to Christ's control.

Multi-media index

This gives a selection of maps, art, photographs, photo-bubbles, dramatic readings and time-lines.

One of the photographs is entitled "Pergamum overview" and is a dramatic shot of the ruins of Pergamum. This church was told to "repent" in Revelation 2:16.

Search facility

By typing in the word "repent" 157 related articles in various programs are listed.

Under the heading of "People and Places" there are 11 matching articles. One of these are the letters to the seven churches, in Revelation chapters 2-3, where you can note that five out of the seven churches are told that the action they need to take is to repent.

51

Good Bible software to consider:

- PC Study Bible (Bible Soft)
- Wordsearch (NavPress software)
- Nelson's Electronic Bible Reference Library (Nelson)
- QuickVerse (Parson's)
- Complete Word Study Bible (AmG Publ.)

How Jesus used Scripture

Our view of Scripture will determine how much we study it

Perhaps the most important reason for studying Scripture is not our own evaluation of it, but Jesus' evaluation. Because we believe that Jesus is the Son of God, we seek to follow his teaching on this subject and his submissive, humble attitude towards Scripture.

"The scripture cannot be broken." *John 10:35*

1. Jesus' behavior was in line with the Old Testament

When Jesus was tempted by Satan, (Matthew 4:1-11), he quoted Scripture in the presence of the devil. What the Scripture said – Jesus did.

When the devil offered Jesus the kingdoms of this world, Jesus replied, "Away from me, Satan! For it is written: 'Worship the Lord your God, and serve him only.'" *Matthew 4:10*

Jesus is quoting from Deuteronomy 6:13. Jesus also quotes Deuteronomy 8:3 and 6:16 in this incident.

Gegraptai ... gegraptai ... gegraptai

In Matthew chapter 4, Jesus uses the same phrase three times in verses 4, 6 and 10: "It is written," or "It stands written." In the Greek this is the single word *gegraptai*. Whatever Scripture said settled the matter for Jesus.

2. Jesus' mission fulfilled Old Testament prophecy

Jesus knew of his role as Messiah from direct revelation, but he also could have learned of this role from the Old Testament Scripture.

- He knew that he was to be Isaiah's suffering servant, see Isaiah 52:13 53:12.
- He knew that he would fulfil the role of Daniel's son of man, see Daniel 7:13.
- This accounts for the sense of compulsion which pervaded Jesus' mission.

"He [Jesus] began to teach them that the Son of Man must

suffer many things and be rejected by the elders, chief priests and teachers of the law, and that he must be killed and after three days rise again." *Mark 8:31*

3. Jesus submitted to the Old Testament's teaching in matters of controversy

When in dispute with the religious leaders of his day Jesus went to the Scriptures as his only court of appeal.

When asked a question to test him, by a teacher of the law, Jesus asked, "What is written in the Law?" and, "How do you read it?" *Luke 10:26*

When the chief priests, the teachers of the law and the elders tried to trip Jesus up with their questions and arguments, Jesus asked them, "Haven't you read this scripture ...?" *Mark 12:10*

Jesus roundly condemned the practice of adding to the Scriptures which the Pharisees were so guilty of. "You have let go of the commands of God and are holding on to the traditions of men. ... You have a fine way of setting aside the commands of God in order to observe your own traditions! ... Thus you nullify the word of God by your tradition that you have handed down." *Mark 7:8-9, 13*

Cruden's prayer

When Alexander Cruden finished his concordance of the King James Version of the Bible in 1737 he wrote the following prayer in the preface to its first edition:

"I conclude this preface with praying that God, who has graciously enabled me to bring this large work to a conclusion, would make it useful to those who seriously and carefully search the Scriptures; and grant that the sacred writings, which are so important and worthy of high esteem, may meet with all that affection and regard which they deserve. May those who profess to believe the Scriptures to be a revelation from God, apply themselves to the reading and study of them; and may they, by the Holy Spirit of God, who inspired the Scriptures, be made wise for salvation through faith which is in Christ Jesus, Amen."

Finding the Old Testament in the New Testament

Watch closely for Old Testament references

In the Gospels there are about 100 different references to the Old Testament.

The letter to the Hebrews, alone, also has about 100 references to the Old Testament.

If you read a New Testament verse and don't realize that a specific quote or teaching is from the Old Testament, you may miss the complete meaning of the verse.

"I am the true vine"

It is not necessary to know the Old Testament background to John 15:1-8 in order to understand what Jesus means when he says in verse one: "I am the true vine."

But your appreciation is enhanced when you realize that Jesus' hearers would have immediately linked up such a thought with Psalm 80:8-11 and Isaiah 5:1-7. "I will sing for the one I love a song about his vineyard ..." *Isaiah 5:1*

"A landowner ... planted a vineyard"

When Jesus spoke about a vineyard in Matthew 21:33-46, his opponents were quick to see that Jesus was speaking against them, because they had such a clear appreciation of the Old Testament. "When the chief priests and the Pharisees heard Jesus' parables, they knew he was talking about them. They looked for a way to arrest him." *Matthew 21:45-46*

The book of Revelation

The book of Revelation has almost three hundred quotations from or allusions to the Old Testament. The more you are aware of them the more you will appreciate the message of Revelation.

Topic	Ref(s)	Old Testament background
1. Seven spirits	1:4	Isaiah 11:2
2. The pierced Jesus	1:7	Zechariah 12:10
3. The Almighty [Christ]	1:8	Isaiah 9:6
4. Lampstands	1:12, 20	Zechariah 4:2
5. Description of Jesus	1:14-15	Daniel 7:9
6. Falling in God's presence	1:17	Ezekiel 1:28; Daniel 8:17-18
7. Tree of life	2:7	Genesis 2:9
8. The First and the Last	2:8	Isaiah 44:6
9. Teaching of Balaam	2:14	Numbers 24:12-14; 25:1-2
10. Searches hearts	2:23	Proverbs 21:2; Jeremiah 17:10
11. Broken pottery	2:27	Isaiah 30:14; Jeremiah 19:11
12. Key of David	3:7	Isaiah 22:22
13. A throne in heaven	4:2-3	Ezekiel 1:26-28
14. Four living creatures	4:6	Ezekiel 1:5
15. Root of David	5:5	Isaiah 11:1, 10
16. Colored horses	6:2-8	Zechariah 1:8-17; 6:1-8
17. Seal on foreheads	7:3	Ezekiel 9:4
18. Tear wiped away	7:17; 21:4	Isaiah 25:8
19. Hand raised to heaven	10:5	Daniel 12:7
20. Eating a scroll	10:9	Ezekiel 3:1-3
21. Dragon	13:1	Daniel 7:1-6
22. Fallen Babylon	14:8	Isaiah 21:9; Jeremiah 51:8
23. Wine of God's fury	14:10	Isaiah 51:17; Jeremiah 25:15
24. Son of man	14:14	Daniel 7:13
25. Judgment books opened	20:12	Daniel 7:9-10
26. New heaven, new earth	21:1	Isaiah 65:17
27. Glory of God's light	21:23; 22:5	Isaiah 60:19-20

Studying a long Old Testament book
An example using Isaiah

A bird's eye view
Before you think of looking at the book in any detail go for a bird's eye view of the whole book. Skim through the book and note how it divides up in the following sections.
- Prophecies for Judah and Jerusalem 1:1–12:6
- Prophecies about foreign nations 13:1–27:13
- Jerusalem under Assyrian rule 28:1–39:8
- The return of the exiles 40:1–66:24

At least this will tell you that the book is full of prophecies and that Jerusalem is a focal point.

Use keys to unlock the meaning of a book

A key verse	Isaiah 9:6-7 It's a good idea to read such key verses and see why you think they are thought to be important.
A key word	Salvation Do a quick study on salvation in Isaiah and look up the following verses. Isaiah 12:2, 3; 25:9; 26:1, 18; 30:15; 33:2, 6; 45:8, 17; 46:13; 49:6, 8; 51:5, 6, 8; 52:7, 10; 56:1; 59:16, 17; 60:18; 61:10; 62:1; 63:5.
A key chapter	Isaiah 52:13–53:12 Compare Isaiah 52:13–53:12 with Psalm 22. Other key chapters about Isaiah's ministry and message 1, 6, 9, 13, 32, 40, 44, 53, 57, 65, 66.
The author	Isaiah has been called the "St Paul of the Old Testament" and his book is often rated as among the greatest of the prophetic writings in the Bible. He started his ministry "in the year that King Uzziah died" Isaiah 6:1, 740 BC. There is a Jewish tradition that he was martyred by being sawn in two. See Hebrews 11:37.

Isaiah's characteristic name for God

Isaiah refers to God as "the Holy One of Israel." It's worth using a concordance to look up this name in Isaiah. It occurs 12 times in Isaiah chapters 1–39, and 14 times in chapters 40–66. The fact that this name for God is used only in six other places through the rest of the Old Testament supports the argument for the unity of and single authorship of the book of Isaiah.

Isaiah's distinctive methods of writing

Isaiah loved using personification.

Who/what is personified	Reference
The moon and the sun will be ashamed.	Isaiah 24:23
Desert and parched land rejoice	Isaiah 35:1
Trees clap, their hands	Isaiah 55:12
Israel is a vineyard	Isaiah 5:7
The winepress is trodden (God's judgment)	Isaiah 51:17
"Rock" is a name given to God	Isaiah 17:10

Isaiah the poet

Isaiah uses 2,200 different Hebrew words in his prophecy: more than any other Old Testament writer, and his rich poetry beautifully conveys his divine message. Read some of Isaiah's poems and hymns of praise.

- A wisdom poem *Isaiah 28:23-29*
- The vineyard song *Isaiah 5:1-7*
- Hymns of praise *Isaiah 12:1-6; 38:10-20*

Key words, key themes and key verses

A list of key verses, key themes and key verses for each book of the Bible are found in a companion book – *The Bible made easy* on pages 8-9, 12-13, 32-33.

Studying the contents of a long Old Testament book
An example using Isaiah

At some stage you must read through the book
It is much more important to expose yourself to God's Word than to read what other people have written about the Bible. Look at the main headings in the contents outline below to get your bearings. Read through Isaiah using the contents outline as your guide.

PART 1 THE BOOK OF JUDGMENT 1–39

1. **Prophecies against Judah 1–12**
   - The judgment of Judah 1:1-31
   - The day of judgment 2:1–4:6
   - The parable of the vineyard 5:1-30
   - Isaiah's commission 6:1-13
   - The destruction of Israel by Assyria 7:1–10:4
   - The destruction of Assyria by God 10:5–12:6

2. **Prophecies against other nations 13–23**
   - Prophecies against Assyria and its ruler 13:1–14:27
   - Prophecies against ten more nations: Philistia, 14:24-27; Moab, 15:1–16:14; Aram and Israel, 17:1-14; Ethiopia, 18:1-7; Egypt, 19:1–20:6; Babylon, 21:1-10; Dumah (Edom), 21:11-12; Arabia, 21:13-17; Jerusalem, 22:1-25; Tyre, 23:1-18

3. **God's word to the world 24–27**
   - Worldwide judgment 24:1-23
   - The triumphs of God's kingdom 25:1–27:13

4. **Woes and blessings 28–35**
   - Five woes on the unfaithful in Israel 28:1–32:20
   - Woe against Assyria 33:1-24
   - Woe to the nations 34:1-17
   - Blessings promised for restored Zion 35:1-10

Studying the links to Jesus in a long Old Testament book

An example using Isaiah

Jesus in the prophets

"Read all the prophetic books without seeing Christ in them, and you will find nothing so insipid and flat. See Christ there, and what you read becomes fragrant."

John Chrysostom, 347-407, bishop of Constantinople

Jesus in Isaiah

Isaiah's prophecies about Jesus being the Messiah are more numerous and more specific than any other Old Testament prophet.

	Prophecy about Jesus		Prophecy fulfilled in the New Testament
1.	Isaiah 7:14	The sign of the virgin	Matthew 1:22-23
2.	Isaiah 9:1-2	Zebulun and Naphtali	Matthew 4:12-16
3.	Isaiah 9:6	A child is born	Luke 2:11
4.	Isaiah 9:6	Prince of Peace	Ephesians 2:14-18
5.	Isaiah 11:1	The stump of Jesse	Luke 3:23
6.	Isaiah 11:2	The Spirit of the Lord	Matthew 3:16
7.	Isaiah 28:16	A precious cornerstone	1 Peter 2:4-6
8.	Isaiah 40:3-5	A voice in the desert	Matthew 3:1-3
9.	Isaiah 42:1-4	A smoldering wick	Matthew 12:15-21
10.	Isaiah 42:6	A light for the Gentiles	Luke 2:29-32
11.	Isaiah 50:6	Mocking and spitting	Matthew 26:67-68
12.	Isaiah 61:1-2	The Spirit of the Lord	Luke 4:16-21

"To proclaim the year of the Lord's favor"

Jesus used words from Isaiah 61:1-2 at the beginning of his ministry to explain what he had been called to do.

> "The Spirit of the Lord is on me,
> because he has anointed me
> to preach good news to the poor.
> He has sent me to proclaim freedom for the prisoners
>   and recovery of sight to the blind,
> to release the oppressed,
>   to proclaim the year of the Lord's favor."
> *Luke 4:17-21*

The "servant songs"

The "servant songs" found in Isaiah are vivid pictures of the coming "servant of the Lord," who can be identified with the promised Messiah.

The "servant songs" of Isaiah

- Isaiah 42:1-4
- Isaiah 45:5-7
- Isaiah 49:1-6
- Isaiah 50:4-11
- Isaiah 52:13–53:12

SOLID
BIBLE STUDY

Make a devotional study of Isaiah 52:13–53:12. Note the numerous references to the death of Jesus. A Study Bible with good cross references will assist in this.

Another approach is to read the following New Testament passages, and see how each one links up with Isaiah 52:13–53:12: Philippians 2:7-11; Luke 23:18; John 1:11; John 7:5; Romans 5:6, 8; Matthew 27:12-14; John 1:29; 1 Peter 1:18-19; Matthew 27:57-60; Mark 15:28.

The necessity of the Holy Spirit in studying Scripture

Two essential truths

Christians believe that the Holy Spirit communicates God's truth in two ways:

- by revelation - to the writer
- by illumination - to the reader

The Bible is "God-breathed" *2 Timothy 3:16*, through the Spirit of God, and so the Bible is referredto as God's revelation to human kind.

All Christians stand in need of illumination from the same Holy Spirit as one reads and studies the Scriptures.

What kind of people does the Holy Spirit enlighten?

- Regenerate people   John 3:3
- Humble people   Matthew 11:25-26
- Obedient people   John 7:17; 14:21
- Witnessing people   Mark 4:21-24

The Holy Spirit in the New Testament

The Holy Spirit has a much more prominent role in the New Testament than in the Old Testament. In the Old Testament the Holy Spirit only came to a few people, whereas in the New Testament after the death of Jesus, he came to all men and women who believe in Jesus. See Acts 2:17.

The Spirit is called "holy" only twice in the Old Testament, (Psalm 51:11 and Isaiah 63:10), but more than 90 times in the New Testament.

SOLID
BIBLE STUDY

Use a Bible concordance to study all the times the Spirit or Holy Spirit is mentioned in the Old and New Testaments.

The centrality of the Holy Spirit in Paul's prayers

Make a study of the work of the Holy Spirit in the life of a Christian from Romans 7; 2 Corinthians 3 and Galatians 5.

"I keep asking that the God of our Lord Jesus Christ, the glorious Father, may give you the Spirit of wisdom and revelation, so that you may know him better. I pray that the eyes of your heart may be enlightened in order that you may know the hope to which he has called you, the riches of his glorious inheritance in the saints, and his incomparably great power for us who believe." *Ephesians 1:17-19*

Also read Ephesians 3:14-19 and Colossians 1:9-14

Titles and names of the Holy Spirit in the Old Testament

Note the variety of names the Holy Spirit is given in the Old Testament. Always ask that you may be illuminated by the Holy Spirit as you study Scripture.

Bible reference	Name or title given to the Holy Spirit
Genesis 1:2	The Spirit of God
2 Chronicles 20:14	The Spirit of the Lord
Job 32:8	The breath of the Almighty
Psalm 51:11	Holy Spirit
Psalm 143:10	[God's] good Spirit
Isaiah 11:2	The Spirit of wisdom
Isaiah 11:2	The Spirit of understanding
Isaiah 11:2	The Spirit of counsel
Isaiah 11:2	The Spirit of power
Isaiah 11:2	The Spirit of knowledge
Isaiah 11:2	The Spirit of the fear of the Lord
Isaiah 61:1	The Spirit of the Sovereign Lord
Isaiah 63:10	His Holy Spirit

The Bible on Bible study

What is the origin of the Bible?
"For prophecy never had its origin in the will of man, but men spoke from God as they were carried along by the Holy Spirit." *2 Peter 1:21*

"All Scripture is God-breathed and is useful for teaching, rebuking, correcting and training in righteousness." *2 Timothy 3:16*

Who does the Bible introduce us to?
"In the past God spoke to our forefathers through the prophets at many times and in various ways, but in these last days he has spoken to us by his Son, whom he appointed heir of all things, and through whom he made the universe." *Hebrews 1:1-2*

Why was the Old Testament written?
"For everything that was written in the past was written to teach us, so that through endurance and the encouragement of the Scriptures we might have hope." *Romans 15:4*

What can the Bible do for us?
"The holy scriptures ... are able to make you wise for salvation through faith in Christ Jesus." *2 Timothy 3:15*

Can God's commands in the Scriptures ever be changed?
"Do not add to what I command you and do not subtract from it,but keep the commands of the LORD your God that I gave you." *Deuteronomy 4:2*

Whom did Jesus say would be blessed?
"Blessed ... are those who hear the word of God and obey it." *Luke 11:28*